Lifting *the* Latch

A Life on the Land

Lifting *the* Latch

A Life on the Land

as told to

SHEILA STEWART

by

Mont Abbott of Enstone,
Oxfordshire

DAY BOOKS
OXFORDSHIRE

ISBN 0 953 2213 3 4
From January 2007, ISBN 978 09532213 32

A catalogue record for this book is available from the British Library

This edition first published by Day Books, January 2003
Reprinted January 2004, January 2006

Text © Sheila Stewart 1987 & 2002, except for
'People and places' © Graham Binns 2002
Etchings © Michael Mattingley 2002
The moral rights of the authors and the artist have been asserted

The verses from Walter de la Mare's 'Nod' are quoted by kind permission of the Literary
Trustees of Walter de la Mare and the Society of Authors as their representative

Printed in the United Kingdom by the Alden Press, Oxford. This publication is printed
on acid-free paper

Day Books, Orchard Piece, Crawborough, Charlbury, Oxfordshire OX7 3TX
www.day-books.com

Contents

Etchings by Michael Mattingley

ix

The crook embellishment on either side of each chapter number is taken from a photograph of Mont Abbott's own crook, also by Michael Mattingley.

Photographs

Lord and Lady Dillon at the opening of Enstone Parish Hall. (By courtesy of Len Reynolds.)

Mrs Sheffield and the 'gracey-pig.' (By courtesy of Len Reynolds.)

Enstone Club Foresters.

The Reverend and Mrs Palmer. (By courtesy of Enstone Local History Circle.)

Enstone Primary School. (Packer Collection; by courtesy of Len Reynolds, Church Enstone.)

Enstone Women's Institute. (By courtesy of Len Reynolds.)

'Little' Johnny Higley. (By courtesy of Enstone Local History Circle.)

Gil in his Buckingham Palace livery.

Mont outside Biddy's Bottom. (Snapshot by Rosa Davies.)

Mont outside Manor Farm, Cleveley. (Snapshot by Rosa Davies.)

Mont at the lych-gate of St Kenelm's, 1977.

Mont in his best wheelbarrow. (Snapshot by Rosa Davies.)

Mont, gardening at Rosa's. (Snapshot by Rosa Davies.)

Mont at Marshall's Fountain. (Snapshot by Rosa Davies.)

'Old Mont.' (Photo by Mark Williamson.)

Preface

SOME YEARS AGO I WROTE a little book, *Country Kate*, based on the conversations of my old daily help, Kate. I wanted to record the richness of the spoken word of ordinary country people before the 'media world' had faded out their own lively observations and perceptions of the real world about us. Such characters are now very rare. I never thought I would have the privilege to meet another.

Several years after Kate had died I happened to go into a butcher's shop in Shipston-on-Stour.

'You're the lady that wrote *Country Kate*,' the butcher and his wife challenged me from behind the counter. '*Somebody* ought to be doing the same job on Old Mont.' It was obvious they meant *me*.

After caring for my elderly mother-in-law for several years I had lost the desire and the discipline for writing; but that challenge niggled me. They didn't even know Old Mont's real name, nor where he lived. They had been out for a drive 'out Enstone way' and 'just happened to lift the latch of a country pub' where they heard this old shepherd singing unaccompanied, and learnt he was known to all as 'Old Mont'.

Through the pub I learnt his name and address and wrote to 'M. Abbott, Esq.' to ask if I might come and see him with a view to writing his life story.

'Thee can come if thee wants,' he wrote back, in careful neat writing. 'I have no transport, only a wheelbarrow.'

'I shall come next Friday at two o'clock. If the wheelbarrow isn't there, I shall know you're out.'

Thus began my friendship with and weekly visits to Mont. The journey was about thirty miles altogether. He lived alone in the tiny hamlet of Fulwell where, apart from a seldom-heard passing tractor, it was so quiet, Mont seemed the only person left alive. I'd take my tape-recorder, place it on the old kitchen table, that same table he'd sat at as a 'bwoy', and he'd converse at random for about two hours. We'd sit either side of the range in his warm kitchen: Mont always in his father's big wooden chair with his back to the window so he could see the light on my face and follow what I was saying; Luke, his little terrier, curled up asleep in his box. When the clock on the mantelpiece struck four Luke would wake up and beg for his walk, pawing my skirt to tell me it was time I went.

I'd play back the tapes when I got home, and make notes on each. He was well enough at the beginning of our friendship to enjoy coming out with me in the car, pointing out his old haunts, sitting with me in Enstone Church, coming home with me to have 'a cup of tay'. I treasured the memory of these outings as it became obvious that his health was deteriorating.

It took me almost two years to write the book, sifting through the wealth of material on fifty tapes, collating random threads and weaving them into a narrative. I left each finished chapter with him for approval. I censored his original 'bloody's from the first chapters, but without them the dialogue lacked 'Mont' and seemed anaemic. I let them stand in the next chapter. Mont was shocked. 'En't we a-sweerin' a bit much, mam?'

I trust we en't, Mont. I just wanted to paint your wonderful character, bloodys and all. I hope I've done you justice.

Acknowledgements

I would like to thank the following: my husband for patience and encouragement with my writing; our daughter, Sarah Dodds, for designing the original map; Nan Neal, for advice and editing; Mont's relatives and friends for photographs and information; and, last but not least, George and Evelyn Peebles of Shipston, who, 'lifting the latch' of a country pub by chance one evening, happened to hear an old shepherd singing unaccompanied, and begged me to seek him out and write his story.

Sheila Stewart, Brailes, 1986

For Mont,
with love
and
great respect

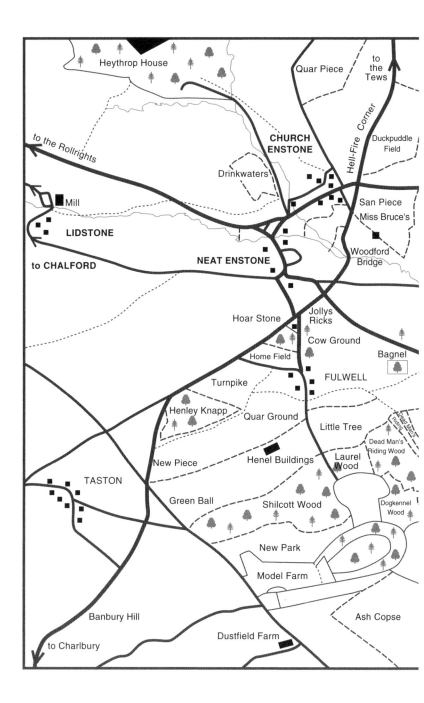

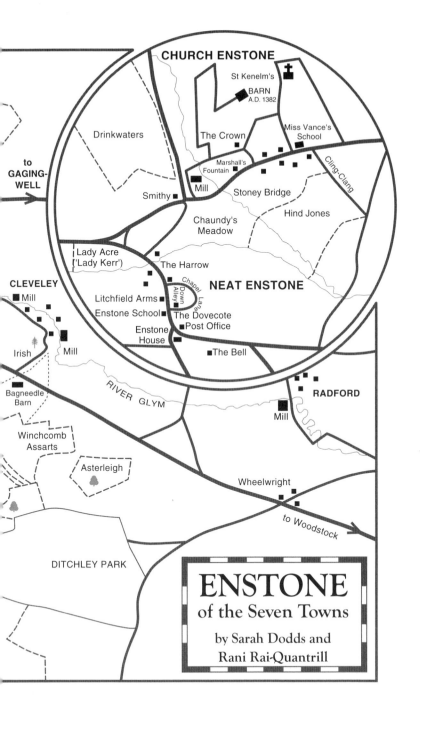

CHURCH ENSTONE

St Kenelm's

BARN
A.D. 1382

Drinkwaters

The Crown

Miss Vance's
School

to
GAGING-
WELL

Marshall's
Fountain

Cling-Clang

Smithy

Mill

Stoney Bridge

Chaundy's
Meadow

Hind Jones

Lady Acre
('Lady Kerr')

The Harrow

CLEVELEY

Mill

NEAT ENSTONE

Litchfield Arms

Chapel Lane

Down Alley

Enstone School

The Dovecote

Irish

Mill

Enstone
House

Post Office

The Bell

RIVER GLYM

RADFORD

Bagneedle
Barn

Mill

Winchcomb
Assarts

Asterleigh

Wheelwright

to Woodstock

DITCHLEY PARK

ENSTONE
of the Seven Towns

by Sarah Dodds and
Rani Rai-Quantrill

— 1 —

The Silver Pocket-Watch

THE DAY 'LORDY' PRESENTED ME with this silver pocket-watch I knowed I were a man. It were 1915, and I were all of thirteen years.

'Lordy' were Lord Dillon, the Seventeenth Viscount, of Ditchley Mansion in Oxfordsheer. He warn't a bit uppish but you could tell he were a lord; he wore a nanny-goat beard sort-of-do and a rich frock-cwoat. He'd come every year at school prize-giving day, give us a bit of a jabber about Christian living and learning, and throw in the odd tale about the Empire.

Sometimes he'd hand out a half-holiday and sometimes a silver watch. Not often a silver watch; you be very lucky indeed in they days of rampant pox, bumps and diphtheria to lift the latch of the schoolroom door 'never absent, never late' all your bwoyhood. I be always a healthy bugger.

Proud as a turkey-cock I be when I opened the back of my brand-new silver pocket-watch and see'd the inscription engraved therein:

Oxfordshire Education Committee
Neat Enstone Council School. Sept. 1915.
Presented to Montague Abbott
for good conduct and perfect attendance for 6 years.

1

Quite a dispatch! Right handsome 'Montague Abbott' stood out on that day in 1915. Bright and unblemished it remains, three-score-year'n'ten later, even though the works be spent, young 'Montague' be now 'Old Mont', and my blunted hands be that ockerd and weather-beat I be apt to blunder when I tries to open it.

These watches was all regulation-made by Rowell's of Oxford. The gals was presented with a more lady-like version, but the boys' was a full man's pocket-watch. A 'turnup' watch, some wags termed it, on account of its turnip shape, and having to turn up on time every day of your schoolhood to get it; and many a row of turnips we've hoved together, me and my watch. We used always to cart our watch on the soft of our belly at work so's it comed to no harm when you leaned across horse'n'hurdle.

A-standing there, a long gangling lad, in Enstone schoolroom in 1915 receiving my turnup watch, I had no blinding revelation of the acres of turnips, herds of cows, teams of horses and flocks of sheep awaiting my future as a farm-labourer. The present were more pressing. With our Jack, George and Horace gone off to the Great War, and our Lottie-Louise and Dora-Beatrice gone out to service, I were now the breadwinner.

Ever since I were a tiddler I'd thought of our Mam and Dad as th'Old Folks. Dad were a good bit older than our Ma. They'd married later in life than most and had gotten ten childern. We Abbotts was definitely 'lower orders' but we was all christened double-barrelled:

John-Henry	born 1887
Lottie-Louise	1893
George-Francis	1894
Horace-Albert	1895

Then comed our Nora. I never knowed our Nora. There be no time to christen the little mite double-barrelled; she died the day she were born, but her brief portion on this earth, '6 May 1897', be all recorded, decent-like, in the family Bible. . . .

Dora-Beatrice	1899
Gilbert-William (our Gil)	1905

James-Robert (our Jim)   1906
Frederick-Ralph (our Fred)   1908

Montague-Archibald comed seventh in this long hierarchy; we was all over six feet.

Dad earned what he could as an outworker, making boots and shoes for Mr Jefferies of Chipping Norton, but it were a pittance. Not that Mr Jefferies were niggardly, but because in they days when Shanks's pony be the main mode of transport there were an army of plodding boot'n'shoe-makers, sometimes two or three in a large village. Though he'd been apprenticed to a London boot-maker I knowed my old Dad, however back-breaking belaboured, harnessed to his last by that big leather strap, would never earn enough to keep the rest of us. By 1915 John, Lottie, George, Horace and Dora had all left home to earn their own living, but there was still me, Gil, Jim and Fred 'down Alley': and our Fred yet only six years old.

Ever since I were a lad of seven I'd been helping out in the harvest holidays on Mr Lennox's farm at Fulwell. At eight I could harness old Bowler, the big roan gelding, providing one of the men would lift the heavy collar and I could scrawf up on top of the manger to get upsides with him. At ten I could plough a straight furrow with old Bowler and old Beauty, though I had to turn fromard all the time 'cos I warn't heavy enough to balance the plough to come t'ward.

As soon as I got home from school on that day in 1915 and proudly showed Dad my new man's pocket-watch, he said, 'Mr Lennox be after thee, Mont. Three more of his men have gone awf to join the War. Thee's to start work on Mr Lennox's farm first thing tomorrow morning, half-past five, *pronto*!'

'*Three men*' and '*pronto*'—me and my silver pocket-watch be going to have to work overtime! Not that there were such a thing as overtime in they days; you done it but they never recognized it. *Pronto* at half-past five the next morning I lifted the latch of the dark cowshed at Fulwell, a tiny patch of a hamlet on the hem of our Enstone, and opened the door on to my careering as a farm-labourer. For the rest of my life as cow-chap, carter, shepherd (thirty years a shepherd), and now gardener, me and my watch were to work the land around our Enstone.

This silver pocket-watch be the most value-blest thing I ever was given in my life, not that I ever was given much. They tells I his old innards—like mine—is beyond repair, they don't make these old bwoys like we anymore; but that old 'Montague' inscription be still there, and I treasures it.

Down Alley

I WERE BORN in ought-two [1902] at St Clement's, Oxford, but when I were three we moved to our Enstone. I can just recall a big horse-drawn removal van a-clattering off away from me over the cobbles in Oxford, and me a-kicking up a shindig 'cos I warn't in it. 'Thee cassen't voyage in *that*,' my big sister, Lottie-Louise, told me. 'It be chock-a-block with our clobber.' And she lifted me high in me petticuts to voyage in a wagonette-set-of-tackle that were chock-a-block with our Mother instead.

It'd come to pass eventually that I'd live in Neat Enstone, Church Enstone and Cleveley, but they be all our Enstone. I'd better explain about our Enstone.

Enstone be the largest parish in Oxfordsheer; over six thousand acres and ten miles square. We lies between Woodstock and Chippy. The old aborigines of these parts named us Enas-stan, after our ancient monument, the Hoar Stwun, still standing among the holly-bushes at the top of Fulwell and the road to Charlbury. They stwuns, all of a yup, is supposed to be the burial chamber of an ancient king, thousands of years before the Romans;

and his body is fabled to have been borned from Ditchley direction all along the trail knowed for centuries as 'Dead King's Ride' or 'Dead Man's Riding'. Our Hoar Stwun and the Whispering Knights at Rollright be the two oldest monuments in Oxfordsheer.

Enstone used to be knowed as Enstone of the Seven Towns: the towns being the hamlets of Neat Enstone, Church Enstone, Chalford, Lidstone, Gagingwell, Radford and Cleveley. Neat Enstone were so called after the small black 'Neat' cattle bred in these parts in the Middle Ages. We all come under the one ancient church, St Kenelm's, founded around AD 830 across the brook at Church Enstone.

Our brook is part of the River Glyme. In my bwoyhood it were a far deeper, swifter, more tumbling course than it is today, giving birth to mills, fords, founts, watering-places and underground springs teeming through the rocks of our oolite soil.

Water and stwun be our Enstone foundation. The very place names, Radford, Woodford, Chalford, Gagingwell, Fulwell, Spring Hill, Drinkwaters Field, Duckpuddle Field, Enstone, Lidstone, and the quarries around declare our standing. All these hamlets in the old days had their own corn- or fulling-mill. The local quarries supplied the great millstwuns and stepping-stwuns; and the brook burst forth from umpteen pumps, fountains, troughs and gissles. A gissle were a field pond fed by an underground spring. No matter how smooth and still the surface, if you listened hard enough you'd hear that tell-tale 'gissle-gissle' hiss of water at the spot where the pond were fed. The whole of Enstone were fed gissle-gissle from the brook in the old days.

In the seventeenth century Enstone were famous for its Fantastical Waterworks, a special attraction built by a chap called Bushell, with grottoes, fountains and nightingales' notes blowing water through underground pipes. It was all so fairy-like that Charles I and Queen Henrietta even visited it, whereupon it became knowed as 'Queen Henrietta's Waterworks'. All this were long before my time. In my young days 'Queen Henrietta's Waterworks' were the privy behind the Harrow Inn. Owen Regan were the landlord. When a charabang party anchored there on their way to the 1924 Wembley Exhibition a snooty passenger complained about the 'disgusting amenities'. 'It were good enough for Queen Henrietta,' Owen says, 'it be good enough for thee!'

It was to the Neat Enstone side of the brook that we was brought in 1905, not in a charabang but in an old wagonette, to a cottage Dad had rented 'down Alley'.

There was eight dwellings down Alley, some short and fat like cottages, others tall and thin like tenements. Ours was tall and thin like the rest of our family, with a small outhouse on the side for Dad's workshop, and was knowed as the Dovecote. From the top of the Dovecote were a panoramic view of the whole Alley every bit as good as your Post Office Tower. The Alley were so narrow you couldn't get a horse and cart down there, and a donkey cart only to the first gate. All our clobber had to be carried a fair distance. Not that us had much: which was just as well, seeing as us was already eight in family and still expecting.

All they properties down Alley was rented from Jinny Wells. Jinny were a funny little body as kept a shop in her house. You just lifted her latch and went in. Her front steps went straight down into the village street in them days (now they'm all stwunned up). If you clombered on top of one of they stwun walls down Alley you could spy into the back-room of her house and see Jinny at night a-counting her glinting wealth in the lamplight. Old Jinny 'ud take any form of payment as long as it rattled true and were coin of the realm. Like Harrods, thee could get anything from a packet of pins to an elephant at Jinny's; if she didn't happen to have an elephant she'd get it for you. Folks used to say Lord Dillon owned half Enstone and Jinny Wells the other. I doubt if that be true but she owned all *my* world, down Alley.

She were a pecksniff biddy, always a-scratting about amongst her dusty stock. Her couldn't talk proper-plain, her spake with a stutter, pinched and nasal, as if her had a tight ring through her nose and wanted to be shut of it. Into the bargain her had a permanent dewdrop running from her nose; not that you ever got a bargain, but you got the odd dewdrop. 'D-dost thee want this?' she once asked old Tom Stevens, her drop pending perilous over his purchase of bacca. Tom eyed it warily, 'If it do, I doun't; if it doun't, I do.'

Buying and selling, pawning and renting, hiring out any mortal thing from a Hudson sack to a cup'n'saucer, thee'd never have fathomed out in a month of Sundays what an empire Jinny ruled over.

Paying Jinny the rent were a weekly do. It were two bob a week for the Dovecote, until inflation struck during the First World War and it shot up to two'n'thripence. The Dovecote with its own chimney, outhouse and privy were in the penthouse bracket; there were lowlier dwellings on Jinny's books for rent at only ninepence. If you couldn't manage in a bad week to pay your rent, she might let it run on for two, but most folks down Alley tried to keep straight; it were a disgrace in them days to run deliberate into debt.

In they days we never heard of millions. If you had a hundred pounds you was a millionaire. You could get eleven big gobstopper sweets or thirteen small sonny-bwoy bars for a farthing at Jinny's; you could have bought the whole of Fulwell, the hamlet where I live now, for a hundred pounds.

Even in the twenties I remember a decent newly thatched three-bedroomed cottage with its own chimney and own latched door, having a job to sell for £50. A goodly company were gathered there just for the entertainment of the auction. Sam Warner comes for a ride up the Chippy Road from Broadstone Hill to Church Enstone in his pony and trap, wonders what all the fuss be about, reins in his pony under the trees, and saunters across. The weary auctioneer were staggering on at ten bob a time. 'Anybody give me more than £49 10s?' he pleads. '*Anybody?*'

Nobody mouthed.

'Fifty!' says Sam, feeling sorry for the bloke: and that were *it.*

Fifty years later that same cot, Forge Cottage, be worth nigher fifty thousand.

Down Alley were my whole world, and the hub of my world were our kitchen. The whole of our kitchen were table. There were just enough room for us to set, Mam to serve, and us to yut. (This be that same table where I sits today; but now I sits alone.) The whitewashed walls was decorated with family photos: Dad as a young man, all togged up and draped nonchalant against a sofa garnished with tassels; long-dead Granny Abbott sitting patient waiting for the last trump in her lace cap and ringlets; Dad and his four brothers, all fine upstanding men, looking as if they owned the whole of Oxford, outside one of they posh colleges where Uncle Frank done the valeting and Uncle Charley looked after Great Tom; and a smattering of other faded, bearded, and bonneted individuals.

Our kitchen were the only room downstairs. You just lifted the latch from the Alley and walked straight in. It were bakehouse, bath-house, wash-house, all flagged into one front room. We was a bit uppish, having our own oven and a proper chimney. Some folks had ovens, but they were built out from the wall of the cottage like a little outside stwun fortress with only a hole in the lean-to roof for the smoke to escape. In the olden days folk had to pay a farthing tax if they had a proper built-in chimney; and the folks of Enstone paid 'Her Majesty Queen Anne' fourteen shillings a year in 'smoake-farthings', which just goes to show what a posh lot we was in our Enstone in the days of Queen Anne. 'I likes history,' I once told our Dad. 'History's orlright,' says Dad, 'but history doun't fill thee belly, bwoy!'

Most cottages in Enstone had only a grate, and folks took their milk puddens and their bits of meat on a Sunday to be cooked at the bakehouse: either to Charlie Collett's in the hollow at the bottom of Road Enstone or to Gregory's at Church Enstone, whichever were the nighest. The baker, not baking bread on a Sunday, was glad to keep his oven hot for Monday and receive a few pence from the flue-less on Sunday. All over Enstone after church on a Sunday morning there were a heavenly aroma of folks a-bearing home from the bakehouse their roasted meats and billy-cans of pudden.

Other aromas were more earthly than celestial. We had five privies down Alley. They were quite a selection. Us Abbotts had a one-holer all to our eight selves; us could turn our nose up higher than the other families. The next three dwellings had to share a two-holer; and the other four cottages had to share two two-holers back to back. It were all very sociable.

It were man's work to empt' the privies once a year, and woman's work to empt' her ashes every day on to a nearby ready ashup. The men would choose a good moonlight night after harvest, come Michaelmas, for the annual event. They'd spread the yup of ashes into a big ring on the garden, and dig a deep pit in the centre. They'd empty the privies with the shitter-scoop, a giant ladle on a long handle, and keach it into the pit, shovelling the soil and ashes in alternate layers, until the privies was empty and the pit was full. Then they'd shovel a good layer of earth and ashes over the top.

Our 'harvest' was sometimes sold to local farmers. There was none of this 'artificial' in they days, just the pure genuine stuff. They'd use it in the water-drills, diluting it on to the land for their root-crops, turnips, swedes, mangolds. But more often we'd garner the precious 'night soil' to we selves, bearing buckets of the black gold up to our allotments.

It be a good thing for our family that our Enstone be on well-draining land, that there be plenty of good thick hedges away from home for we old bwoys to answer the call of nature, and that we had only the one set of Old Folks to hold up proceedings to our hovel. It were a long-winded do in some big families with only a one-holer if they was forced to accommodate a trot of modesty-vested maiden aunts or a doddle of grannies with their umpteen petticuts.

I never remembers having a granny nor a grampy. With our Old Folks a-marrying late in life, *their* Old Folks had already snuffed it. I knowed I had a Granny Abbott up on the kitchen wall; and on our Mother's birth certificate *her* mother's signed, 'x Ann Smith her mark', so I must have had a Granny Smith too once upon a time. I faintly remembers one or two spare aunts a-knocking about. An Aunt Em cropped up once from out Stan' Harcourt way, a fair distance in they days, to visit us in a hired pony'n'trap. But the horse be restless and the hire expensive, so her only lifted the latch and then her sleered off. It were just as well, her couldn't have stopped the night; we had only two bedrooms down Alley and they was chock-a-block.

The stairs went straight up out of the kitchen to the bedroom. The Old Folks slept in there in the double bed, with baby Gil in the bottom drawer and our Dora in the camp-bed tucked under the stairs winding up out of the bedroom to the loft. Us old bwoys slept in two double beds in the loft. (In they days an 'old bwoy' were a young lad; an old man were called 'Master'.)

There be just enough headspace to clamber over the near bed to get to the nether, but no room to caper about. Us growing giants was always a-groaning, knocking our bwoons on the purlins and pinions. But the view from the two low casements on either side of these cramped quarters was well worth it; right up to the allotments on one side and right down the street on t'other.

My earliest recall of sleeping in the loft was hearing one morning the distant heavy horses and wagons a-tomping all the way up from Broadstone Hill, nearer and nearer, and all us bwoys a-scrambling over the two double beds to crowd at the opened casement for a bird's-eye view of Brassey's prize sheep a-being carted to Oxford Ram Fair.

Albert Brassey were a big GWR man, made his brass on the railway, lived on the grand scale—with everything to match—at Heythrop Mansion. His horses was massive Cleveland bays, all to match; and his coaches, carriages, broughams, wagons, was all decked out in the Brassey colours, with cockaded coachmen and liveried grooms to match. Each of his prize sheep on this Olympic morn, packed individual in his Brassey sheet into these two great wagons, had a back as broad and flat as a table, with cloth to match. Now that I be older I knows it be the ewes in one wagon, the rams in t'other: their fleeces fulled, their horns polished, their long snooty noses pointed straight for Oxford and that First Prize cup.

The horses and showmen was all toffed up too, with a goodly array of curling tongs, rags and polishes, and teazy-weazy brushes a-stowed under the driving board for all the final crimping and buffing-up of men and sheep when they gets there. In Oxfordsheer we always calls sheep 'ship'. I once warned this posh woman in Woodstock, 'There be an old ship stuck up by the Bear.' Her thought they'd stranded the bloody *Queen Mary*.

From that same lofty eyrie as the years went by we cheered the progress of they steam-engines a-skidding up the hill on they newly tarred 'arch'lls. They had a bevelled pin to help they wheels grip, but they'd cut the road about summat awful. The choking smell of the smoke 'ud make our flannel chests heave, and the smuts of soot 'ud make our eyes stream, but us couldn't resist they clanking dragons.

On dark frosty nights, bedded down tight in our lofty roost, we'd hear they old steam Foden lorries thrusting slowly up the hill below, spitting enough sparks, flames, fireworks to set the whole of Enstone alight, and flickering through our leaded casement on all we snoozing Shadrachs, Meshachs and Abednegos in our raftered fiery furnace.

Our John never lived down Alley. I'd never see'd my eldest brother. When I were born our John were already sixteen and earning King Edward's shilling out in India. In they days of overextended childbearing the eldest were often moved out into the world by the time the younger ones were born.

Our Lottie-Louise moved out at thirteen years into service at a boarding-house in Oxford. Our Old Folks conveniently wangled Jim and Fred into our world as George and Horace moved out. But we was all big, and it were always a tight fit for us clambering lads in the Dovecote.

There was always plenty of kids to play with down Alley. Next door to we were the Faulkners, three gals and two bwoys; and next door to they, the Harrises produced five gals and four bwoys for our benefit.

We missed out on the bottom cottage; no childern there, only an old bachelor-bloke, Billy 'Bunny' Hemmings, and he produced only rabbits. Rabbits galore Bunny bred in his hovel. He were a shy self-effacing chap, a sensitive whiskery creature, growed more like a rabbit every day. Not that we often see'd him by day; he were a nocturnal Bunny, always a-bobbing in and out of the verges after dark, a-foraging for rabbit grub.

There were two more lads and a wench in the Huckinses' opposite to we. Then comed old Em Wearing with a growed-up son. He were a love-child, born out of wedlock. He married happily later and borned three legal childern, but they be all dead now.

Next to the Huckins comed the Stevens. Over the years as I growed older and lankier I were always being sent to run and fetch the doctor for Mrs Stevens. Not only for Mrs Stevens's jobs but for other accidentals as well. For most of life's ailments and tragedies it were usually, 'Send for Mrs Abbott'; then if our Mam were stumped it were always, 'Fetch the doctor, our Mont.' I were a good cross-country runner in my young days, and 'fetching the doctor' usually meant being dragged out of my warm bed in the middle of the night to run in the pitch dark four miles to Charlbury to knock up old Doctor Croly in the big house at the top of Station Hill, or Doctor McNeight next to the White Hart. They wasn't butties, each worked off his own bat.

They say one doctor be as good as another; they learns it from the same bloody book. But to me Doctor Croly were the better of the two. When Mrs Faulkner had her second bwoy her had milk-block. Our Mam tried to help but her breast-pump be busted, so I be sent off in the middle of the night to fetch Doctor McNeight. He set off in his posh brass-lamped motor and never even offered I a lift. To cap it all, when I runs in home he sends I straight back to fetch *his* breast-pump which he'd forgot, *and* passes me again in his motor on his way home. If that had been Doctor Croly he'd have stopped his horse'n'trap, 'Hop in the back, bwoy!' he'd have said, no matter which way the pony be pointing nor how full he be loaded to the tailboard. Doctor Croly be too dedicated to forget a necessary breast-pump. He be thoughtful for everybody. His coachman, Strickland, lived at Number One, Station Hill, in the cottage next to Doctor Croly's gate, but he'd try never to disturb Strickland to harness the pony if he were called out in the middle of the night. Doctor Croly be a gentleman and a surgeon to boot.

Besides 'fetching the doctor' I were always our Mam's right hand when it come to the laying-out. Our Mam showed a care and dignity in her ministrations that were much appreciated among the bereaved. Thomas Hawtin, sexton and coffin-maker for years, were the traditional trestle of support to the bereaved in the village. I can just recall Thomas's father, old Joseph Hawtin, who had held the same office, as had *his* father before him. But old Joseph were out of joint by the time I were a bwoy, a splinter of his former strength, no longer capable of raising the dead in an oak coffin, only a shaking handful of hens' corn in a wicker punnet. Thomas, his son, were village carpenter and worked hard about the district. He'd load as much wood on his bike as a pony 'ud draw on a cart, and dovetail all his parish duties as sexton, clerk, bellringer and boiler-tender in with his main joinery. His demeanour and the nature of his standing in the parish were such that he were hardly ever 'Tom', always 'Thomas'.

As soon as anybody died the family 'ud send for our Mam, and to Thomas to toll the church bell. Our St Kenelm's has six bells. They was recast in 1831 but some retain their original inscriptions. Thomas's favourite was 'I to the church the living call, and to the grave do summon all.' It were widely believed in the old days that the sound of bells 'broke the power of lightnings' and 'drove away thunder', and that the air were the great highway of evil spirits waiting to snatch the soul of a dead person before it could reach the haven of heaven. Thomas's tolling kept 'em all at bay. He'd let you know which soul had fled by giving three lone knells before tolling regular for a man, two lone knells before tolling for a woman, and one for a child. How long he went on tolling 'ud tell everybody the status of the dead person in the parish. Thomas were a proper ringer, tolling full-bell, ringing on the sally. If he warn't able to ring, swinging the whole bell, he'd tie the rope on the clapper for a volunteer toller to hit the clapper against the bell, waiting a whole minute between claps for the note to die away. I done that for him many a time.

If Thomas couldn't come to measure the body straightaway I'd fetch the laying-out plank and help Mother to tend and dress the body all decent for burial in clean shirt or nightgown, socks or stockings, and lift them on to the plank. They'd stay in the house with a night-light for company until Thomas brought the coffin on the bier. He'd bring a posh silky-looking shroud, and Mam 'ud put it on the body.

Our Mam never charged for her services, and Thomas charged precious little for his. He didn't have no Rolls-Royce hearse, just our Enstone bier. It were a good'un, craftsman-made by one of Thomas's ancestors for good balance and ease of running. He knowed it 'ud have to bear him to rest one day, so he made a good job of it. There were no hired bearers; the men of the family or a man's workmates generally acted as bearers. There warn't no money for funeral outfits; the chaps 'ud wear their poshest black bowler or cap. There warn't no money for wreaths; the coffin were often bare or, at times, strewn with a few wild flowers from the verge or 'the grinserd' as we used to call it, as the company of bearers and mourners wended their way alongside the bier up to the lych-gate. The family usually gived Thomas a couple of bob to give to the bearers, but it usually went back, they 'udn't take it. Come the following Sunday, you'd always see they self-same bearers come to church and sit together, a last testimony of respect on behalf of the whole community.

Death and birth were of close concern to us all down Alley. Even though I became accustomed to fetching the doctor almost annually for Mrs Stevens it were still a great event. Despite having one child living permanently in a wheelchair, Mrs Stevens were a wonderful conscientious mother. She kept her increasing brood close to her apron-strings, always knowed exactly where each one be, all except the seventh, Alec; he were always missing, the odd one out. 'Our Odd' she always called him.

Our Odd were a little masterpiece; he never crawled as a baby, he bottom-shuffled, walking one hand on the ground in front and shunting his rump along the ground to keep up with it. Moy-hoy! Our Odd could bottom-shuffle! It were as much as you could do to keep up with him.

'Hast seen our Odd?' Mrs Stevens 'ud enquire anxiously umpteen times a day, a-pushing this wheelchair up and down Alley; and reports of last sightings of the champion bottom-shuffler 'ud come flashing back from all directions. He once shuffled under a passing motor. Luckily motors be higher off the ground in they days, and he shuffled out, unscathed, the other side. I rescued the little chap and restored him to home on that occasion. Throughout my life I be nursemaid to some poor wandering soul or creature. Many of they I fetched the doctor for at birth be dead and gone now, yet Old Mont lumbers on. (Our Odd be still alive, praise the Lord. He be still our Odd to me, and I be his lifelong friend.)

In the last cottage down Alley lived Jesse Bennett, an old walking postman, all parcelled up in his braided GPO uniform with his polished boots, gaiters, long black waterproof cape, and peaked chimney-pot hat. You'd see that hat a-pecking along the hedgerows all over the district. He were a crusty old pwoosty to us childern, frit the life out of us with his cussin'n'cloutin'—bore a grudge against everything. He could never pass an innocent bush nor rail without giving it a bash with anything he had to hand. Great Tew Cricket Club ordered a brand-new bat once to come by post. Jesse cut every 'arch'll for six from Enstone to Tew with this posh new bat, and chip-shot all the bottom out. There was a smartish score to settle with the GPO over that.

In his spare time Jesse would improve the shining hour going up and down Enstone with a wicker skip on his back a-picking up all the horse-muck for his allotment. Pick it up with his bare hands, he 'ud, then shy it hard at his cabbage-stalks, '*Veg*etable! *Veg*etable', venting his pent-up ire and manure on his harmless patch. For years after old Jesse were dead and gone his old pwoosty's hat were stuck up on a scarecrow mounted among the manure and *veg*etables up on the allotments, and us kids dussen't go near it on moonlight nights in case old pwoosty's gwoosty suddenly lashed out at us with a fourpenny one.

Yet even Jesse, grumpy old stick, were accepted as part of life down Alley. We was all one in they days. There was nobody down Alley to envy; if pity were needed we'd all rally round. It were hard do's but fair do's for all. 'Trate 'im as thee own,' our Dad would say to anybody down Alley as had dealings with me as a lad.

'I 'spec thee desarved it,' he'd chide if I came back crying with a clip round the ear-'ole. 'There's another to kayp it company,' were all the coddling I'd get. Thee soon learnt not to come crying home if thee'd been up to mischief.

In the same way an invalid or a hero belonged to us all; as in later years when our Jack came home a broken man from the Great War, or our Horace came home on leave from HMS *Agincourt*, or our George came home from 'guarding the King', bearing a photo of himself in his dazzling Life Guards uniform. I have that same photo yet, with all the details of his military dress pencilled on the back for the admiring benefit of all us rustic Alley greenhorns: 'Steel cuirass, brass scales, white slings, white gauntlets, steel helmet, white plume, scarlet coat, blue edgings, high jackboots and white pantaloons.' '*High jackboots and white pantaloons*'—moy hoy! I still feel now as I felt then—a bloody far cry from this old bwoy's clathoppers and corduroy breeches!

Down Alley were a passport for life; if in later years you introduced a friend as coming from 'down Alley', it were spake with the same pride as 'from Eton'. Down Alley our door were on the latch to anybody in need, but we minded our own business. Down Alley our George belonged to everybody that could touch the tails of his scarlet cwoat, but once inside the Dovecote he belonged to we. Down Alley us all shared the same well, but us each respected the t'other's water-butt.

'Jump, Jinny-Wagtail, One, Two, Three!'

I DONE ALL ME SCHOOLING at Enstone. At three years old I were
pared out of petticuts into breeches and toddled off to Miss
Vance's, the little governess school at Church Enstone. This little
school were run by the Church but it belonged to Lord Dillon, so
I suppose it were private, but us never paid nothing.

Miss Vance were plump, neat and clean, dressed respectable with
button boots. Winnie Bennett were her assistant. Winnie's bosom
always glinted with a silver watch on a long silver chain. Winnie
were a good teacher, her went up to London at it later. Always
comed home to Enstone in a posh new hat. Antiquated the village
bonnets no end, Winnie Bennett's posh hats.

All I can remember about Church Enstone School is playing
round about the stone fountain where we used to drink from the
ever-flowing ice-cold water in the summer and break off icicles to
suck in winter. It were a memorial affair, built in memory of some
chap's wife. There was length enough for hosts of us runny-nosed,

barefoot littl'uns to gather at the splashing shrine; and when in later life I used to sing

Shall we gather at the river
That flows by the throne of God?

I'd think of Church Enstone fountain. Nowadays I looks down upon it from the dwindle of old age, the spout be silent, the waters all ceased since they brought the mains and altered the water-levels in the village; but before the First World War, when most water were hard-won from the pump, it seemed to my splashed uplifted eyes a tumbling torrent, a majestic monument, fit to be the 'throne of God'.

At five years of age me and my mates was marshalled into line and marched two by two to the big school at Neat Enstone. Nowadays that great trek be only a few hundred yards and a lollipop-lady across the A34 which runs from Oxford to Chippy through the middle of Enstone; but down Alley and Miss Vance's, the whole of my known world in they days, be on one side of the road, and it be like being launched into space to cross the great divide to the big school on t'other side.

Mr Glover were the boss-chap at the big school; and Mrs Glover, the boss-chap's wife, taught in the first two Standards. I can't remember much about her 'cept her had a lovely contralto voice and always gived a good rendering in church. Her were very strict, a different kettle of teacher from Miss Vance and Winnie Bennett. Thee soon see'd thee be on a different roundybout with Ma Glover and that there'd be no splashing about with fountains. Still, I got around to all her set I to, and usually enjoyed it.

Master Glover ceremoniously unlocked that school gate at eight o'clock every weekday morn, and the minute you stepped on to that playground you was on hallowed school ground. There was no skiving out and sleering back in. The minute that school gate was shut of a morn you warn't allowed out without asking until four o'clock. Us brought bread'n'lard or bread'n'brown sugar for school dinner. When that gate was locked after you'd left on a Friday you dussen't set boot again on school ground until Master Glover unlocked it again at eight o'clock on Monday morning. And woe betide thee Monday morning if he'd copped you playing up in church on Sunday: for Master Glover were also churchwarden. Thee dussen't swap marbles nor nod off with his beadle eye upon you for he were a keen marble-catcher and sluggard-waker too. He were all enthroned on his churchwarden's vantage-point, in his judicial black warden's gown, umpiring we old bwoys in the stalls and the gals separate; backed up by the ancient Roll of Parochial Administrators dating as far back as I dare peek—from dusty 'Churchwardns. W. Soudon and R. Boulton. Anno 1632' to the Saxon cobwebbed 'Monks of Winchcombe Abbey' centuries beyond.

I took to learning. Reading, writing, reckoning come easy to me. Folks be amazed that I, a labourer and eighty-two, can spell and reckon straight off. All credit be to my schooling. Many a time in my life I've stood patiently by, the answer all buttoned up in my head, while my master's run out of fingers.

There were seven Standards in Enstone School. The middle classes was always forty or fifty strong. Only when you'd mastered one Standard of learning you was put up to the next'un. I hotched up a Standard every year with a mounting pile of prize books for History, Arithmetic, Dictation and so forth, presented by Lord Dillon. Our Old Folks thought the world of they books but I give 'em all away to the soldiers in the Second World War. They was a-pleading for books for our homesick lads in the Forces in the Far East. I often wondered which cheesed-off Chindit in the jungle ended up with *Children of the New Forest* presented at Neat Enstone School, 1910, to Montague bloody Abbott.

I becomed the biggest lad in the school as I growed older, a spare rule to the staff and a hero to the littl'uns, rescuing kites off weathervanes and kittens from water-vents.

Master Glover be a good teacher. He were a tall chap, military in bearing, with a clipped moustache and clean boots. (Clean boots ranked smartish in they days.) He kept a cane on show but it were seldom used—hung on the bottom of the easel for weeks sometimes, a-gathering chalk-dust. Glover kept us at it, kept us up to time, made us walk orderly and sober. 'Stop scortin' about, Abbott, and pick they boots up!'

No end of better-off bwoys and gals he coached through to the grammar schools. The bwoys 'ud go to Bloxham or Burford, and the gals to Witney. 'There is a happy land far, far away,' I used to sing in assembly, gazing up at that Roll of Honour on the schoolroom wall with they magic realms, 'Bloxham', 'Burford', blazoned in gold over and over alongside they lucky names of scholarship kids.

Master Glover be quite advanced for his time in the theory of education. He reckoned, with so many of us clathoppers destined for the land and the allotment, a bit of horticulture 'udn't come amiss. He cajoled this posh landscape-keeper-chap at Blenheim Palace to come and give us a few tips. Come all the way from Woodstock, this posh keeper did, to show us how to prune this old apple-tree. The tree hadn't borne for years—it be hardly worth his horseshoes to trot over—but the trunk be quite a girth and the timber be sound. He preached if the roots be pruned the tree 'ud perk up new heart to fruit. He were all for we old bwoys a-poking polite all round it with a spade. I could see it were going to be a bloody boring long-winded effort. The keeper soon realized he'd bitten off more than us 'ud prune. 'Let's have the bugger over,' I says. The keeper agrees. Giant Monty pulls it back a bit at a time and we both co-operates. He were all for giving I a job at Blenheim Palace. I reckon he visioned in I a future JCB, excavating his noble landscapes, but I couldn't see Blenheim Palace a-fitting in with th'Old Folks, so I declined. The tree turned out to be a good cropper, half-Blenheim, half-russet, a bloody good keeper and a bloody good eater. That's what I call team-work.

Team-work: that's what I misses most today. It were all team-work in they days, on the land, in the home, even at play; bwoy or gal didn't make no odds, us played together as one. Some of they gals could chuck a stwun as straight as a gun, and some of we old bwoys was a dab hand at the hopscotch. 'Jump, Jinny-wagtail, one, two, three!' us old bwoys 'ud cry, bending our backs, inviting any hoyden or hobbledehoy to leap over. 'Jump, Jinny-wagtail, one, two, three!' they'd leap and bend in their turn according.

Bwoys as well as gals 'ud run down to the brook early on May Morning to gather 'jillies', as we called the mayblossom, kingcups and cuckoo-pints, which we tied in a mop on the end of a stick, and we'd plod in a band round the houses before school, carolling:

> *Gentlemen and ladies I wish you a happy May*
> *I've come to show me garland because it is the day.*
> *The day do come but once a year,*
> *So please give to the poor.*
> *With a pocketful of money and a cellar full of beer,*
> *I hope you won't be angry for me a-coming here.*

Or:

> *A bunch of May*
> *I have brought you*
> *And at your door I stand.*
> *It is but a sprout*
> *It will spread about*
> *It's the gift of Our Lord's hand.*

Our Enstone wasn't posh enough to have a proper May Queen nor a maypole: just our jillies on a stick and a fair share-out of the precious ha'pennies and pennies, or megs'n'clods as we used to call them, at the end of the long day. Our May jinks warn't nothing to do with school, just a bit o' begging on our own account. We used to hope that Master Glover would let us out early from school on that day, but he never did. During haymaking and harvest he'd sometimes let you out early if you asked, to take the tea up to the men in the field. Sometimes he'd be a bit uppish even about that, if he copped you playing up in school that day, but he usually relented.

We had a whole half-holiday for Empire Day. We'd chant on the way to school:

> *Twenty-fourth of May!*
> *Empire day!*
> *If you don't give us a holiday*
> *We'll all run away.*

We wore a daisy in our buttonholes, and prayed at long length for all the peoples of the British Empire, 'from Greenland's icy mountains to India's coral strands', a-shunting along in their queue in their buffs and Eskimo hoods, on the big varnished geography poster on the blackboard in the big room. 'Afric's sunny fountains' always conjured up visions of old Zulu Harris, left over from the Zulu War, down the Lidstone Road. His 'sunny fountains' was the pints of golden larrup he and his tun-barrel of a wife, Mrs Bumper Harris, used to down once a month at the Litchfield Arms of a Saturday night.

Zulu were a native Zulu, a big fuzzy-wuzzy bronzed chap with a mop of frizzy grey hair, smouldering dark eyes and a broad flat nose. He always walked about, even in a heatwave, in an old tatty Dragoon uniform with all his medals up. He'd fought on the British side in the Zulu War, having a personal grudge against the Zulu chieftain of that time. When the Zulus won back Zululand he'd been shipped to safety in England. How he landed in Enstone from Africa I shall never know, but he landed a war pension: and on the last Saturday in the month, he and his wife, old Bumper, would mooch along to the post office to draw this bounty. It warn't a great lot, but good beer were only eightpence a gallon. They'd live it up at the Litchfield for this one night, and for the rest of the month reside properly sober in their little cottage in Lidstone.

Us called her 'Bumper' 'cos her were such a big piece. When her were three parts sozzled it used to take three or four of we old bwoys to haul her along the road past the Litchfield Farm—where the Higgs be now. In they days Edward Bolton farmed it and he were a chapel parson and JP. It were up to we old bwoys to be sporting and bump her out of trouble past Bolton's afore she were had up for drunkedness and fined half-a-dollar at Chippy Court. She warn't disorderly, but she were a hell of a lump to get your arms round, and if her fell down her old guts 'ud rattle like water slopping in a sink.

I liked old Zulu; he could talk sensible and interesting when he were sober, and in a more educated voice than we. But he'd never tell us how he won his Empire medals, nor about his faraway native Zulu land.

After praying for old Zulu and the rest of the Empire still

straggling across the yellowing plains of the geography poster, the whole school 'ud line up in the playground for 'the Salute'. The old battle-flag, Enstone School Union Jack, 'ud be waft-wafting with the lilac in the breeze of an Oxfordsheer May morning, fixed to a makeshift pole on the Infants' swing. We'd march, we old bwoys leading the littl'uns, to the ring of our hobnail boots and the smell of Hitchman's hops being brewed at Chipping Norton, right round the yard: looking up at the flag and saluting as we passed, and belting out in loyal tradition the old Boer War songs what was still—years after the Boer War—top of the pops on Enstone Empire Day:

> *So put my chair to the window*
> *And see them passing by.*
> *'Long live the Queen!'—that's the song they sing,*
> *'Long live the Queen!'—o'er her glorious throne ascend.*

Somewhere along the line somebody must have passed the word that the old Queen had snuffed it and Edward VII had ascended to the throne, 'cos the lyric were updated to 'King' just in time to fit George V.

Us were a right royalist lot in our Enstone. Five days after Empire Day we'd chant on the way to school:

> *Twenty-ninth of May!*
> *Royal Oak Day!*
> *If you don't give us a holiday*
> *We'll all run away.*

But they never gave us a holiday for Royal Oak or 'Shick-shack Day' as we called it. Yet we was entitled to one. When Charles II made his triumphal entry back to London and the throne on 29 May 1660, it were exactly nine years to the day after his narrow escape from old Cromwell's troopers by hiding in the oak-tree at Boscobel as they rode beneath. The king declared that 29 May, Restoration Day, would ever after be a public holiday. Somehow, over the years, our Enstone had missed out; but, faithful and forgiving to the end, we all sported a Royal Oak-apple in our buttonhole that day. If it were a Sunday you warn't properly togged up without the sprig in the lapel of your Sunday best. If it were a school day and us spotted a traitor in the playground who warn't sporting the Royal Oak we'd taunt:

> *Shick-shack! Shig-shag!*
> *Put old Crom'ell's head in a bag!*
> *Royal Oak*
> *The Whigs provoke!*

and whip 'em with stinging nettles. We was a roughish lot! But it was mostly in fun. You never hears of Shick-shack Day now. In my opinion the coming of the Liberals stopped a lot of fun. Some folks thought Lloyd George done well by the poor:

> *Hark, Lloyd George, the angels sing,*
> *Insurance tax is just the thing.*
> *Peace on earth and mercy mild*
> *Thirty bob for every child.*

but they mothers down Alley never handled that birth allowance; they just signed the doctor's paper and the doctor had it.

Another team effort when I were at school were on the Feast of Stephen, Boxing Day. Us young buggers 'ud get up a band and go niggering. They tells I 'bugger' and 'nigger' be swear-words nowadays. In my opinion any word be a swear-word if it's spake with malice; but in our country talk 'bugger' and 'nigger' be equal 'chaps'. You could get a decent bugger or a rotten bugger. We only knowed one nigger, old Zulu, and he were decent; there warn't no more about. (Cokey Smith once see'd an amazing sight. Early one summer morn, afore the birds was up, he walked along a green lane and stumbled upon a whole ring of darkies, fast asleep upon the dewy ground, their bare feet pointing to the dying embers of a camp-fire. Old Cokey were the biggest barnum for miles around. He'd see'd some fancy sideshows in his time, but he'd never see'd a sight so curious as this in all his life. In they days in deepest Oxfordsheer it be phenomenal to see *one* darky, let alone a whole

25

bunch. When Cokey sleered back with another chap to witness the vision, the chap never believed him. There be only dead embers; they'd all stealed away.)

Negro minstrels, Jolly Jack Coons, we was supposed to be when we went niggering. One 'ud play the fiddle, another the squeeze-box, or the mouth-organ, the bwoons, the triangle or the whistle— whatever spare talent were tootling around on Boxing Day. We'd black up our faces with burnt cork and go round the outlying hamlets, farms and pubs, a-singing, playing and clathopping. Even old Zulu enjoyed us and gave us a whole two-penn'orth of encouragement. We'd get a fortune, half-a-crown or more, at the big houses with their Christmas house-parties. The ditties we sang was traditional to us and made little sense, but as everybody was full of good Christmas spirits, they never noticed. 'Radford Jack' was our favourite; it had a good beat and warmed us up in the bitter cold:

> *My name is Joseph Boston*
> *I'm the fun man left in town*
> *I'm up to all the spree, my lads,*
> *In the village or in town.*
> *I'll spend thy money freely*
> *Wherever I may rove*
> *But if you ask me to stand one*
> *I'll say, 'No, not for Joe!'*
> *Not for Joe*
> *Not for Joe*
> *Not for Jo-ziff*
> *If I know-ziff!*

Joe and John were often 'Jack' in they days. Radford Jack were also the name given to the bell on the convent at Radford, in the parish of Enstone. If we could hear Radford Jack striking clear early in the morning when we was down Alley, the wind be in the east and we be in for a freezer.

Some bands of kids went niggering with a Jenny-wren in a cage, asking for 'a mite for Jinny's funeral', a tradition connected to St Stephen; but us never. Some calls her Jinny Bunt, but we always calls her Jinny Pug 'cos she holds up her little tail over her back like a pug dog.

In these days of plenty, folks shudders when you tells 'em you was glad to yut wrens as a kid. We walked afar on little food, our boots was always miles from our stomachs. We was glad to yut anything; going hunting at night with a lantern or carbide lamp, netting 'the poor man's game', the roosting blackies, thrushers and spajits. In they days the bird world were overcrowded, chock-a-block; it be truly a miracle for Our Lord to mark the fall of a spajit. Nowadays, with the spread of machines and the lack of cover, it 'ud be a bloody miracle *not* to spot it.

Our niggering money 'ud eke out the bleak midwinter with a penn'orth of humbugs, ju-jubes or blackjacks from the big glass jars in Jinny's shop. Each sweet 'ud be counted out careful by Jinny into a stiff blue cone of sugar-paper; and each meg or clod 'ud be counted out equally careful from our hankercher in payment. But the takings from the May garlanding we'd save for the greatest event of the whole year, 'Enstone Club'.

When I be older I learnt the more serious side of the Club and its providence for men who be ill and unable to work; but when I were a child I thought it be one glorious day to go on the spree with the band and the funfair.

The last Thursday in May be always Enstone Club. That date meant so much to me as a child that even today, in old age, on waking on the last Thursday in May, my first happy thought be Enstone Club. We'd count the days beforehand, gloating in private over our precious hoard of May garland megs'n'clods, resisting the terrible temptation to blow the lot at Jinny's. If you had a shilling on Club Day you be a millionaire, with your fortune, twenty-four goes on the funfair, tied up in the corner of your hankercher.

On the Tuesday evening the funfair 'ud start rumbling into Owen's fields. Owen did a lot for the fun of the village. The fair didn't crop up overnight like Banbury Fair does nowadays. There be no electric. It be all drawed and worked by horses and manpower, and took two nights and a day to set up and two nights and a day to take away. In they days that little field at the back of the Harrow and all where they council-housen be now belonged to

Owen. He'd let they showfolk graze their horses in one field and set up camp in the other, spilling out their rides and sideshows from the field all the way up the side of the road, around the giant elm that used to be outside Adams's shop, right up to the post office and up by Venvell's. They swingboats outside Venvell's 'ud swing right out across the road. There might be the odd motor, even in they days, but you'd hear him coming, hiccuping a mile off, and soon send him out the road.

The three main families of showfolk be the Cokey Smiths, the Hatwells and the Phippses. Cokey Smith had twenty-one childern twice, so he had plenty of family to run his sideshows. (Jesse Smith of Bloxham, knowed for miles around in the twenties and thirties as a good judge of horseflesh, were one of the youngest of Cokey's childern.) There were about seven in the Hatwell family. They hailed from out Cassington way. Thee'd never have associated Pa and Ma Hatwell with showfolks: always togged up to the nines like Milord and Milady, never rigged up rough as their childern was for work.

The Phippses numbered seven too; a close-knit family, on a quieter scale, sticking together with their home-made rock, knick-knack stall, and hand-turned whirligig for the littlest ones.

As soon as all the cavalcades had rumbled in to Owen's fields on the Tuesday evening, they showfolk parleyed in a ring, drawing lots out of their traditional worn leather bag for the different sites. There be no falling out; all be amicable. By general consent, chaps with roundybouts and swingboats ought to be on the level to be on the safe side; and the hoop-la and other contests involving skill ought to be on the next levels. They'd have to lop-side and skew-whiff the other stalls and sideshows 'as best as us can'. Us kids followed this important summit with nosey interest and impatience, longing for 'em to get down to the real business of unloading the rides so we could 'help', and lighting their camp-fires so we could smell the fleshpots of their roving life.

Master Glover be hard put to it to keep our wayfaring wits to the grindstone all the next long day at school: prising us off the long low school wall where we clung at playtime like limpets, looking over and down upon the billowing tide of tarpaulin and waves of bunting rising all the way up the main street, swirling round the old elm, and filling the Lidstone Road inlet. There be as yet no music till the band and the barrel-organ swelled forth on the morrow; but the paeans of preparation, the pounding of mallets, the chink of chains, the shouts and whinnies of the fairground foreigners in our midst be all wild music to our Enstone ears. As soon as us kids capered out of school at four o'clock the women of the village charged in bearing mops, brooms, bunches of Union Jacks, baskets of grub and buckets of wild flowers. Buttercups, keck, campion 'ud be plonked to overflowing in they big mustard-coloured stone jam-jars and set on the starched white table-cloths. Further jars, decked with Union Jacks on sticks, 'ud be ranged along the shelf at the foot of the Roll of Honour in remembrance of our poor growed-up scholarship kids, deprived of Club Day, stuck out in the wide wide world, a-running the Empire.

Us kids 'ud dash home from school to our own skinny backwater down Alley, polish off our tea and roly-poly pudden in record time, and clatter back up to the mainstream keeping well out of earshot of our Mam's following bellow, 'BACK BY *EIGHT*, REMEMBER!'

By nine they'd come searching for us. Maybe they'd spot us 'all ears', listening to the cluster of showfolk in the paraffin lamplight outside the pub, or nosing in at the school porch to the arch of the schoolroom beyond where the women, all the main feast prepared, was setting up a final breakfast table ready for the band's arrival first thing in the morning. But most likely they'd cop us out in the dark field gawping spellbound at the Phippses concocting one last batch of rock outside their lamplit caravan. They'd come to scold, then stay to watch the slow twisting magic of they swarthy firelit hands spelling up strings of cobwebbed sugar from the steaming cauldron below.

At last, bedded down along of my brothers in the moonlit attic, it seemed as if the whole village were hushed, lying in wait for the dawn of that golden 'Fourth Thursday in May'—Enstone Club.

First comed the band. They be hired, after much weighing of tenders (whichever were cheapest!) from Sibford or Hooky or one of they distant villages. Close on nine o'clock they'd arrive in two big wagonettes, chock-a-block with gilded braid on bright uniforms and instruments disguised in weird-shaped black cases, and pull up outside the Litchfield. They'd jump down in their best polished boots and clatter through the flagged stone porch of the school into the 'Infants' to have their breakfast and a pick-me-up. There be ample accommodation for their horses and wagons in the coaching stables behind the Litchfield.

Duly sustained, the band 'ud get fell-in outside the school. Then, led by the banner and the band, and the officials in their broad Lincoln-green or red shoulder-sashes and official Club insignia, everybody 'ud parade in their best caps and hats all down the main street to the church at Church Enstone.

It were a corking banner—took two stalwart Foresters and four Juveniles to carry it. It warn't the same banner every year—just depended on what they dished you out from headquarters at Oxford. It comed on the carrier's cart the day before and were always unfurled with deep suspense to see which one they'd sent; but it always had billowing scrolls of 'ANCIENT ORDER OF FORESTERS' and 'OXFORD' worked into it somewhere. I liked our 'JUVENILE SOCIETY no. 242' banner best. The centrepiece were a topping cwoat of arms supported by two plumed and sashed cavalier Foresters in Lincoln-green doublet and hose, with a rampant angel in swirling robes hovering overhead from the rosy sunset clouds above, and the sun itself in the form of the all-seeing eyeball of the Almighty, blazing out at you from the awe-full fiery rays, meriting every trumpeting blast of 'Thine be the glory' blown by the accompanying marching band.

Sometimes Club Day 'ud clash with Ascension Day or a threatening shower when 'Lo, He comes with clouds descending' were deemed a more appropriate approach for the banner to the church. If it were a blustery day it were a case of 'Rescue the perishing' with that giant banner acting like a mainsail, the two Rangers hanging on to the masts for dear life and the Juveniles snatching at the heavy tasselled ropes whipped from their beseeching hands.

Our old church, St Kenelm's, be filled with the moist sweet air of more jam-jars of wild flowers, with posher homage paid in garden flowers to the altar and the monuments of 'Old Wisdom', 'The Meat Charity', and other ancient parish benefactors. The organ and the band 'ud combine, swelling forth in glorious praise. (Enstone Church be always a good sounder.) The banner 'ud be blessed and prayers made for the thriving of the Club. If it were Ascension Day too the hymns 'ud be shared, fair'n'square, between the more lofty 'Come down, o love divine' and the more down-to-earth 'Oft in danger, oft in woe'. But 'Thine be the glory' be our main Club signature tune. Even today that hymn, heard anywhere in the world, from Woodstock to Chippy, on the wireless or the telly, be instantly recognized by old Enstone folk as 'Enstone Club'.

After the service the band 'ud play all round Church Enstone and down to Woodford with the banner and the parade, collecting a bob or two from all the big houses and farms. The Juveniles in their smart silk shoulder-sashes, special badges and Ancient Order of Foresters collecting-boxes 'ud have the honour of carrying the takings, which would all be used in the course of the next year to help sick workers over a bad patch. We'd work it so's we all paraded back to the school just in time for the dinner at one o'clock.

Members paid through their Club dues to go to the dinner, but the band were gived it chuck-free because they'd earned it, marching and puffing up hill and down dale. Their horses behind the Litchfield wasn't forgot, with a good drink at the trough and a special Club nosebag too. Quite a few nobs 'ud feed at the Club Dinner, honouring the occasion with their presence and a whole ten-bob note or a golden guinea on the enamel tin collecting-plate.

After all the speechifying and rendering of annual reports, the Chief Ranger 'ud extend the hand of friendship to all and declare the Club Dinner over for another year. The hard-working band 'ud resume their tour of the rest of the village, and the rest of us 'ud be free to go on the spree.

If you had no money you could still have your spree, following the band, or sitting, listening all ears to they old carters and shepherds recalling other Club Days outside the pubs, or spectatoring at the coconut-shy or the hoop-la, the swingboats or the roundybout. There warn't no generator for the roundybout, just a stout-hearted cob treading round and round, doing his shift, breeched to a frame of wooden horses. The music was made by one of they Phippses doing *his* shift on the handle of the barrel-organ.

My vice were swingboats. They swingboats were the nearest I ever got to heaven in my childhood: working yourself up with they plush velvety ropes, rushing up and back through the air, higher and higher, till you nearly went over the top and hardly knowed your head from your boots. You could feign not to notice the end of your go and sneak an extra bout, racked with the foolish fancy that he might let you have an extra go for nothing; but he'd soon skid you to a halt on that thick board strapped to the front of his shoulder, and he'd grab your best cap for hostage or soon tip you out if you was cheeky. But to the ladies he were Sir Walter Raleigh, laying down his little set of gaudy-painted steps for their dainty best shoon to step out on.

Even when you was all spun out by the late afternoon, with nary a meg left, however many times you checked in the corner of your hankercher, there were still plenty of folk to watch. The littlest 'uns having their last rides on the Phippses' hand-turned whirligig. The new wave of workers, home early from work, reviving a flagging interest in the sideshows and a fluster of late teas among the valiant women still plodding between the two tortoise stoves boiling water in the schoolroom.

Soon it were coming on for dusk. The women, puce as campion, flaked out like buttercups, gave in at last to their poor old feet. The hard-worked band, returned from the outlying parish, reassembled in our midst outside the Litchfield, and blowed their old paunch out for their traditional final tune, 'Abide with me', a signal to Mr Peachey, the landlord, that they and their horses was ready for a final topping-up drink before the long trek home.

At last they clopped away to their far-flung villages for another year, the braid on their uniforms striking one last glint in the lamps swinging gently away all along the side of the wagon into the Dark Unknown.

Back in our Enstone they garish showlamps was being strung up. They were cylindrical, made of metal, with a handle at the top and a long spout curved up from the bottom where the naked flame 'ud blaze. They was lit by a coven of showfolk huddled round the pile of lamps in the dark. Suddenly a wicked flare of flame 'ud shoot out from their midst along the ground like a fiery dragon coming to lick you up. Once they lamps was strung up, the fun of the fair hotted up.

By nine o'clock the respectable women and tiny tots was gone home. The young daredevils 'ud come out of their hides, forcing the pace faster and faster, making they flares on the roundybout whiff'n'whirl like a Catherine-wheel, working they wenches up in they swingboats, higher and higher, till they screamed like banshees, their faces flashing through the smoky sky over and under the rising moon. The noisy throng 'ud swell and jostle for turns and the showfolk 'ud shorten the rides according. If us kids could dish th'Old Folks we'd go hunting under cover of darkness for marbles in lemonade bottles, or abandoned coconuts, cocking a snook at the grown-up world at large; but they generally comed and collared 'ee home by the scruff of your limp collar by ten o'clock. 'Up the wooden hill and down Sheet Lane!' our Mam 'ud order smartish, bundling us bwoys to bed up both sets of stairs to the attic.

Fighting my drooping eyelids, lying alongside my little brother Jim clutching an empty coconut, I'd hang on for dear life to the velvet handle of distant barrel-organ music until sleep swung me out from our Mam, far below, hanging out sheets down an endless lane. My May Day megs'n'clods be all spent, but I had a hoard of precious memories that 'ud never, even in old age, be forgot.

Enstone Club Day were abandoned during the First World War but revived again during the early twenties. By then I was a fully paid-up Forester and a young carter, bloody tired from being up since four o'clock of a May morning trailing behind a horse-mower haymaking all day, but still game enough, on one occasion, to plod home on Club Day to catch the official photo being took'd. Jack Shuffel turned up that very photo the other day, and there be I, Carter Mont, bold and tieless in me working togs, grinning at the back of all they sober Foresters in their Sunday best.

The rise of motor traffic polished off the street-fair. Up till 1915 it be perfectly safe and natural to play in the street. In that heyday of the railways, before many motors come about, the main roads through villages was often deserted for hours on end. We'd stretch the skipping-rope right across, boys as well as gals all skipping in together, slacking off for the odd horse'n'cart. All the usuals, hoops, marbles, jacks, whip'n'top was played in the road. There were always at least one hopscotch marked out. Holey-holey was always played on the village green outside Adams's shop. There were a pickèd piece ideal to dig the holey pitch to cast our pebbles into. About four yards from the peck there were a telegraph pole into which we'd pull our victim in a tug-of-war. It were a roughish do—hurt 'ee if they pulled you into it—but thee dussen't flinch.

Us knowed there be motors but they was few and far between, and so slow and noisy there was ample time to finish our game of ducks'n'drakes and beat the old bone-shaker too. Squire Faulkner is supposed to have had the first motor in Enstone. It were called a 'Quad'. The driver sat at the rear and the passenger in the upholstered armchair in front. It terrified horses, so whenever a horse approached he had to stop, and his gardener ran behind to push and help him to start it again. The corner up at top end by the post office were even sharper and narrower in they days; even horse traffic was forced to travel carefully. The siccy-tree now standing free on the pavement were then enclosed deep in Johnny Adams's garden behind the wall. Mrs Adams had an old horseshoe rammed into it to anchor her washing-line. The middle section of the street were narrower too, with the village green almost creeping across to the Litchfield. It be a tightish work of art for they drays and wagonettes to wheel in one fell swoop into the inn yard. The ascent too from bottom end were steep enough to slow the traffic, though not as steep as some of the old carters remembered it when there be no bridge but a ford in the deep hollow.

As we growed older and into Top Standard at school our games ranged further afield. Fox'n'hounds were a great favourite. The two foxes 'ud go on ahead and the rest of us hounds 'ud follow. When we hollered 'Tally-ho!' they was supposed to answer. We'd run like hell. If you was too little to jump the bloody hedge the big'uns 'ud grab you by the arms and lug you over. The gals 'ud drop out if the going got tough. The foxes could part for a chain or so, if they was running either side of a path or the brook, but they was supposed to come together again soon after. Their echo 'ud play devilish tricks in these valleys and hills, and sometimes it be a job to fathom where their holler be coming from. Cricket and football we bwoys often played separate in the Adamses' fields, but we'd all congregate back on the road before nightfall for one last game of 'Jump, Jinny-wagtail' or 'Bum-the-barrel-bum'. Finally, 'Last tag top end!' somebody 'ud cry in the gloaming and we'd all chase, eyes widening like cats in the fading light, from one end of the street to t'other, dodging the catcher between.

I can just remember in 1915, the last year of my schoolhood, playing 'Jump, Jinny' all down the street in the dusk one evening when the old Super comed down the Lidstone Road in his horse-drawn police vehicle. It were a smart little four-wheeled varnished wagonette with room for four behind and two up front drawn by a brisk grey pony. The way he reined in his nag by the village school and plodded slow and heavy across to us childern, summoning us to all gather round, us knowed he were about to make an important announcement. 'Childern! Motors is coming. After tonight all you childern must no longer play in this 'ere road.'

He warn't upset over the job; he were just solemnly a-warning us like, for our own safety. But somehow, all us 'Jinny-wagtails' knowed it be the end of an era. Us didn't want to go in that night; and our mothers seemed to leave us out later than usual, bwoys and gals, Nature's childern, chasing up and down the road defying the gathering gloom, challenging 'Last tag top end!' until us couldn't see to ready-steady-go another dusty foot.

— 4 —

Bits o' Ditties

FRIDAY NIGHT WERE tubbing night. Tubbing night were the weekly bath and singing night in our family, and one of my happiest memories of childhood down Alley.

Mother and Dad 'ud work in harness, yoking the buckets of water from the well, tipping them into the big iron kettle-cauldron to heat on the range, and filling the zinc tub in front of the fire. There were no end of a steamy array of bodies, jugs and utensils a-flashing'n'flushing about in our kitchen of a Friday night. Mother 'ud tub us and Dad 'ud dry; lifting each dripping kid from the tub and plonking us on the towel on the kitchen table, he'd learn us no end of songs, or 'bits o' ditties' as he always called them.

'Over the garden wall,' 'Miner's dream of home,' 'Count your blessings.' You learnt to take no notice of the captive audience photo'd on the walls in their Oxford frames, and look straight at Dad a-drying you; holding true to your words and tune no matter what towels was buffeting, arms splashing, or jugs was spouting round you. 'Singin' costs nowt,' Dad used to say. 'When a man's a-singin' he needs no help; when a man's a-cussin', *that's* when the bugger's got trouble.'

All my life I've loved to sing. I got my love of singing from my father. And my blue eyes and open good looks—so they tells I!—from my mother.

Dad always sang at his work. I can picture him now, a-sitting in the doorway of his workshop in the hovel next to the Dovecote with that wide stirrup-leather strapped over the last on his knee and down under his instep, a-trotting out all they old Sankey hymns, tautening and slackening the strap over the last by working his foot up and down as if he were playing the harmonium.

You often heerd a man a-singing at his work in they days; singing was one of life's free pleasures. A man 'ud sing out unabashed as he strode down the village street. If thee was to sing out like that down Enstone nowadays they'd think thee'd just come out the Bell and lock 'ee up in Oxford Castle.

From earliest years most of us lifted the latch to church or chapel where choral singing was cultivated and trained. At school Master Glover could grockle fairish. He taught us tonic sol-fa, broadened us with four-part ditties from *The National Song Book*; and us was carried away at the pub on a more popular strain. In my young days the pub were the village community centre, open seven days a week, from six in the morning to ten o'clock at night, and we childern had only to lift the latch to enter. Mr Keen, the landlord of the Litchfield, and his wife and daughter were good souls unto us childern. You could always be sure of a meg or a clod if you went May-garlanding or carol-singing round the back of the Litchfield. Mr Keen never gived the whole lot to the first click, he'd always spin out his bounty so us each had a meg.

Mr Keen were a fine bass singer. When it were a wet miserable morning in the school holidays he'd have us childern in off the village green and teach us to sing unaccompanied roundelays and part-songs, just for the joy of it. Broke his heart no end when that no-childern-under-fourteen-in-a-pub law come in just in front of the First World War and us couldn't 'Row-row-row your boat' in his smoke-room no more.

He died soon after; and a pair of non-musicals, interlopers from London, took over. I missed out on the singing then but I had many a meg to make up for it, a-carrying hot love-letters between their luscious barmaid and Harold Crawford, the chauffeur up at Enstone House. She'd beckon I with melting looks to take this letter up; and he'd briben I with ha'pence to take another down. I were rattling moony-eyed up and down Road Enstone like a yo-yo. It were one in the eye for me and poor Harold when after about a year they all upped and went back to London and the flighty piece married another.

The Peacheys comed next. They was some good old sorts; comed out from Kingham way and knowed the needs of country folk. It were Mr Fred Peachey as understood the needs of old Zulu and his Bumper once a month and wangled her safe conveyance back home past the law to Lidstone. Mr and Mrs Peachey were family folk with a son, Horace (he went out to Canada but comed home years later to take over as landlord in his father's footsteps), and two daughters, Doll and Mary, nice gals who'd always talk to 'ee. Doll married Jimmy Rathbone, the blacksmith, and went back to live with him in Kingham; but Mary never married.

Mary were a topping piano-player; any snatch of tune thee sang to her, any torn sheet of music thee set before her, her 'ud pick up the remnant, full-chord, and tack on the twiddly bits. Her must have spent a fortune on sheet-music. Any new song that come out, her sought after it. 'Mary's got the latest!' 'ud travel like pop-fever round the village, and that same night a fair crowd 'ud gather around the piano in the smoke-room, fair enough to agree when Mary insisted the window should be opened so all us banished kids listening outside could join in too. As I growed into a man of fifteen and sixteen I had nice talks with Mary about the land and politics, stopping off after work to collar her before she got busy. Looking back now, I expect her was only tolerating a raw lad, struggling to fathom out what all the world be about, but her 'ud listen to I as if I were Lloyd George hisself and serve I a drink with 'You're welcome.' Ah, Mary! how welcome all they songs be that sweetened my harsh work all they years out in the fields, warming my frozen fingers and toes and making the long drudging hours to pass so much more quickly.

My favourite of all the many songs Mary taught me was 'In an old-fashioned town', because the second verse,

In an old-fashioned house in an old-fashioned street
Dwells a quaint little old-fashioned pair

reminded me of th'Old Folks, Mam and Dad. That song were number one in the charts for the whole of Oxfordsheer. It were knowed for miles around as the Witney National Anthem because the woman as wrote it were supposed to be a Miss Harris of West End, Witney. My voice bean't the same strength now I'm eighty-two, but the words be all there in my head same as Mary learnt them to me all they years ago, and I often sings them to myself to cheer me up when I'm alone. The Litchfield be all gone now and a posh housen-estate be risen in its stead. If any of ye present Litchfielders hears gwostly singing arising from your ashup of a moonlight night, don't be frit: just join in and holler along o' Mary and Mont and all they old-fashion songsters of the Litchfield Past.

Organs, harmoniums and pianos cropped up all over the place in they days. They knowed thee be in fine singing company when thee see'd they ivories worn right down to their wooden bwoons. Many a church and chapel organ were reduced to such honourable estate.

It were like putting your name down for Eton to get into the choir in my young days. Right up to the 1930s Enstone Church Choir be very choice, with Mr Thornett, the organist and choir-master, dedicating a healthy two evenings a week to choir practice, with an extra booster-shot for anthems. A far cry from later years when Enstone Choir dwindled right away to only old Zicky Harris, still faithfully holding the fort after sixty years, with a volunteer organist and 'Any difficult bits tonight, Miss Parsons? 'cos I'm on me own'—five minutes before Evensong.

Before the Great War, Enstone Church Choir were in full boom. Chisel Hawtin, one of my mates from Miss Vance's, were lucky to be in the choir from a very early age. His dad were the afore-mentioned Thomas, master-joiner, parish clerk, undertaker, captain of the bell-tower, stoker of the church boiler, and sexton in between. Chisel were lucky to have this overwhelming birthright that placed him next to the altar in the choir-stalls. True, next to the altar were the least of the choirboys, but Sunday after Sunday

I'd envy him piping away up there, exalted. It warn't his pitch but his privilege of being amongst all that fine singing that I envied.

Ted Bennett were the lead-tenor at that time and his word as a man were highly thought of by Mr Thornett, the organist. Ted's allotment run alongside of our Dad's. From a nipper I had helped Dad on our allotment, singing together, taking parts, as we worked. One day we was working in harmony, counting our blessings and planting our Brussels, when out of the blue Ted joined in. Ted's quality tenor weaving in and out of our homespun effort suddenly brought out a new fullness in my voice. At last we all stood enchanted, revelling in our final well-held note lingering over the cabbage-stumps.

'Tom,' Ted says to my Dad, 'that lad of youern sings very true for his age; why don't you let him try for the choir?'

'Trying's one thing,' says Dad, 'getting in's another.'

'Tell you what, the choir's rehearsing the Harvest Anthem tonight. I'll smuggle the lad in and try and get Mr Thornett to bend an ear to him.'

I were skulking behind this pillar for ages. The next time they stops for a post-mortem on their hallelujahs—out I pops. Up I pipes, 'Count yer blessings, name them one by one. . . .'

Mr Thornett just did peek; and so did the choir, straining their necks out of their cassocks to see who was daring to trill forth in the midst of their sacred choir practice. Mr Thornett slowly advanced towards me down the aisle. I remembered what my Dad taught me, keeping my eye without falter on Mr Thornett and holding true—even when he bent his ear that close I could have bitten it off. 'And it will surprise you what the Lord hath done!'

Mr Thornett were very surprised indeed. After a few questions he hauled me up into the chancel and stuck me at the tail end next to the altar, opposite Chisel. It were the start of a friendly rivalry between me and old Chisel that were to last all our bwoyhood, not only working our way up the choir-stalls but up to Top Standard at school as well.

I rushed from church and lifted the latch of the Crown across the way. Dad looked up from drowning his suspense. 'I'm *in*, Dad!'

Dad were that proud. 'Give my lad half a pint!' he ordered.

I joined the choir and had my first half on that same day in 1909. It be only small beer, fit for childern, but by lifting the latch of the church and the pub at the ripe old age of seven I had the deep solace over the years of having a voice and a boot in both camps. From that day forth the stwun flags of both domains were to echo my bootsteps and my bits o' ditties over the next seventy-odd years. And my faithful silver time-piece, presented to me at school when I were thirteen, clocked my coming in and my going out.

— 5 —

Bwoy–Chap

PRONTO AT HALF-PAST FIVE that morning in 1915 me and my watch turned up to work for Mr Lennox at Fulwell. I be thirteen, no longer bwoy and not yet a man. I be what they used to call on the farm 'bwoy–chap'.

I be bwoy–chap under the cowman, Mr Hopcroft. He be all right for his job, but nothing ever be all right for Mr Hopcroft. He kept his north eye on me. No matter how hard I worked or tried to please, not a word of praise nor encouragement ever passed his lips. It were 'Here, bwoy!' 'Fetch, bwoy!' just for the power of it. But he knowed his stock and he knowed his tackle; pitchforks, sheppicks, shovels, every tool in that yard had its allotted space under the ladder in the stable. If you left any tool about the byre or manger you be for it. Old Hopcroft be right in that respect; they tines be that sharp and shiny from hardwork, if stock run amok they'd stab theyselves just by glinting at 'em.

Thanks to all I had learnt in my harvest holidays in the years before the War, there warn't many jobs I didn't know how to tackle on the farm, though I lacked the speed for some and the strength for others. Then I be carefree, schoolbwoy Monty; now I be

42

'bwoy–chap' in earnest. From half-past five in the morning to half-past five at night I were lifting the latch of cowshed, stable, barn to help with the milking, the feeding, the mucking out, the ploughing and drilling too. At the end of my seven-day week I'd line up with my little candle-lantern in the dark stable alongside Franky and Polly a-stamping and snorting in their stalls, awaiting my turn to go up to the tollert in the harness room. There Mr Lennox always paid us our wages of a Friday night.

Before the War he employed a lot more, but now he were down to eight for his 350 acres. The chaps who had miles to walk home, like Shoddy Hall to Taston or Walt Freeman to Charlbury, 'ud be let to go in first. Then, before the master got down to discussing next week's important work, with the carter and the stockman, they'd shovel I out the road. 'There you be, bwoy'—Mr Lennox gave I half-a-crown. I'd take it straight back home to th'Old Folks and they'd give I tuppence back.

My first chore of a morning were to get the cows in for milking. Mr Lennox usually run a herd of forty to fifty dairy short-horns. I'd been tit-pulling since I were seven. Abel Newman, 'old Pommel', learnt me for fun. There warn't no fun about it now with old Hopcroft pitching into me at every chance: and old Pommel, with no chance at all, away at the War a-pommelling the Germans.

Abel had been in the Terriers before the War. He had been one of the first to go, on one of Mr Lennox's best horses, when war was declared on 4 August last year. Mr Lennox had no say in the matter; like all other farmers, bakers, tradesmen, he'd had his best men and nags collared by the War Office. The first British Expeditionary Force to be sent to the War was ill equipped. The Kaiser dubbed them 'a contemptible little army': but our lads fought bravely against tremendous odds, and Abel was one of they valiant 'Contemptibles'.

I were still at school when all they young men went from our Enstone. Before the War us had often mocked that gangly-legged assortment of agricultural clathoppers and broken-down nags a-playing at being soldiers in the Yeomanry. The Queen's Own Oxfordshire Hussars were their official title, but us dubbed 'em 'Queer Objects On Horses'.

Now they be mustering in earnest under the old elm on the green opposite the Litchfield: the best of labourers, the best of horses, the cream of the land. I can see them still as they were on that summer's day in 1914, laughing and calling their farewells, under starter's orders, then clattering off in a band up the village, charging for foreign parts and Charlbury Station.

I warn't as quick as a man at milking. I had to milk Lady, Daisy, Strawberry, Nell, Gertie, and last but not least have a go at Rosy. Rosy were a kicker. Her 'udn't let none of the men come nigh her. I suppose I didn't count for a man in Rosy's wild eye: but even I didn't dare milk her without a kicking strap on her. Rosy were an old roan'n'white Ayrsheer Mr Lennox had brought down from the wilds of Scotland when he came to live in Fulwell. She belonged to his old mother, and he'd brought *her* down from the wilds of Scotland too. Both of 'em resented being exiled to the wilds of Oxfordsheer.

I treated both with respect, especially Rosy. I never let her, nor any other cow, see the stool. 'Always show her the bucket, laddie,' Mr Lennox had taught me. 'A stool to a coo be too much like three sticks to beat her by.' With any other cow I had only to set down beside her, tuck my head into her old rump, and say 'Step, foot!'

'Help yourself,' her seemed to reply, stepping her dainty hind-foot out of the way to make her bag more accessible. With Rosy it'd more likely be 'bugger off' if I hadn't got that old kicking strap on her. I'd always start on her two front teats first, as Mr Lennox taught me with all the other cows; when they be in full profit, emptying the two front quarters first makes the back'uns more accessible. I *won't*! I *won't*!' Rosy 'ud squirt, resentful at first; but I'd squeeze on, regardless, until her give in—'Och! You-can-have-it. You-can-have-it'—frothing it all down into the tinted pail.

I don't know how old Rosy were, but old Mother Lennox were ninety-two and couldn't spake a word of Oxfordsheer. Whenever her fancied a touch of milking at tea-time her 'ud come tottering across the yard on her pattens with her little snow-white lace cap tied under the chin carrying her own wooden pail and milking-stool. Her 'ud whisper sweet Scottish nothings in Rosy's twitching ear, set down beside her, give her udder a pat, and get stuck in: and there they'd be, pretty as a picture. Two Scottish old'uns, all of a piece, no kicking, no strait-jacket, just the lilt of ideal milk.

I were man enough to milk but not to tip the heavy buckets of milk into the cooler. They buckets held ten or twelve gallon. While the cowmen were tipping the milk through the cooler and into the churns I'd get Polly harnessed and shut into the shafts of the float ready to take the churns to catch the milk-train at Charlbury. The regular milk-nag had gone to the War. Poor Polly were like me, new on the job and the long hard road; but us was getting over it.

All the milk was carted on they old-fashioned wide-bottomed milk-churns what you used to see in the nursery-rhyme House that Jack Built. I'd help to load them, rolling them along the yard on their strong bottom rim and up the ribbed sloping tailboard into the float.

No time to dawdle. Go-go-go! Trotting along the narrow leafy Fulwell Lane, up to the ancient Hoar Stwun, left along the turnpike. 'CHARLBURY 3 mls' spake the milestwun half-way along the Furze; 'CHARLBURY 2 mls' down New Piece. Other milk-floats swelled the rattling cavalcade, from Dean, Taston, Spelsbury, until we slowed at 'CHARLBURY 1 ml' at the top of Banbury Hill and put the drag on if it were slippery before we descended into the waking market-town of Charlbury. Wheeling right at the Bull and left at the White Hart, we'd clatter down the last lap between the high-banked houses on Station Hill, with their smart sash windows and early-morning smoke uncurling from their tall stone chimneys. Smoke rising too from the distant waiting-room chimney at the station in the sleepy hollow beyond the river; and far to the right along the valley, past Mr Townsend's high farm at Walcot, wisps of smoke threading in and out of the racketing landscape from the invisible train diddle-dee-dumming along the water-meadows from the Vale of Evesham.

Floats, horses, cowmen crowded into the station-yard from the surrounding countryside, clocking in to the booking-office as the train steamed under the arched bridge and into the busy station. It were all very official. They'd record in a big ledger how many churns you was sending and collecting; you signed and they signed. It were the same pallyaver all over again in the evening. The clatter of churns, shouts of men and hiss of steam were all very exciting: but there were no time to be sociable. The GWR milk-train waited for no man; all they posh London folks was waiting at the other end, billy-cans poised, for fresh country milk with their porridge.

As soon as I got back from the milk-run I had to feed the calves, learning them to feed from a bucket by offering them my fingers dipped in milk. Their rough tongues were sore on my chaps and chilblains, and their butting horns were hard on my skinny ribs: but us got over it.

Calves fed, I harnessed Bowler, the big roan gelding, into the water-cart to fetch the water for the cooler. I had to watch old Bowler; he were a biter. He'd waggle his old ears fairish at me whenever I comed near, but I warn't a-feared of him. I had to pump the water from the well half-way down the road from the farm. There be thirteen wells in Fulwell, none of 'em much cop. This one had two spouts, a low one for normal filling and a high one for filling tanks on wagons. You pumped easy and short to work the bottom spout, and swept high and down hard to force the water out the top one. It took me no time at all to discover you had to stuff a sock up the bottom spout; a bit longer to realize it were best to park old Bowler facing downhill away from the farm, else he were apt to take off if he saw the rest of his team being led out to the field and leave you high and dry on the end of the handle; and much longer to discover it averaged thirteen hundred 'pumps' to fill the cooler. It weren't much of a holiday: but us got over it.

From nine to half-past we was signalled to eat our bite of lunch. Then comed the farming-out, thoroughly brushing down and sluicing the cowsheds and byres. I'd done it all with Abel's cheerful whistling accompaniment before the War, but now it were Mr Hopcroft's surly 'Bwoy! Come 'ere! Be you deaf?' and a box on the ear to send I lumbering across the yard. By twelve o'clock I were that knackered I hadn't had time to glance at my watch. I were more than ready for my bit of tucker.

Keeping as far off as I could from old Hopcroft I'd sit with the men, fish in my tucker-bag and open up my tommy-cloth hoping to find 'man's grub'—a hunk of bread and cold bacon with a thumbpiece of bread—so's I could be a man like the others, cutting off a tidy piece of bread and bacon from under my thumb to eat with my pocket-knife. But more often than not it 'ud be bwoy–chap's grub, bread'n'lard'n'onion or a cold end of roly-poly pudden, anything th'Old Folks wanted yut out of the road, and a bottle of cold tea. Always cold tea, even in the middle of winter. Warn't no use putting in hot tea; hot tea always frez quicker than cold.

Most winter afternoons was devoted to making the feed for the cows. A proper concoction of a feed it were: breaking up the cake, cutting up the chaff, pulping the turnips, swedes, mangel-wurzels with the cutter or the shredder or the pulper. A layer of chaff, a layer of pulp, and so on, in a big juicy yup on the yard.

On a Saturday I'd have to work twice as hard to pulp enough feed for Sunday because though Mr Lennox believed in keeping holy the Sabbath-day, the animals had to be fed, and I worked a seven-day week. The trouble was, instead of developing into Mr Universe I were more like the Long Lad of Enstone, with me navel stuck to me back-bwoon and me aching boots ever distant from me aching stomach.

You just accepted life as it comed in they days. All over England there was bwoy–chaps like me a-getting on with it and over it. Despite old Hopcroft, work warn't all misery. Mr Lennox bean't bad as bosses go. He were what us called 'a daycent bugger'. He'd gained his farming the hard way, picking it up from harsh experience in the wilds of Scotland and learning from his mistakes; and he warn't averse to imparting his hard-won knowledge to a raw lad as was eager to learn. 'Come on, Mont,' he'd say, 'I'll learn ye to thetch a rick' or 'calve a coo'. Since I were only eight or nine he'd liked me to help him with the calving because my hands was smaller than his.

It were thanks to Mr Lennox giving I the chances that I became all-round on the farm. Most farm-labourers was fashioned to be handy all round in they days. It were Shepherd Akers as learnt I to plough when I be still at school.

It were in the harvest holidays, culling time, and I were up in

Henel Field helping Shep to cull the ewes for market. All I knows about good shepherding I learned as a bwoy with Shepherd Akers, or 'old Spurgeon' as the men called him. He lived across the fields in the lone Henel Cottage, but it be all pulled down now. On that day in 1910 I were catching the sheep with a handy lasso he'd fashioned out of a leather strap; and he were examining their mouths, udders and feet, and a-stamping them for market. We'd got old Bowler up there giving us a hand, humping all the hurdles and whatnots. Mr Lennox came up very near dinner-time. 'Finished, Tommy?' he asks old Shep, and they has a jabber over the culled ewes. Then he announces, 'I've brought old Beauty up with the geo-tack. Take Mont to New Piece with Bowler and Beauty and learn him how to plough this afternoon.'

It took two afternoons. It warn't hard to learn once I'd got the feel of the plough. You hadn't got to push'n'twist'n'do, you had to let Bowler and Beauty do most of the work.

'Thee cetch holt and let 'em go,' Shep says. 'If it doan't kayp to the furra, us can alter the cock.' Patient old soul! He took no end of trouble with me, showed I how to alter the cock, gave I insight into all they little tactics, and cheered I on to the end of the furrow. Most of these fields around Enstone be on the big oolite rock. You can't set a plough at one end of the field and have it right for t'other. You start on maybe only four or five inches of soil, then have it brashy, with stwuns getting stuck in your coulter, and then go beautiful down in the hollow.

I had to turn fromard all the time, 'cos that were the side of the big plough-wheel and I'd got the shellboard to help me keep the balance. If I comed t'ward I be on the little wheel and I warn't man enough—you had to sit skew-whiff with that old plough-handle up behind your rump and bear down with the weight of your body—to turn the horses without the plough tipping over. It were easier when he taught I to baulk taters; I could turn either way then 'cos the wheels on a baulker be both the same size.

I soon got the quiff on it. Proud as a turkey-cock I be when I surveyed my first few wobbly furrows. Moy-hoy! my legs be wobbly too, and my arms that weak and useless. Shepherd Akers had to help me on to old Beauty's back to cadge a lift back to the farm with Bowler-the-Biter in tow at a safe distance.

By the time I were thirteen I were already working the land regular by myself between my cow work. There warn't so much feed to be concocted at times and I'd be set to the plough, sometimes on my own with not a soul in sight, sometimes with other teams in concert. A strong bond was felt between bwoy, man, and carter, and with those who had trod the earth before us; and on a crisp morning when the tilth were turning easy, and we could lift our eyes at times from the dark earth to the sunlit uplands, a leading voice 'ud launch on the still, frosty air:

> *When the trumpet of the Lord shall sound*
> *   and time shall be no more*
> *And the morning breaks eternal, bright and fair*
> *When the saved of earth shall gather over on the farther shore,*
> *And the roll is called up yonder we'll be there . . .*

and we *were* there, soprano, tenor, bass, schooled to harmonize in church, chapel and pub, turning our steaming teams in jingling unison. Snatching a breath to give our last echo a chance to catch up over the new-ploughed furrow, we'd roll forth again across the listening landscape:

> *When the roll (when the roll) is called up yonder*
> *When the roll (when the roll) is called up yonder*
> *When the roll is called up yonder—WE'LL BE THERE!*

When the going were bad there were not a snatch of breath to spare. It took the concerted effort of four horses, Carter Maycock and me on the one plough to draw a single furrow. Carter Maycock 'ud have *his* hands full, wrestling with the plough, and I'd have *my* hands full, leading the two foremost horses, my hands high in the air between them, my legs yanked to earth by the weight of the mud on my boots, my arms yanked from their sockets every time the horses tossed their dripping heads in extra effort. It were a long hard day for a growing lad, and my body were racked and sore at the end of it; but us got over it.

Mr Lennox reckoned I were good with horses. He used to put

me in with the colts when they was being weaned. They was less frightened with me than with a grown man. I supposed they sensed I were but a young colt too. Carter Maycock liked to start to wean them when they was about three months old, easing the mares back into one or two hours' work in the hay or harvest field. I had to black out the light in the little stable and keep the colts shut in there. They'd be clombering up the stalls, raring to get out to their mothers. If I neglected but a chink of daysight they'd have been through the window. I had to stay in with them to stop them harming theyselves. It were like a madhouse at times. No sooner had I calmed one down off the manger, another'un 'ud be on its hind-legs clobbering the hayrack. One colt on its own were often more of a battle, relentless: whereas a calming effect on one 'ud gradually spread to the whole nuzzling bunch.

Then they'd smell their mothers coming back from their work in the fields, and the whole shenanikin 'ud start all over again. I had the devil of a job to slip out to milk each mare a little by hand before her colt could be let to suck. It were important to get rid of any stale, overheated milk in her teats and to stop the colt over-gorging to make up for its fast. Gradually the colts came to look on me as a comforter, smelling of mother's milk and all, but weaning 'em were a painful process.

Another job I hated when the cows was out in the summer was fetching down the odd calves. When a cow were going to calve her 'ud sleer off away from the herd to confine herself in private. 'BWOY!' the dreaded clarion call 'ud sound from Mr Hopcroft. 'Take that wheelbarrow up to top field and fetch that fresh calf.'

Have you ever tried loading an animated set of bagpipes? A calf be worse. No sooner had I folded one leg on board than another half-dozen hit I in the face. The mother be no help, specially if she be a heifer: attacking I black'n'blue with her horns, no matter how hard I tried to explain that I be succouring not stealing her first-born. Her 'ud keep up the attack, bunting I in the backside, sending I stumbling all the way down the hillside to the bottom gate. As soon as I set the barrow down to open the gate her 'ud tip him out. By the time I'd scooped him all up again, the gate had shut. I be all on me own as usual. It were much easier if Polly were available: then us went together with the cart, loaded the calf so its front legs flopped over the tailboard, and the mother 'ud follow, nuzzling it, with Polly and me safe up front. *That* were a rare luxury. Collecting one calf in a barrow all by myself when I were thirteen be more knackering than culling a whole flock of sheep with Shepherd Akers. Even fetching in the bull were an easier task than fetching in the calf—or it *were*, until I had a near-do with George the Third.

I were fourteen by then. Mr Hopcroft had moved on at the hirings, as most agricultural workers did in them days, and a new cowman had come. It were my job to feed and clean the bulls. Mr Lennox usually kept two bulls, a young'un he'd reared from a calf, and an old'un he'd bought in from elsewhere.

George the Third were the old'un. He were good on the job: a big red-roan fellow, a smartish Bovril-looking chap. Like his regal namesake, he had periods of insanity when he had to be kept shut up, but between whiles he were docile enough. He were even turned out to graze with the cows when none of 'em was in an interesting condition. 'All right to turn the bull oot with the coos this morning?' Mr Lennox 'ud ask the head cowman. The cowman 'ud consider careful. It be always a tricky question; most weeks there was a cow calving, and her usually come back into service, or 'bulling' as we calls it, after one month.

That morning the new cowman had sounded the all-clear, and George were grazing in the meadow with the herd. Meanwhile a man from Church Enstone had brought his cow, Delilah, into the yard to be served. The cowman had got the little bull in all ready. There were some misunderstanding; the man didn't want the littl'un, he wanted George the Third. 'Run and fetch George the Third, bwoy!' And off I sets.

I couldn't understand it. I'd brought the old bwoy along to serve many a time, good as gold, on my bull-stick; he be usually only too willing to be led to the altar. But today he were stubborn, 'udn't let me fasten the stick to his ring, snorting his big beefy nose away, stomping the ground. The men down on the far gate into the yard could see I were having trouble. George were getting nastier and nastier. Even the cows were backing off. Except Maudie, hot little

Maudie, her were BACKING ON! George put his head down at me and bellowed. I fled, hooves pounding after me.

'Stand behind the tree, laddie!' Mr Lennox's strained voice stabbed the jolting landscape. I see'd—clump of trees in middle of field—lone tree nearer gate—men on gate—Mr Lennox starting up the field. If I stopped at the clump George 'ud turn and chase back. I made for the tree nearest the men, doubled back round and stood trembling. George thundered past and stopped, sensing I were there and he'd been double-crossed. Goodness knows what'ud have happened next if Delilah hadn't bellowed, 'Come on, Gorgeous!' And her 'Samson', swishing his tail, swaggered through the opened gate.

Poor George! Mr Lennox never again allowed him to graze with the herd—said never again 'ud he subject his men to such risk. I felt proud to be dubbed 'men'; but I felt sad, taking such a powerful chap for walkies up and down the dusty lane at Fulwell, chained to a bull-stick. Very like they must have felt who fettered the real George the Third at the end of his royal tether.

There was days as a bwoy–chap when you be dogsbody part of a team, haymaking, harvesting, threshing; and there was days when you was dogsbody slaving all on your own and never see'd nor heerd a soul. I were working the land all on me own one day when I were fourteen; it must have been first Monday in June, 'cos it were Charlbury Market. I were working with two mares, Daisy and Violet. Mr Lennox had bought them as a new team some months before, and when we broke 'em in and collared 'em we discovered that they both be in foal. Mr Lennox had told I to keep working 'em at their own pace, giving 'em a rest whenever they wanted. It were best for 'em to keep working rather than standing in a stall swelling their legs, or grazing all day getting over-fat. It was obvious they was getting near their time, but not knowing the date they was served, us didn't know when they was due.

Daisy were a slow patient plodder, but Violet were a kicker and apt to get het up. They was good for each other; Violet 'ud chivvy dozy Daisy, and Daisy 'ud calm her, gazing round at her with her big velvety eyes as if to say, 'What's the fuss? *Plenty* of time!'

Us stopped for grub at twelve o'clock, dinner-time. They had their nose-bags and I had my tommy-cloth. We was all unharnessed, lying down in the shade for a rest, when I noticed that Daisy were discharging fairish. I led her back down to the farm, put her in the stable with plenty of fresh straw, and went to fetch Mr Lennox.

I couldn't find a soul. We was getting less and less on the farm, with every able-bodied man nabbed for the War; but the barn, the byre, the bothy were that silent and medieval, it were like every serf had gone to the Crusade. Nobody in the stables, the cowhouse, the pigsty, the rickerd. I were worried about Daisy and getting more and more het up. I ran to the farmhouse and lifted the latch of the Lennoxes' kitchen.

Mrs Lennox, up to her elbows in flour at the kitchen table, looked up in surprise.

'Daisy's having her foal, mam. Where be marster?'

'Gone to Charlbury Market. Carter and Shup have gone too. They'll be hame for the milking at three.'

'Three!' I glanced at my shaking watch. It were only half-past twelve.

'Her can't manage all on her own, mam,' I pleaded. '*Thee*'ll have to come.'

'Me? I'm not coming. I'm afeard of horses. 'Sides I wouldn't know the first thing about it.'

'But thee's had childern.'

'I haven't had *horses*.' She calmly began to roll out her pastry. 'You'll have to manage on your own. You've helped the marster calving often enough.'

My belly sank to my boots. True, I'd helped the master, but never all on me own. I'd never see'd a foal borned—didn't even know if it comed from the same quarter.

'Away wi' ye,' she chivvied. 'You know where he keeps the 'pothecary box. Get on with it!'

Snivelling like a four-year-old, I blundered out into the bright day. I ran with the battered old leather 'pothecary box to the stable, praying hard to the Lord to make Daisy all right and I 'udn't have to use any of the contents.

The stables were strangely quiet as if waiting for a performance.

Daisy were lying patient in the straw just as I'd left her. I sank down at her bottom end. There were a terrible amount of it. I opened the 'pothecary box. There was a terrible amount of *that* too: tinctures of this and spirits of that, each in its own glass-stoppered bottle. 'Linctus,' 'Lotion,' 'Poison,' 'Potion,' instruments, cords, siphons, help-meets for every catastrophe, each in its own rigid compartment. All I recognized were a little bottle of iodine and another of smelling-salts; both spelt calamity. I shoved my face on my fists and blubbed like a babby. Daisy slowly lifted her head and looked round at me with her velvety eyes. 'What's the fuss?' her seemed to say. 'Us'll get over it.'

And us did. I wish I could say that but for my heroic skill the greatest little grey foal in all the world 'ud never have been borned, but the truth is Daisy doned most of the job. I *think* I made his entry into the world a bit easier by sponging away the sticky veil over his nose so he could breathe, and getting the extra tongue out of the way so's he didn't suck it back and choke; but I expect she'd have got over that too. The sweetest music to my ears be the contented snuffles, snorts and licks Daisy made over her first-born. How proud I be later, when I took Mr Lennox into the stable to show him, and the foal came tottering, not to my master but to me, as if to say, 'Thanks, Mont, for helping me into the world.' Mrs Lennox rewarded me with a fresh-baked apple-turnover.

And I come home.

～— 6 —～

Home

IN THE EARLY MORN OF THIS CENTURY you'd see Frank Packer cycling with his tripod and tackle all over the district, photographing the picturesque and peculiar. He had his studio by the Horse Fair at Chipping Norton. At the beginning of 1915 he came upon our Mother and a motley muster of men, women and childern doing the oak-barking in the depths of Heythrop Forest.

All over the land the mighty oaks, like the valiant horses, was being requisitioned by the War Office. They was needed for warships, wedging them up on our Oxfordsheer oaks for repairs and refits; and their bark was needed for all they 'Sam Brownes', millions of 'em, destined despite Mother's gigantic saw and the Sergeant-Major's spit and polish to be finished in Flanders mud. The term 'Sam Browne' were Army slang for only the wide 'Sam Browne's Cavalry' belt at first, but 'to Sam' and 'to finish' be old terms for leather dressing, and sam-browne were the shade achieved by tanning to the Army's requirements with oak-bark, so

'Sam Browne' later engirthed the whole of an officer's leather harness and his mount's as well.

The only protective head-gear for this dangerous task in the forest were your own hat and common sense. Mother wore no hat, not that she belittled the danger; she had only one hat, her wide black straw best, but she had more than her share of common sense. For the laying in of babies and the laying out of bodies it were always, 'Fetch Mrs Abbott,' and our Mother went. Her bare grey head, dusty, defiant little nose and still lissom figure were caught working in the wedge of sunlight slanting through the trees, and Mr Packer singled her out for one of his photos.

Mother were that flattered at being sought for this unusual purpose she determined to snap up the chance for her childern as well. After hearing how much a proper studio group would cost, she set about saving a little of her oak-barking every week until Christmas when me, Gil, Jim and Fred found ourselves all togged up at Mr Packer's: me in a real man's collar'n'tie and my silver watch, the others in starched 'dinner-plates', as we used to call they wide starched collars lads wore outside their jackets, tied with a black bow. There we was, standing solemn, eyeing Mr Packer; at least, we assumed it were Mr Packer, a body bobbing about under a black cloth all over the shop.

'*To Horace from Home,*' Mam wrote on the back of that photo, his first Christmas away from home in the Navy in the War, to prove that home in the remnant of we four boys was still existing: for it were thanks to her beloved Horace as breadwinner when *he* were thirteen that home had survived at all.

In ought-eight [1908] our Dad were very ill and our Mam had just had baby Fred. Jim were two years old, Gil were three, and I were just five. Our Dora were second-mother at nine, and our Horace had just left school. All Mam had coming in for the eight of us to live on were Horace's five bob a week. This was double the usual wage for bwoy–chap, but we was lucky that he were working for Magistrate Bolton on the Litchfield Farm. Mr Bolton dispensed strict justice in the court, but he were also a Methodist minister and tried to dispense Christian charity at home. Despite Horace's support, our Mam were at the end of her tether, trying to breast-feed the baby, keep Dad alive, and the family together. She disdained charity but in the end there were nothing for it but to go to the Parish. The Parish Relief were connected to the Board of Guardians at the workhouse in Chipping Norton. Leaving my big sister Dora to look after Dad and us three bwoys, she took baby Fred with her in case he needed a feed on the way, and trudged the five miles to Chippy to plead our case.

The Board of Guardians be mostly formed of local tradesmen. The majority were on it for the public good, the rest for their private pocket. Unfortunately a local miller were on duty that day. He sold pig-feed to the poor; most families struggled to keep a pig in they days. If our Mam had kept a pig he'd have awarded her enough relief, providing it were spent on his food, and a bit over. Mam told him she were sorry she couldn't afford to keep a pig, she were struggling to keep childern. He awarded her one loaf a week, and she trudged all the way home again.

Without our Horace's five bob a week, our Dad 'ud have been under the ground and we'd all have ended up in the workhouse. The workhouse were the ultimate disgrace in they days. We owed so much to our Horace. Mother always had a soft spot for him, and so did we old bwoys. He were worth every tortured moment of standing stiff and still in our best serge Norfolk jackets and knickerbockers to have our picture took'd for his Christmas present.

By ought-nine Dad were well over his illness and back to his boot-making. Working harder than ever before, determined that never again would his family be reduced to the Box, he subscribed to the Club, the Ancient Order of Foresters Friendly Society, a Friend in Need is a Friend Indeed. We bwoys was subscribed for too as Juveniles until we be swore in to full Foresters at sixteen.

By ought-ten things was a bit easier. I were eight, earning a penny or two driving home the wagons from the fields for Mr Lennox or running all over the place with medicines for babies and missives for barmaids. Our Dora, wise beyond her years, were a capable eleven-year-old, skivvying out of school hours for busy farmers' wives and harassed mothers. Horace, still ploughing his all into Mr Bolton's acres, suddenly decided he were fed up with the land, he were off to the Navy. Enstone be about the furthest from the sea you can get in Great Britain. Dad couldn't have been more surprised if he'd announced he were off to the moon; 'What thee wants to join the Navy for?'

'To see the world. I see'd enough of our Enstone.'

Horace started the rot to the Navy in our village. By 1913, that last Christmas before the Great War, I counted *twelve* sailors, all Enstone lads, skating in their bellbottoms on the ice in Chaundy's Meadow. The brook used to flood fairish in they days and when it frez it made a topping lake for sliding and skating. All of 'em had HMS and the name of their ship woven in capitals on their hatband; later, during the War, for reasons of security, it were docked to only HMS.

Christmas 1913 the War hadn't started. I can see our Horace now, HMS AGINCOURT, a proud figurehead, sailing along on the ice, leg raised to the side, towing George Knight, Jack Jones, Frank Benfield and Phil Regan, all stringing along in his wake like a line of bunting; our Enstone Navy dressed over all on the frozen brook before the icy sea swallowed 'em up in the War.

Our Horace were the only one to survive his ducking; and so did Mam's photo of us bwoys with her washed-out writing on the back: '*To Horace from Home, a merry Xmas, and a bright New Year.*' But 1916 warn't all that bright for Horace: and we old bwoys never recovered clarity, still surviving in that photo, faded youths preserved in brine, having been dunked with Horace several times in the bitter North Sea, as one ship after another were sunk in the Battle of Jutland. At one time, milling around in the water, were crews from three different vessels.

'Wheer yer from?' asked Horace, hauling yet another half-conscious body into the lifeboat.

'Church Enstone,' came the wistful reply.

'I joined the Navy to see the world,' says Horace, 'not another silly bugger from our Enstone.'

The trouble was, our Horace be only a signaller and the other silly bugger be Petty Officer, Frank Bennett, but I reckon rank gave precedence to rescue on that occasion.

With fourteen of our ships sunk in the Battle of Jutland and so many of our skaters lost at sea, th'Old Folks could hardly believe it when our Horace and his photo won through.

'It's a miracle,' said Dad.

'It's that fota,' said our Mam.

Mother were Mary Ann and Dad were Thomas Henry. As I said before, we Abbotts was definitely lower orders, rough and ready, but we was brought up in the straight and narrow, according to the Good Book.

Mother kept us clean and mended. Her hands was quick and deft, always patching patches, passing our tackle down to the next, and turning the good bits of remnants to further use and reach-me-downs; worn sheets to new tommy-cloths, old sugar-bags to fresh aprons. Sugar was sold loose at the shop from long narrow close-woven sacks. Mother 'ud beg the empty sack for thripence, cut it open careful, wash it, stitch it, and iron it into a long strong coarse apron for doing her chores. She never went up to the hovel without returning with a load of treen, small offcuts of wood, in her coarse apron. Nothing were ever wasted, time, treen, twine. The strong sugar string from round the top of the sack were cherished for tying the cloth of the daily roly-poly pudden.

> *O for a roly-poly Mother used to make.*
> *Roly-poly, treacle-duff,*
> *Roly-poly, that's the stuff.*
> *Only to think about it makes my tummy ache*
> *O Lor' lummee! I wants my Mummee*
> *And the puddens she used to make.*

How they used to laugh when I sang that solo unaccompanied for fun in the crowded tap-room at the pub! Now there be no tap-room, no Mother, and no roly-poly, and I means every word.

Mother's roly-poly every day for dinner in some form or other were the staff of life to we growing lads. Sometimes, if we was lucky, it were savoury 'be-acon jack' with a bit of bacon and herbs wrapped in it, sometimes it were sweet with a few plums and treacle, but more often it were plain, tied in a clean cloth and cooked in the big iron kettle-pan with the vegetables. Moy-hoy!

That was good! 'Specially in July time with all the new young veggies, and the new potatoes sweating out their pearly bubbles. Thank God for Dad's allotment and that Act of William IV that had set aside land for the relief of the poor in our parish. How they women of Mother's generation worked to prepare and stretch enough food for their families! Our Mother 'ud cook a whole nourishing meal for her big family in one pot over the one hob. Now they has umpteen pots, hobs, and even ovens to serve a dollop of frozen peas and one fish finger.

For Christmas dinner Mother 'ud get a rabbit from old Jack Claridge. He were official vermin-catcher, earth-stopper and walnut-basher to the Heythrop Estate. He walked with a limp and a stick, and always a sack of something, often *moving*, on his back. He'd catch live rats and carry them, often to the dismay of other passengers, on the carrier's cart to Oxford and sell them to the undergraduates for their terrier hunts. He'd bash the walnut-trees to raise their sap, and collar all the walnuts on the trees around Enstone. There were loads of walnut-trees around Enstone in my young days, but they was mostly felled for valuable timber and veneers for wireless cabinets, radiograms and television cabinets in the thirties, forties and fifties. Many an early posh car was fitted out inside with walnut too. Jack sold the nuts, counted by the penn'orth or measured by the gallon, 'cos a penn'orth were all we childern could afford and a gallon were the only measure Jack possessed.

Owen Regan, the landlord of the Harrow, saved us several times from starving when I were a bwoy. Owen were a giant among landlords. He were six foot or more. He growed the biggest belly I ever see'd, not from beer—he hardly ever drank—but from grub. You never see'd such yups of tack as Owen could knock back. As a boy I used to clean out his pigsties on a Saturday. He thought the greatest reward he could give a chap were to feed him. He'd sit me down before a mount of victuals. 'Set thee chair back, bwoy! Lave room for thee belly! Yut till thee navel reaches the table!' and what I couldn't vanquish he'd let me take prisoner, home to the others.

He were knowed as Pouch or Paunch Owen. He kept the Harrow for forty years and when he died at twenty-two stwun they had to launch him out of the bedroom window. He were 'born on the strength', as we used to say in they days, when your father were in the regular Army and carted his wife and childern with him around the world. I knowed him first when I were only a little lad and he used to keep the half-pub, the off-licence, at Barton. (Barton were sometime knowed as Bereton, 'bere' being the Old English word for barley.) He were thin as a whippet in they days, which was just as well, his half-pub being the Hole in the Wall where he'd pass out the beer from his limited premises. When he wanted to expand he moved to Enstone and the ever-open Harrow.

His log fires in the smoke-room and the taproom were like him: roaring, generous, with great trunks stuck out into the room. He had huge hands with tremendous strength in his fingers. It were quite a sight to see a foaming gallon of beer, four pints in each great hand, ascending from the cellar followed by the rest of giant Owen. He'd warn any troublemaker only once, 'Sup up and get up.' Any further trouble, they huge hands 'ud swoop like grabs and lift the startled offender in one almighty chuck up six steps and into the street.

The best Christmas we ever had as childern were thanks to Owen. I were a starving bwoy of ten before the First World War. We was still feeling the pinch badly at home. Owen asked Dad if I could go up to the mansion at Heythrop on Christmas morning to accompany his wife back home through the forest. Mrs Regan were a good cook, and whenever the Brasseys had more guests than their chef could cope with, he'd send word to Owen for her to come and give him a hand.

It were another world up there. Everything were done on the grand scale with an army of servants and workmen. The stables and coach-houses was that posh and employed such a multitude the stud groom were allowed to run his own pub on the premises. There were a team to man the gas-house where they made all their own fuel to light the mansion: and a bothy, a sort of hostel, where all the under-gardeners lived. There was several head gardeners, toffed up to the nines like lords, holding sway over their 'ticular territories, the glasshouses, the mile-long borders of fantastical plants, the nuttery, the bowling-green, the croquet lawn. There was two lakes, one cascading into the other, where perch 'ud gather in a herd in the summer and men 'ud gather in a barge in the winter to collect the ice to build the rick to supply the ice to make ice-cream and cool the wine. That rick 'ud stand, well covered with straw and bracken, to last all summer to cool the fevered brow and shrink swellings if needs be. Mrs Brassey retained a trained nurse full-time for the parish, and bought every bwoy a new pair of boots and every gal a new warm cloak every Christmas. Them Heythrop red riding-hoods was the envy of every little gal in Enstone parish: and the boots 'ud have been a godsend, especially that Christmas, in our family.

I crept inside the back portal to wait for Mrs Regan. The chef were Italian, hadn't a word of English. He were like a tight round bomb about to go off through his high hat at any moment. He tasted everything, rolling his eyes, smacking his lips, flashing his big white teeth, flinging his arms about, jabbering off the top of his head, swivelling on his heels and darting off in all directions for further flavours. His hands were podgy yet swift and nimble. He had a wicked knife and a clanging steel hung from hooks on his broad leather belt, and with these he ruled supreme. I were terrified of him at first. I could see him chopping up little bwoys into puppy-dogs' tails and relishing 'em like nobody's business.

Mrs Regan warn't quite ready. A butler-chap asked me if I'd like to earn a bob or two sweeping the snow off the front-door steps. The chef yells at me, jabbering in Italian. I couldn't understand a word but I got the gist: I were to come straight back to the kitchen when I finished.

I had a job to fathom which were the front-door steps, the mansion were built to face equally posh in all four directions. I done 'em all. It were biting cold and the soles of me boots warn't all that special, but us got over it. The butler-chap were that pleased at the way I done 'em he gived me *fifteen* bob. And when he showed the chef my work *he* loaded me up with two brown-paper carrier-bags stuffed with apples and pears, nuts and oranges, and half a cooked ham. I were a laden godsend that Christmas to our Mam eking out her one rabbit.

Despite Owen's ladling out, Dad's allotment and Mother's thrift, there were never enough. All our young lives we knowed what it were to go hungry; and there were many more families in the same boat. No matter how much we giants fee-fi-fo-fumm'd we had only our ration of tucker out in the fields all day; and when we crowded round the kitchen table for our one main meal there were only our one helping of pudden in the pot. I've always been tall and thin. 'Give it the long bloke,' strangers used to say if there be any victuals left over, 'he looks as if he could do with some stuffing!' I couldn't; my belly warn't used to it. Even today, when I can more afford, I don't stint, but I can't stuff.

Yet it never harmed we much to do without, apart from the usual colds and coughs. Our Mam 'ud use that black-jack-tack made with boiling water, and we'd sit, boots and elbows in a tangle, huddled round the big bowl on the kitchen table, breathing in the healing fumes with a sheet over our heads. At night she'd leave a raw onion downstairs to draw the germs and give her and Dad a bit of peace in their room from us a-coughing, on and on, up aloft.

Mam never had enough money for us all to have a haircut together, even though Teddy Capes only charged a penny. We had to have it done at lengthy intervals. Teddy 'ud shape us up outside his back door along of his prize sweet-peas in the summer. In winter we'd lift the latch and have it done in his candlelit hovel. They littl'uns in petticuts having their first haircut 'ud yell like hell, and the old'uns having their penny Saturday-night shave 'ud sit there, solemn as prophets as he shaved 'em with a cut-throat, raked out their beards with a comb, and trimmed 'em with the shears. He were Gardener Capes up at Braybrooke's, so he knowed well how to prune.

I don't know how our Mam managed on so little. She kept everything very clean, loved to make poor things look their best, and was in great demand for corpses, convalescents and confinements. Yet she had very little of much cop in the way of chattels. Her two best treasures be Mother's plaques and Mother's tea-caddy. These plaques be a set of carved clay pictures of decent country folk, reapers and gleaners, stopping in the midst of their labours to say their prayers. Wherever home shifted over the years it warn't home for our Mother till they plaques was fixed up on the best wall. Took a whole family gathering to nail 'em up with due reverence.

Mother's tea-caddy be a home in itself, a Swiss chalet with log roof for lid and a slim bottom drawer with a precious hoard of shirt-buttons. Shirt-buttons was like gold-dust in our house. I have that caddy yet; it still houses my bit of tea, and amongst they old linen buttons, one of Mother's best jet.

Jet were all the rage when Mother were young: buttons, beads, brooches, bracelets were fashioned in this hard glossy stone, polished and cut like black diamonds. Mother had jet buttons all down the bodice of her best frock, and a posh row of jet beads from her Granny for special occasions. Her had grace, good skin and bright blue eyes; her could look the real lady, togged up for best in her old-fashioned tackle of a Sunday. With her smooth silver-grey hair braided up at the back, her silver brooch with 'Mother' on it, and all her jet, her 'ud glow and sparkle lovely when her moved in the lamplight. Our old Dad were lucky to cop his Mary Ann.

It warn't difficult to see, looking at that photo of Dad in his younger days, draped nonchalant against the tasselled sofa, what Mother saw in her Thomas. In later years when the young blade had blunted into the shuffling, thicker-set, white-haired 'Lloyd George', so much less sprightly than Mother, strangers used to wonder. But he were kind in his dealings with Mother and his daughters, taught us bwoys to respect women, couldn't bear to hear of a man knocking a woman about. Yet he knocked us bwoys about fairish! But only when we told lies, or pinched the pears from the Pound or the spigots from the baskets hanging under the back of the brewers' drays. How they draymen used to crack their whalebone whips at us thieving monkeys clinging under the back as the pounding Shires gathered speed and the spinning wheels crushed dangerously close to our cropped heads!

We all respected his devotion to his trade. His workshop next to the Dovecote were his private den. He'd sometimes allow one of us in there with him, but he didn't want the lot of us clombering in and out. I loved to help heat his glazing irons to melt the wax for his thread and the heel-ball to gloss all round the rim of the sole and in the instep. I used to heat it on a candle when he hadn't got a fire. I never hankered after learning the trade, but I never tired of watching a master at it. First the insole on the last, then the welt, a narrow band of leather, cut skilful, athert, from the width of thickness of the band on one side to the thinnest nothing on the other. He'd use his curved awl for this, dropping it back without looking into its own pocket in his tool-bench. Every tool had its pocket, hand-made awls and fudges, their blades and wheels well tempered to their purpose, their oak handles smoothed and honed by years of work. In the summer he'd sit at the open doorway, singing and working in the sun: sometimes working his stirrup-leather, sometimes stitching blind, with pigs' bristles for needles, the two waxed threads casting in and out of the same hole, crossing each other, tautening with a swift squeak, and on to the next hole as if by instinct. He used a groove in the handle of his awl to tauten one thread and his hand with a leather on it for the other. He knew from experience exactly how long each thread needed to be to complete the boot without a join. He always had some pieces of leather soaking in a bucket by the door. All the dogs relished that leather ale, even though it be black as ink and there be plenty of other spring-water nearby.

Dad hardly ever had a decent pair of boots. He couldn't afford for hisself the hours of work, the fine leathers and fudges he handled so well for Mr Jefferies and his customers. They say the cobbler's childern go the worst shod; Dad made sure we childern went dry-shod by giving us a penny a week for the boot-fund run by Mrs Palmer, the vicar's wife. She purchased factory boots wholesale and supplied the village childern cheaper than the shops.

He not only measured feet, he sculpted their every corn and callus, building up small bumps of leather on to the basic last. He always sent up to London for the last. They was made of beech or hornbeam, took nails easily without splitting, and never warped. Each last were unique, faithful to its owner—and I mean *owner*. When you pays for a last to be made, then that last is youern. You can keep it in a glass case if you wants, corns and all, or you can cart it off to another boot-maker.

Dad clozed some queer feet in his time. He once made a pair of kid-boots for a Japanese lady at Oxford. All her life before she burst from education her feet had been bound. Her smaller toes never recovered, and her two big toes and the ones next to them, set free like two little forward claws on a parakeet, were fragile as a butterfly's feelers; yet Dad's boots clozed 'em comfortably.

Harry Venvell had the ockerdest set of feet Dad had ever shod. Harry were the mailman, comed to Enstone from Milton-under-Wychwood at the turn of the century. Our Enstone be set on one of the great post-roads from London to Worcester, Hereford, Birmingham and other important places. Despite the importance of the railway at Charlbury, letters be always addressed until quite recently, 'Charlbury, Near *Enstone*'. The spirit of that famous mail-coach, the Brummagen Tantivy, with its thundering four-in-hand, trotted on in Harry's brisk little mail-cart and pony. He used to get up at 3.30 a.m. to get all his chores done, feed and groom his pony, pick up the mail from Enstone Post Office and deliver it to the Wychwoods—Milton-under-Wychwood, Shipton and Ascott—at top speed.

He were a tetchy impatient fellow, bad on his pins; his feet was hen-toed and curved into a circle when he put them together. Yet he were always on the go—wanted everything done with the fastest dispatch—an excellent mailman—tottered everywhere at the double. Said he could never find a man to make him a pair of boots.

'T'en't only yer fayt,' Dad told him. 'Thee never stands still long enough!'

Asked Dad to make him a pair.

Dad reached down his big measuring-book.

'What thee wants a book for?'

'To measure yer fayt'—Harry offered a foot—'*both* of 'em!'

'What for?'

'Yer LAST!'

Harry bristled, 'VENVELL'S *never* last!'—a slogan on which he later founded his famous international trucking fleet of 'VENVELL. ENSTONE. OXON. ENGLAND.' Moy-hoy! We was proud years later to first see that a-blazoned on a truck in our village.

The first pair Dad made for him Harry tossed straight back: 'Don't fit!'

'Don't chuck 'em about,' said Dad. 'Give 'em a few more seconds; thee hasn't had 'em *on* yet!' Dad showed him how to ease his 'crescents' round the bend to sink 'em home, comfortable, to base.

Harry gave a rare smile. 'Like a glove,' he said. And stalked off.

He were a rummy old chap to fall out with, but to us kids he be a godsend. On his return journey from Charlbury each day he'd collect parcels, trunks, portmanteaux from the station, and prescriptions from the doctors. If anybody in poor circumstances called at his place to collect their medicine he 'udn't charge. For other local deliveries he'd call us bwoys in from the street.

'Here, bwoy! Take this medicine to So'n'So. Charge him tuppence, and thee kayp the tuppence.'

He'd spread his bread upon the waters, sending different bwoys to different places. One snowy Christmas Eve I were that bundled up against the cold he couldn't see at first who I was.

'Whose old bwoy bist thee?'—nearly banging my nose with his lantern—'Got a wheelbarrow down home, bwoy? Thee fetch it up here.'

I fetched our Dad's old wooden wheelbarrow, and helped Harry to heave this posh portmanteau into it. It be a leaden, wooden-ribbed trunk affair, well fortified with brass and steel. 'Thee take this to that snooty old snapdragon that's stopping up at Mrs ———. Charge her eighteen pence.'

Eighteen pence! A fortune to an eight-year-old on Christmas Eve, but I could see from the pretty labels in the light of Harry's lantern it had already been carted all round the fleshpots of the Riviera to Charlbury, and pushing it on a wooden wheel in the snow all the way up our Enstone were no picnic. I reckon it were over half a mile, and her never said thank you, let alone Merry Christmas, just a haughty 'How much?'

I swallowed. 'Eighteen pence.'

Her nearly swallowed *me*, barrow and all. Her haggled. I huffed. In the end us settled for half.

Dad and Harry were sparring partners. Dad fell out with him so badly once he took his last elsewhere. Feet alter over the years and your last has to be updated according. The fresh boot-maker, stunned by Dad's jiggery-pokery to make Harry's last fit, hadn't the courage to tamper. The new boots pinched. Harry swallowed his pride and brought 'em to Dad.

'Make 'em fit, Tom.'

'Thee cassen't make a boot fit, Harry. Thee makes a *last* fit; the boot follas after.'

None of us followed in Dad's bootsteps. Jack couldn't have been interested, else he 'udn't have enlisted all they years ago. I had never seen my legendary eldest soldier–brother. In the Army in India, in the Police, back in the Army again. The first time I see'd him in 1916, when he came home wounded to stay for a while, I could hardly believe this thin old man, who were close on thirty and shuffling so slowly, leaning on my arm up and down Alley, were the dashing hero that had wild-rovered all through my bwoyhood and into my teens.

My big sister Lottie left home to skivvy at a boarding-house in Oxford. Her worked there all her life, and hardly ever managed to get home in the early years. I can remember going there with our Mam once when I was a nipper. We had to ask a Miss Knight and a Miss Stevens permission to see her. It were a biggish old place— took 'em some while to ferret out our Lottie. She come in to see us laden with two full scuttles of coal. She were hardly in there five minutes before she were scuttled back out again down to her servants' hole.

I see'd her again several times in later years when her were more highly installed on the staff; a tall elegant gal with her dark heavy hair braided up at the back, so like what our Mam must have looked as a gal, yet her never wed. They was all 'Miss' that mothered that boarding-house. There were a permanent shortage of escorts for gals of our Lottie's age after the First World War.

George had just left school when we first came to Enstone. Mr Adams, the postmaster, took him on as a telegraph-bwoy with a smart red solid-tyred bike, a little poked GPO cap and a uniform. Sometimes life were hectic for George, with catastrophes coming in thicker than he could carry them in his important leather pouch; and sometimes it were flat and empty with nobody dying at all. Mr Adams didn't mind how George passed the time between sallies as long as he remained within call.

Colonel Eric Dillon's stables at Enstone House were right opposite the post office; and old Alf Aries was often in there a-grooming the colonel's fine horses. Alf were a topping groom, knowed all there was to know about presentation and riding. George stood on the public footpath, watching and worshipping, from a respectful distance at first: but gradually he worked his way in until he was learning everything he could about smart grooming, correct riding, and good mounts. The colonel took to him, and soon every moment George were off duty from his telegraph job he were exercising and grooming the colonel's horses.

'George,' the colonel says one day, 'you're getting too big for my horses, how d'ye like to mount a fine career in the Life Guards?' And he wangled him from a public education at the stable door into the famous regiment.

Dora went out to service when she were thirteen. I missed my big sister, Dora; she'd often been second mother to me when our Mam went out to earn a few extra pence at seasonal jobs like tater-picking. She'd been second-mother to so many of us village childern, she looked twice her age at thirteen. She were skivvying as a tweeny-maid at a big house near Oxford. She had her photo tooked soon after she left home, at Norman Taylor's Day and Electric Studios in Oxford. The new electric light had so opened up Norman's shutters he were advertising 'Portraits taken Day or Night'—very convenient for our Dora; she had a handy half-day off 'tween 4 p.m. and 9 p.m. once a week.

'*To Horace from Home*'. . . HOME, with all its links to these older brothers and sisters who had passed through, and th'Old Folk, and my three younger brothers in the Dovecote, meant a lot to me when I were bwoy–chap and breadwinner aged fourteen in 1916.

7

Taking a Pride

I STUCK THE COW JOB for two years until I were fifteen. I en't that wrapt up in cows. Cows be full of sweet–sour outpourings of milk and muck, and not much given to team-work. Oxen may be more congenial. I en't never worked with oxen, though there be still teams of oxen working the land in Oxfordsheer when I was a lad. They be mostly on the Hereford side. Jim Ivings were the last in Enstone within living memory to plough with oxen. He had a four-ox team: Drummer, Dumpling, Prince and Rattler. There were other old men at the pub that could recall oxen being bred at the Malt Shovel at Cleveley. You can still see the ox-harness pokes in the walls of the barn there.

Our 'Oxenfordsheer' symbol be a mighty ox crossing a ford, and many a go-ahead Oxfordsheer mechanical firm has been proud to blazon it as their trademark. Mr Morris bagged it when he were fed up waiting for the Oxford Electric Tramcar Company to shilly-shally into existence, and got on with making his motor-car instead. Before the Morris motor I mind a big steamroller from

Cowley (I think it be Allen's firm now) with a fine brass ox-head on the front; and there was a steam-engined furniture-removal pantechnicon, Archer Cowley it were called, that bulldozed its way from Oxford with a brass ox mascot and great iron wheels to shift the chattels for the posh folk at Enstone House to another mansion before the First World War. It travelled nowheres without its little guardian 'Mr Angel' engine-driver, a bow-legged chap, who never deigned to lift a stick of furniture, sending his middle-aged bwoy–chaps to do that while he kept outside the house, pottering and tottering about that huge engine, sparkling up its brass girths and brass ox on the front. Driving this iron-shod monster over the years had palsied his shaking hands and pins, yet he never stopped cosseting his beloved pride and downfall, and us kids 'ud gawp in awe at its massive sheen.

It were the Sunday work that finally browned me off with the cows. The day of rest were my busiest day of the week. When I warn't milking or feeding the cows at Fulwell, I were putting me working boot forward to get home to the Dovecote to put me best boot forward to get to choir on time at Church Enstone. It were the same pair of boots, they just had an extra clean in between. It didn't help neither to be always on work bent, running the gauntlet of all the other village lads of my own age in their Sunday togs having the traditional mooch'n'chat along the wall at top of Alley or along Cling-Clang Lane at Church Enstone. Us choir called it 'Ting-Tang', 'cos if the final bell, the ting-tang, were being rung down as you run along the lane you knowed you had just enough time to get into your surplice and your straight face for proceeding into service.

In 1917 when I were fifteen I were just plucking up courage to give in my notice and face th'Old Folks and Mr Lennox when, out of the blue, Mr Lennox faces *me*:

'How d'ye like to be my carter, Mont?'

CARTER! In they days on the land, carter were king.

'But, sir, I be only fifteen.' I felt var' like the Princess Victoria when they offered her the throne of England: 'cept her warn't exactly bwoy–chap at the time.

'Carter Maycock be leaving to go on the war work in Banbury.'

I were sorry to hear that. I owed a lot of my knowledge of handling horses to Joe Maycock. He had kept his weather-eye on me ever since I came on my first harvest holiday to help on the farm before the War. He were well trained under Carter Eden up at the Model. 'The Model' were the posh farm on the Ditchley Mansion Estate where everything, husbandry and accommodation, be modelled on the ideal. The stables was Buckingham Palace, all under one vast roof where you could parade under cover and shovel out the muck in wagons. Joe were a family man with four childern, but he be too old to fight in the War. He'd been slogging short-handed on the farm ever since war were declared and three of his men had quit to join the Forces. I didn't blame him, after years and acres of plodding, for wanting a job with less responsibility, less hours, and no doubt more money.

I loved the old farm-horses. I'd been working with them more and more of late, and thanks to Carter Maycock, Shepherd Akers and Mr Lennox I knowed I had enough gumption to do the job.

'But, sir, theer's an awful lot I *don't* know about carterin'. Is theer a book?'

'Sit along of they old carters, Carter Atkins, Carter Sheffield, Carter Newman, when ye gangs to the pub, Mont,' Mr Lennox strongly advised me. 'Keep your mouth shut and your ears wide open. Thee'll glean far more aboot horses from they old carters than thee'll ever sift from a book.'

So, at fifteen, I becomed Carter Abbott with two bwoy–chaps and a grampy under me, and nine great cart-horses rattling their bins for grub when I turned up all alone on my first morning. I didn't know it then, but I were up to my eyes in clover compared to they poor devils in Flanders up to their knees in mud. The Third Battle of Ypres were in full flood.

One of the perks of being carter were choosing your own team of horses. Most carters 'ud go for youth and beauty, but I collared old Jolly and Prince because I'd worked with them before and knowed their even temperament. They warn't a matching pair; Jolly were a mahogany, and Prince—borned at Woodstock like his royal namesake—were the Black Prince. Jolly were seventeen hands and

Prince were sixteen and a half. With Jolly in the furrow and Prince on the ridge, us was working all on the level.

First job as carter, lifting the latch of the stable all by myself at five o'clock of a dark winter's morn, be to light the stable lamp. It were a hurricane-lamp, hung on the beam, and I'd light it as I'd seen Joe Maycock light it, with one of they old brimstone lucifers, striking it one-handed across the rump of me ridge'n'furrowed corduroy breeches. Its soft swinging glow 'ud alight upon Jolly—Violet—Prince—Daisy—and come to rest over Bowler-the-Biter and others beyond, their rumps glimpsed glossy in their knowed stalls in the stable. They was all over sixteen hands: mostly the old Suffolk, with one or two Canadian Punch, and Boxer the heavyweight Shire.

I'd fill the sidlip, the large round shallow rush-basket we used to use when sowing seed by hand, and bait the horses, teasing the mixed corn and chaff thinly along the manger so's they licked rather than scoffed. Baiting stopped 'em bolting their food, made 'em give each mouthful thirty chews—good for 'em on an empty stomach. Good for *my* empty stomach too—gave I a bit o' peace to eat my breakfast without 'em all standing round, cadging.

There was four pairs, and Polly for the odd jobs: carting swedes to the sheep or churns to the station. I'd turn 'em out in pairs to drink at the trough in the yard while I swept the muck into a ready-yup for old Gramp, Bartholomew Chaundy, to do the farming-out. Then I'd put out a fuller feed. They'd saunter back of their own accord, knowing they was due for their main course.

While waiting for the men to turn up I'd start grooming my team and polishing their harness. Even when I had only old Bartholomew and a couple of bwoy–chaps as labour, us took a pride in our teams and harness, often turning up early or staying a bit late. You warn't paid for the extra time spent on spit'n'polish, you took a pride in being all ready and well-turned-out in the yard with your team by the time Mr Lennox came at seven to give the carter his orders.

'*Et!*'—it were a powerful moment for me, my first time as carter, giving the traditional Oxfordsheer carter's command for the teams to set forth. They talks of a pride of lions; us had a 'pride of

Punches' (and mighty Boxer done us proud on the Shire). The true Suffolk Punch be always 'chesnut', spelled just as it were writ in 1768 when the first foal were recorded. There be seven shades of chesnut from Captain's 'bright golden' to Prince's 'deep brown–black', all still identifiable today as they was first classed in the 1877 stud-book.

The Canadian Punch be all colours; ours were grey. Some slave-driving farmers had only grey or light-coloured horses on their farms so they could spy from a distance if their men be still toiling, nose to the plough, traipsing across the landscape.

Mr Lennox warn't that harsh a taskmaster. After he'd gived the orders for the day he'd trust us to collect our tucker-bags, top-cwoats and nosebags from the pile by the trough and go and plod on with it. When I were short-handed he'd come and take a team hisself, working alongside. The farmer were often one on you in they days.

If we was going to plough afresh we'd have a fairish walk, driving the implement behind our team along the muddy road, down Fulwell, past 'lotment Hill and up on the hill to Henel Field; or, in the other direction, along the narrow Fulwell Lane up to the turnpike along the Charlbury Road to New Piece. If we was carrying on from the day before, our implements was already up in the field and we'd ride to work. Dropping into step with the horse we'd catch hold the hames and hotch ourselves 'UP' to sit side-saddle—with no saddle. It were a fair old hotch to land up there, but you soon got the quiff on it. It'd fall to the youngest bwoy–chap to slide down to open the gates, and the toffee-nosed carter 'ud sail through right royally, chewing his straw.

You took a pride in setting a straight furrow, often following the same line of stubble seeded with pride by the man that had trod the earth before you. You become var' close to the land and they who have toiled before when you plants your soul and plods your strength into every inch of it. A carter's reputation—and ofttimes his epitaph—be laid bare, writ in furrow and framed in 'adlands, for all the world to see, peeking over the hedgerow. And woe betide 'ee in the pub that night with they old carters if they'd spotted a dingy turnout or a skewed furrow.

We'd crane our necks likewise over the hedges of passing acres, critical, particularly of the posh estates, from our vantage seat driving the wagon to Charlbury or Woodstock. One old carter were once 'gone right awf Blenheim 'cos the Duke of Marlborough 'adn't got 'is 'adlands roight.' He must be tossin'n'turnin' in his grave at some of today's tantrum'd earth and tractor-crazy capers.

There warn't many tractors about when I started off cartering. Mr Lennox had a Titan a year or two later: a cumbersome iron-wheeled monster, viewed then as a giant 'copter in the jungle might be viewed today, wonderful useful for aiding the ground forces providing you could find an uncomplaining spot to let it down. It were a marathon task to shift it up and down the furrow; even then the ground forces, old Uncle Mont, Jolly and all had come to its aid and finish off the 'adlands. If you wanted my valuable opinion, as a fifteen-year-old carter, tractors 'ud never catch on, and the Titan were var' like to end up like that other modern marvel, the late *Titanic*.

Meanwhile us ploughed on with our Ransom or our Ball, down to earth in every sense, knowing every field, every furrow could differ from one end to the other on our big oolite soil; altering the cock according to the varying depths from the brashy banks to the rich hollows, coping with the elements, cleaning the coulters, commanding the horses, claypering our noses, boots and gaiters, until my watch said it were time for nine o'clock lunch or twelve o'clock dinner.

The nine o'clock lunch were a moveable feast, depending on which end of the long furrow you'd left yer bacca; but it were politic to stick to twelve o'clock dinner for your dinner-hour, specially if the master were working with you. Twelve o'clock prompt he went home for his dinner; if you was to carry on for an extra bout he'd be back before you'd had your hour, and it'd look as if you was swinging the lead. Twelve o'clock prompt, out came the nosebags.

The youngest bwoy–chap 'ud fetch me my tucker-bag. I'd open up my tommy-cloth to find real man's grub which I yet with my real man's pocket-knife, rounded off with a drink of cold tea, and a roll of bacca for my pipe. I hadn't quite mastered a pipe when I first started cartering, but I soon got the quiff on it. Everybody smoked in they days. Over the years my pipe became my companion, a solace for long hours alone out in the fields. I 'udn't advise anybody to take it up now; smoking be a silly job, but at eighty-two I be too old to change for the better.

By the time you'd walked back and forth all day, battling with the elements, you was ready to shut off at four o'clock. They used to reckon if a chap ploughed an acre with a nine-inch-wide furrow he'd walked fourteen miles, let alone all the homping of the plough and the weight on his boots. You didn't hotch up quite so lissom on to the horse's back for the ride back to the stables. First stop— the horse-trough, to give the horses a long, long drink. How they enjoyed that end-of-work drink! They'd sink their old noses right under the water, and the level 'ud plummet like billy-o. If one had a touch of colic you'd leave the bit in his mouth so's he couldn't gollop the water so fast. Now I be carter, one of the bwoy–chaps filled the troughs. He be lucky; no more thirteen hundred 'pumps'; by now there were piped water brought overland from Spelsbury to the Fulwell farm buildings. Only to the farm buildings, not to the cottages. On the farm, animals comes first.

After I'd racked up, I'd walk home for my tea. By the time I'd walked back after tea the men be all gone. It were their job to do all the skivvying for the carter, to curve a ready supply of hay for feed and straw for bedding, to fill the corn bins and cut the chaff. We always used oat-straw for chaff, the wheat-straw be too knotty and bad for the horses' bellies. I'd end the day as I began, baiting the horses, cleaning my team and harness, watering and feeding, and bedding them down for the night. You'd soon tell if a horse 'udn't lie down in a stall and was standing all night, his droppings 'ud be all in one spot and he'd have 'Monday-morning leg', as we called it, because their legs swelled the same if they stood all weekend. After a spell on his own out of the stall, lying in an open hovel, he'd usually take to sharing again and lying down with the rest.

I always talked to animals as I worked among 'em; never approached from behind or between without having a quiet word, cultivating trust on their part and vigilance on mine. I never went home without casting a keen eye over my charges and along the row of harness in the harness room.

You took a pride in keeping your horses and harness in good working condition: hardening the horses off after they'd been out to pasture for a day or two, with a day in the stable on dry grub so's they warn't too green and sweat into a sore when they started work again. Making sure they had ample time to clear their windpipe of food before they set off, else they'd start a cough. Keeping an eye out for worn or weak harness. A small worn patch on a collar, no bigger than a silver thripenny bit, 'ud rub a terrible hole in a horse's shoulder by the end of a working day. A few broken stitches could weaken a whole breeching, making it suddenly snap—as it did once going down to Charlbury Station, sending a cart into a horse's hind-quarters and nearly crushing old Shoddy Hall to death. I warn't carter then, but it taught I a lesson.

The collier 'ud come from Barton regular, once a month, bringing back the repaired harness and collecting the next batch. He'd re-line and re-stuff collars. We'd collect all the sheep's wool from the hedges and the horsehair from the combs, and do a swap with him for leather bootlaces. He'd cut 'em for you there and then, straight down the leather, one swift long sliver. They was wonderful strong and long-lasting, much sought-after for working on the land.

You kept your horses shod and their feet sound. A horse's hoof be always growing, like a big toenail. Working horses needs their shoes off and their nails cut about once a month. If his shoes en't worn out they goes back on, otherwise it means new shoes. The Suffolk has clean legs, not a lot of feathering like the Shire, so you can keep a good eye on his hoofs, and he doesn't so much pick up the clats of mud. But it were my job to clean out stwuns and thrush, and to have the right shoes for working in the fields or on the roads. In slippery weather, drawing wagons to and from Charlbury Station I'd ask the farrier to shoe 'em with frost-nail-holes, or rough 'em with turned-down flanges to grip the road. But you dussen't leave they same shoes on for working in the field; if they happened to step on another horse they'd rip his leg. A loose shoe be like a bicycle puncture, a horse can't go far on it without doing a lot of further damage. He needs it off and another fitted as soon as possible.

There were three blacksmiths in the village. I used to take our horses to Jack Sansbury, top of Spring Hill. He were a strapping chap, carried hisself strong and wide in his long leather apron, ready to take on all-comers, man or horse. He were a brisk hand at shoeing, turning each operation into a slick performance, singing and playing his irons on his anvil like a pop drummer:

> *I to Monte Carlo went*
> *Just to raise my weekly rent*
> *Biff-bang! Biff-bang!*
> *Pom-tiddly-om-pom clang! clang!*

His premises was ample, room for two great cart-horses to stand under cover; and his jackets was ample, several of them hanging in a row like outsize armour, ready to take on the elements outside whenever he left the heat of the forge. Jack's butty, or 'striker' as they was called, 'ud prepare the horse's feet while Jack set to work to give his performance on the anvil. Once he'd shod a horse he never forgot what size shoe it took, from a nine-inch-wide cart-horse to a two-inch-wide donkey, he knowed by heart exactly how much iron was needed. Shod a horse in no time. All round. Seven and a tanner!

I once heard another blacksmith, old Hedges, choked off for refusing to shoe a horse. In his prime, before I were born, old Hedges had 'relieved Mafeking' by mafficking under the old elm on the village green, making explosions on his anvil with gunpowder, so he must have been a bit of a spark at one time. But in older years he were an ockerd, yummery fellow. A stranger came riding from Kidlington one sharp frosty morning, and as he approached the village the road became more and more slippery, so he stopped at the blacksmith's to have his horse's shoes roughed up. Old Hedges refused to do't. 'Look at that sign over your shop,' pointed the stranger, '"Blacksmith and *Farrier*". Shoe my horse, farrier.'

The man was a lawyer. By law a farrier could not refuse to shoe a horse, just as an inn must always accommodate a traveller. These laws be vital to the traveller in the olden days.

The vet be a rarity then; now they comes in bunches. In they days, by the time you'd snuffed one out he were probably out already, gone for miles on his bike or in his pony and trap. There was few motors and few phones, so you had to cope as best you could. Jack Walker, the horse-doctor from Long Compton, 'ud usually come to castrate the colts. Amazing fellow! Never needed no help. Rounded 'em up from the fields, castrated 'em standing up, working blind from round their back-quarters. No ether, no halter, no trouble, all done! How they colts trusted him, I shall never know, but they did.

I dosed all the horses once a month with a physic-ball, a solid aperient about as thick and long as four inches of candle. I had to open their great mouths and shove it right to the back of their gullet and snatch my hand out quick before I were swallowed up like Jonah. At first I were so frit I'd snatch my hand out that fast my forearm 'ud be ripped to bits on the horse's sharp teeth. I tried not to flinch, but I were ashamed of my bungling and tried to hide my wounds. Mr Lennox soon noticed and taught me to draw my hand out straight and down. A horse's side teeth be sharp as razzers and, like their toenails, they goes on growing. Sometimes as they gets older they grows such uneven fangs they can't chew their food and has to have 'em filed down. Even today, after all they years of being exposed to all weathers, my forearms still carry the scars of learning the hard way to ball a horse when I were fifteen.

I soon learned to spot a horse that warn't feeding properly or up to form. One away from the rest of the gang, wrapt up in hisself, be usually middling. That goes for most herd animals. Animals, like man, be sociable creatures. One horse in a field be often a nuisance, trying to get out to find company. Put a goat, or a donkey, or even a few hens in with it and it's more content. In the main my horses needed little doctoring. The best doctor of all be old Johnny Greengrass—a bit of good pasture done 'em a power of good.

Fulwell pastures and farm buildings, grouped round the rickerd, be that ancient you sensed on a still, hazy morn the centuries of men and horses, workers on the land, that had been there before. I were only seven when the old stable, built of faggots, wattle and daub, with a bit of old thatch, were pulled down and rebuilt next to the chaff-house in ought-nine. They old stwun-masons, Ted Huckin, Walt and Harry Benfield from Taston, and old Joe Benfield from Gagingwell, gauged from its construction, and from details of all they other structures that there were once quite an important settlement at Fulwell. Part of the barn were plastered inside like a church, with a narrow stwun-mullioned window, and another ruined foundation, properly pitched and rounded, like a bell-tower, nearby. The old masons told me there be no burial ground, just a deep well where they poked the dead folks—'And some was poked for dead, alive!'

They opened that well once just to show me. It were terrifying dank, dark, fathomless. 'Dayp enough,' old Joe Benfield spake in his deep bass voice, 'for 'ee to drop in a stwun and run all the way to Enstone and back before it full-stopped.' I don't know if they was fritting the life out of a seven-year-old bwoy, but I were jolly glad when they put the cover back. Even so, for years I suffered terrible nightmares of being poked for dead, alive, down a well, making me leap awake in a lather of sweat and making our Jim scream for 'Mam!' in the middle of the night.

I can still picture the colossal slabs of stwun they old miner–masons dug out of Quar Ground and the way they dressed them into massive quoins, adzing them to channel off the rain. I still marvel, as I did as a bwoy, watching them build that stable, that they knowed exactly where each stwun were destined, picking each for purpose and never putting it back. In they days all craftsmen, be they boot-makers or blacksmiths, colliers or masons, appeared to me to be mastermen. I can see they masons on a Sunday, proudly walking to church in their mason's 'uniform', jacket and breeches of cream corduroy, the colour of stwun dust, and a smart bowler-hat. By fifteen I be steeped in a man's pride in his calling and his craft, and I be proud to be carter with that fine new stable they masons had stwunned with such skill.

Looking back, I reckoned I achieved quite a bit in my fifteenth year. I envy now my stamina as a young man, walking to and from work, up at the stable by five, ploughing all day, sometimes singing my heart out; choir, or cross-country running, or the Thripenny Hop by night.

The Thripenny Hop were the dancing-classes Mr Lowe and his phonograph 'ud run once a week in the top room at the Litchfield. Cost you thripence to go in, and an extra spit'n'dubbin on your working-boots and gaiters. They old buttoned gaiters 'ud trap the air, wiffle-wuffling like mad as you capered through 'The dashing white sergeant', the lancers and the military two-step. I discovered that as long as I kept my hobnailed boots to myself the female form enjoyed being handled. I enjoyed it too. I enjoyed the music, and the crowd Mr Lowe had managed to conscript into the wagonette on its way through Charlbury and the villages around, helping us to forget for a while how miserably empty our Enstone and the choir were with all they young chaps, good fun lads, and many of our lasses too, away at the War and the munitions.

The trouble was, I were such a big chap for my age, the wenches thought I were home on leave from the Front. I had quite a job to handle their response when they discovered I warn't doing my bit. Worst of all were the 'Canaries', the gals who worked in the munitions factories, defiantly flaunting their yellow skin and hair wreaked upon them by the TNT they was constantly having to handle. In some villages the Canaries was turning quite nasty, throwing white feathers, the symbol of cowardice, at chaps not in the War. There were a too-handy supply of white feathers free-ranging in the countryside in they days. I didn't want no wench doubting my manhood.

I dussen't think how Mr Lennox 'ud manage with the cartering if I went in the Army. He were already scraping the bottom of the barrel having a fifteen-year-old as head carter. Like so many other farmers, he had faced up so many times to having his men shipped off to the War and his latest well-broke-in colts being constantly requisitioned by the chaps from the Remount Depot. Horses too was giving their lives in thousands to the carnage. I couldn't bear to think of deserting my old faithfuls. I couldn't think of anybody to take them over. Mr Lennox were desperate all round for labour. He'd just taken on our old bwoy, our Gil, straight from school to help with the cows. Our Gil were hopeless on the farm, more wench than bloke. He were no good roughing it as a clathopper like me. Too timid to milk, he'd been put to feed the calves: but it were like feeding Daniel to the lions.

As for home . . . our Gil were earning—just!—but our Jim and Fred were still at school. My wage as a carter had shot up to fifteen shillun a week, a win on the pools for our Old Folks. If 'our Mont' were away at the Front, who 'ud keep the Old Folks at home? But when you're a big chap with more than your share of strength, and you've been used to 'rescuing the perishing', and your country's hollering out for help, you feel you ought to go.

The gwoost of Kitchener had been fading his finger at me for some time on they washed-out posters outside the post office. 'Your King and Country NEED YOU.' Being up to me eyes the last few years in 'Rosy's rump', lone calves, mad bulls and hungry horses out at Fulwell I hadn't had time to list to Kitchener. But by 1918 the old gwoost were cropping up afresh, pointing at me from barn doors and tree-trunks, 'Your King and Country NEED YOU.' The Germans were hammering yet again at our exhausted lads in the Fifth Army, ninety thousand of our men and thirteen hundred of our guns taken at Lys. I'd be sixteen in July. I only hoped the lads could hold out till I got there.

— 8 —

Empty Heroes

ON MY SIXTEENTH BIRTHDAY, 16 July 1918, I went to enlist with four other bwoys from our Enstone. I'd been quite open and above-board with home and Mr Lennox. Nobody had backed me up. Nobody had backed any of us up. All of us had fought lone battles on several fronts in the village already. People were low in body and spirit; the shortage of food and basic necessities at home, the terrible loss of men, ships, and battles, was turning everybody against us. 'Daft! What d'ye want to enlist for? You'll be called up anyway when you're eighteen. All of yer, throwin' yer lives away!'

Two was seventeen, the rest of us was sixteen. We'd knowed each other all our schoolhood. At the last minute, still torn between us in so many directions, we went, an almost guilty bunch of deserters, into the school to seek final word of advice from our old school boss, Mr Glover.

Nothing had changed. The old varnished Empire were still straggling across the old Geography poster, a bit more cracked, a bit more fly-blown. Mr Glover were proud to see his 'new men', shook hands with each of us, and directed us straightway to the new recruiting-office that had opened up in St Giles, Oxford.

We pushed off in our best suits on our motley bikes. Our Mam never came out of the Dovecote to say goodbye. I don't know if she even 'put her chair to the window to see them passing by'. I couldn't bear to look.

My bike were a mongrel, but I were very proud of it. Shoddy Hall had miracled him out of various transplants he'd found abandoned in hedges and quarries, ditches and haystacks. Cost me ten bob. He must have had some pedigree about him, 'cos when I treated him to a brake at Walt Paxford's bicycle-shop in his hovel at the top of Spring Hill, Walt offered I *three quid*! And when I traded him in for a bigger frame after the War, he were still being ridden years later, cropping up with amazing stamina all over the district.

Goodness knows where the rest of the gang had picked up theirs. There were Smiler Simms, Alex Hunt, Diddy Beale and old Coggy. Coggy were only little, couldn't sing a note—grommeted in his boots and always fitted in the middle of us. We'd kept him in the middle ever since we used to go carol-singing as kids, trudging right up through Heythrop Forest in the pitch dark. He were feared a bogey-man 'ud grab him—and *we* was feared he were a bit light-fingered with the collecting-box. He were biking in the middle of us now, petrified of all the horse-drawn traffic squeezing us into the gutter as we entered Oxford. Goodness knows where he'd got his bike from, it were far too posh for the likes of his pocket, probably pinched it. We was still going to have to keep our eye on Coggy one way and another in the Army.

The Army welcomed us with smartish-opened doors, took down our 'ticulars, examined us all over, and pronounced us fighting fit. We was half-way there already. As an afterthought they asked us our jobs.

We was all on the land. We was 'fighting a more important battle there', they said, 'with food so short and harvest coming up'—and sent us straight back.

Mr Glover were looking out for us, prouder than ever to see us come back. He guessed they 'udn't take us away from the land, he said; but every lad should be encouraged to face up to taking his own decisions and grow into a man.

Next day I were a hero, back at Fulwell, clathopping behind my horses. I felt an empty hero behind our brave lads at the real Front; but it were nice to be appreciated. Food had gotten so scarce, the farm-labourer were a case for extra rations. For some time now the Food Office had been issuing small food-parcels to farmers, and Mr Lennox had been doling 'em out to us with our wages every week.

Mr Lennox were so glad to see I back, he upped me wages another whole ten bob a week. I were now earning twenty-five bob, over half the top wartime agricultural weekly wage, and I were still only sixteen; but in the eyes of Mr Lennox I were fully a man.

Our Gil had become a man too in his fashion, faced up to his true nature, left the land, and found his role in service at Stratton Audley Hall. Our old bwoy were in his element, liveried in plush, wearing a wig, powdering hisself up and flouncing about as a flunkey. Proper pantomime! It takes all sorts to make a world, but *that* sort of caper 'udn't do for the likes of *this* clathopper. I likes to keep a civil tongue, but I en't a one for the bowin'n'scrapin'.

How history repeats itself! Gil started his career as a six-year-old page to the village 'Queen Mary' at the 1911 Coronation Concert in the barn at Church Enstone. He were to end up footman for years to the real Queen Mary at Buckingham Palace.

All through the War the memory of that wonderful coronation celebration in Rectory Barn at Church Enstone were becoming more and more distant and golden. It were a topping barn, held the whole parish. Village feasts had been held in there for centuries. It's supposed to be one of the oldest tithe barns in England, and says in Latin on a stone tablet outside:

> This barn was founded and built in the year 1382
> by Walter of Wyniforton Abbot of Winchcombe at the
> petition of Robert Mason, bailiff of this place

In 1911 it were a bit dilapidated after 529 years, but we was all too merry to notice. Memories of the old Queen's jubilees in '87 and '97 was being swapped; and one old carter could remember her coronation revels when, for a wager of ale, a young carter drove a wagon and three horses in and round and out of the barn in one fell sweep. That must have been a breathtaking feat; but he must have had a 'turn-under' wagon, he 'udn't have managed it with one of our high-wheeled Oxfordsheer wagons.

They gave us kids a spiffing booze-up in 1911: four bottles of lemonade for each nipper. They gived you this ticket and cut off a corner each time you had your drink. They done the same arrangement with the beer for the grown-ups. Our Gil were only half-cut when he felt sick 'cos he were going to act the page in this here concert, so I had the rest of his ticket. We had a mug with the new King and Queen on it. It were the first time I'd see'd 'em close up, and they looked all right.

We had rides in the field on Neddy Claridge's donkeys, and one black donkey careered off home with somebody's lollipop, but nobody were bothered; there were plenty more lollipops and donkeys to go round. There was plenty of everything to go round, drink and food and entertainment. And in the evening, the grand village concert, winding up with a pretend King George and Queen Mary, and our Gil and another nipper as pages, solemnly bearing plush cushions with the silver-paper crowns of Great Britain and all her Dominions and Empire—stuck with ju-jube jewels. I can still feel the deep hush of the crowning moment, and then the wild cheers and rejoicing when, as if by magic, the real church bells pealed out next door. Our Enstone ringers be a topping team before the War.

Where be all they brave ringers now, we wondered, whenever we talked of those far-away golden days before the War. 'When the War ends we'll have another "1911 Coronation",' we promised ourselves. 'When the War ends . . .' were the only dream we had left in 1918.

It were fine but raw on 11 November. We was tatering in Turnpike, with eighteen women, several of them war-widows, picking taters, and a little lad of three years squawking miserable because he were cold. His mam had done her best, pulling his dead dad's socks over his boots and coddling him up to his little raw red nose in scarves, but her needed the money and he'd have to put up with it. Seemed he was crying for all of us, up to our necks in mud and war, sick to death of the waste of lives and the want of men. Turnpike were heavy sticky ground. It needed four horses on the digger, with heavyweight Jolly as thiller between the shafts, and George Snow the baker helping out, leading them. Another horse and bwoy–chap were on the harrow, turning up the taters the digger had missed; and another three carts and teams was manned by older chaps for loading the sacks of taters on to the carts.

I were on the drawing out. The women filled the sacks. The men loaded 'em on to the cart. I stacked 'em, drove the full cart into the barn with a trace-horse and a thiller, backed the full cart into the barn for old Shoddy Hall and his son to unload, unhitched my trace-horse, hitched him to another thiller waiting in the empty cart, and drove back to the field. 'It's what we call 'team-work'.

The little chap were still crying when we stopped for dinner at noon. Clatted with earth up to his runny nose, pinned to the land by the weight of his feet, I dubbed him 'Little Tater' and carted him across the baulks to his back-aching mam. We'd just decided to yet our dinner out of the field on the verge of the road, away from the endless mud and out of the wind, when we spotted Postmaster Adams sailing down the road from Charlbury on his wicker mail-cart cycle. He'd been to collect the midday mail from the station.

He usually dismounted and pushed up the next rise, but today he kept cycling post-haste up the rise towards us and wobbled to a halt, breathless with excitement.

'It's over. They called it awf, 'leven o'clock this morning.'

We gawped. We couldn't take it in. The War had dragged on for so long.

'It's over! It's OVER!' Everybody were suddenly hugging each other, laughing and crying. Little Tater stopped crying, looking up at us bewildered. He'd known nothing but war. He started to bawl again.

I swung him up, again and again, 'All better! All better!' until at last he gave me a smile.

But his mam warn't smiling. For her, and for thousands of others, it'd never be 'all better'.

No more taters was picked that day. But how could we celebrate? We couldn't even gather in the great barn; after years of neglect it were no longer safe. There was no lollipops for the kiddies in the shops, no beer for the chaps in the pubs, and no bellringers.

No bells? Already I could hear Charlbury bells pealing out in the distance. They must have roped in a team from somewhere. Our Enstone bells be jolly good sounders. Our champion bellringers 'ud never forgive us if their rivals, Charlbury, Spelsbury, Tew and all the towers around gave tongue and our Enstone didn't bellow at all.

We must muster up some sort of a team between us. I hurried up to Church Enstone, whipping in two other chaps on the way. Coggy were one. Said he couldn't come 'cos he were in his best boots. Told him he always sang 'in his boots', so he could pull in 'em.

Parson Palmer and Chisel were already in the tower. Chisel were the only true ringer among us so we made him yedsirag, captain of the tower. Parson Palmer were bouncing about on his broad feet full of no experience and dangerous enthusiasm. I were cursing to myself that with so much Sunday work to do on the farm I'd never had time to learn to ring properly, but I'd often chimed in with a bit of a pull for fun before choir. The others had no idea at all. Chisel looked at his team in despair. 'I'll have a job with you lot. . . .'

There be six bells at St Kenelm's. Chisel could change-ring, two of us could down-ring, Coggy were too scared to pull at all, so Parson pulled three, 'long–tail–sow!' with one in each hand and one looped round his foot. 'Cling-CLANG! BONG! BONG!' 'Long–tail–sow! Long–tail–sow!' Thee never heerd such a pandemonium in your life. More like ringing a new scare in than ringing the old war out. Chisel called us off. It were too dangerous. The lads 'udn't have thanked us if they'd come home to find Parson and we had wrecked the bell-tower in their absence. Ah well! we consoled ourselves, at least we'd made the effort.

It were an even greater effort to find a pint of beer. There were no consolation at all in our Enstone. Word spread that they'd got a drop in at the Albion Tavern at Chippy. It were worth a walk. If the Albion were dry we'd have a chance at the twenty-nine other pubs in the town. So we walked to Chippy the back way, through the swirling fog, to find—no beer; and the lamps was all out—no paraffin. So me and the other empty heroes celebrated Armistice Day 1918 by walking the five miles home to our Enstone in the pitch dark, carolling, 'Theer en't no be-er in the town,' with Coggy grommeting '*In the town*', in his best boots, between us.

— 9 —

Troopers All

IT WERE JULY 1919 before the Germans finally settled the Peace Treaty. A day of jubilation was declared throughout the land, and we could officially welcome our lads home as a village. Mr Bolton shifted his threshing-drum out of his Litchfield barn and we had a real posh do with a hot dinner in there. I sat with Albert Beck and the rest of the farm-labourer 'heroes'. We was uncomfortable being classed with the fighting troops and waited upon by all they old comrades of the Boer War. We was troopers too, they insisted; and Albert Stevens, a colour-sergeant in the South African War, said in his opening speech they 'deemed it an honour to wait upon all those who had served their country in the Great War, *including our valiant farm-labourers.*' Albert Beck were that overcome he drank a whole jug of broth thinking it were beer. I can recall being stunned by the term 'Great' War; heerd for the first time from a respected old campaigner like Albert Stevens it brought home to *this* green old bwoy the scale of it.

None of us was classed as heroes for long. The Agricultural Wages Board was set up to standardize farm wages, and straightway cut the top wartime wages from forty-five to twenty-five bob. You was mostly paid according to your age. Even though I were still doing the same full carter's job, Mr Lennox were ordered to dock my wage back to fifteen bob, the national wage for a sixteen-year-old, and the dole for our unemployed soldier heroes. Many of them with families to support was forced to troop to Chippy for Parish Relief, but all the relief they got was 'Join the Army'.

Some joined the growing army of unemployed taking to the road in search of work. Unlike the true roader—the lone vagrant at home on the road—this new breed were a sad strained sight, trailing their women and kiddies, struggling to string together their last pathetic parcel of family life.

The true roader, hardened by the elements, dossing down over a network of familiar barns and ditches, were a seasoned pilgrim to our village, knowed by name, 'Uncle Mace' and 'Holy Joe', catching up on the local news, enquiring like a visiting distant relation into the state of crops and the health of the inhabitants.

They was mostly men, meeting up with each other haphazard. Uncle Mace were fabled to be of noble descent, born out of wedlock. He had a guilty fund from somewhere providing him with the means to line his old keeper's jacket with a warm weskut, and his poacher's pockets with lollipops for the kiddies. You'd hear snatches of his pleasant voice wafting up from the other side of the hedge with the whiff of smoke from his camp-fire, serenading his billy-can:

> . . . *My old black Bill-y*
> *Whether the wind be warm or chill-y*
> *I always say when the shadows fall*
> *My old black Billy be the best mate of all.*

Holy Joe were a different kettle of tea, not so homely a brew as Uncle Mace, fused with religion and rarefied blends of conversation. Couldn't come down to we earthbound farm-labourers. Sought to discuss high-flown Trinities and sacramental dogma. He'd draw Holy Families on the whitewashed inside-walls of barns and hovels, and scribe beautiful texts, 'Though my sins be as scarlet they shall be whiter than the driven snow.' It were hard to picture Holy Joe, driven to black charcoal and a shabby bowler-hat, committing anything scarlet.

'Old Brummy' were one of the few that had a Missis with him. Her were more of a Mission than a Missis, sent on foraging expeditions by him among the natives in the village. Her knowed all the womenfolk, shopping around with her big wicker-basket, playing each off against her neighbour. 'Mrs Venvell gave I lump o' cake and Mrs Benfield twist o' sugar.' Everybody were sorry for her 'cos her were punch-simple; old Brummy knocked her about if her come back empty-basket. He'd been a prize-fighter in his time; his nose had travelled about a bit and his ears warn't all that special.

Bagnel Barn were a mecca for the roaders. Sometimes there were a gathering of the clan in there; but 'Redskin', a doctor's son, ruddy from drink, with women's stockings round his throat and a hatchet at his waist, never roosted in the barn with the others. It warn't that he were stuck up, it were just that if he fell out with folks he were apt to fell 'em with his axe; it were safer all round if he parleyed at a distance and made his roost in the adjoining cart-hovel. He were warm enough in there even if it were open on one side. The true roader were used to dossing in the open, hated to be completely closed in under a roof, only deigned to burrow into Bagnel because it were already half-ruined to the sky, handy to the familiar road, with a clear spring nearby in the slinkit called 'Irish' for filling his precious billy-can.

Some vagrants craved a roof. They had their wandering life all mapped out by the statutory mileage to be tramped from one spike to the next. They sought public shelter at night, even though it went hard against their grain next morning to have to skivvy towards its upkeep before setting off on the next harsh lap of their skiving existence.

The Romanies kept their aristocracy intact, hauling and

hawking their stately hump-backed homes around with them, doing their 'seasons' all over the land.

Roaders, vagrants, Romanies all had a settled life of sorts, and mostly by choice. But the new crop of vagrants was cut down by chance, the lattermath of war, littered across the country, bundled they knew not whither.

'WANTED!' posters began to appear and increase outside PC Hudson's police-house. Before the War, crime had been mostly local, light and primitive, scrumping Adams's apples or playing pranks on Hallows' Eve. PC Messenger, Mr Hudson's predecessor, knowed exactly which of we old bwoys he wanted, and meted out rough justice on our rumps with the little rod he kept tucked down beside his truncheon. He never spared the rod, but once administered your trespass were forgiven, and he were just as ready next day to help you out—or hand you out another.

Our village bobby pounded his beat, plodding for miles around the parish, trusted to be on point duty at different outlying signposts, crossroads and turnpikes, keeping vigil at set times of the day and night. For the more serious crimes of poaching or drunk'n'disorderly, set penalties were dished out from the Magistrates' Court at Chippy. Murder were so rare the precious newspaper-cutting, a whole page of every gory detail, 'ud be kept pressed, handed down like an heirloom, to be aired only at nostalgic family reunions.

PC Hudson were a more feared enforcer of the law than Mr Messenger, a keen confiscator of catapults, banning four-on-a-bike and other innocent suicidal pranks. It were good fun, one standing on the front wheelnuts facing the handlebars, one standing on the pedals, one sitting on the seat, and one mounted on the little step at the back—hurtling down from Top End of Road Enstone to Bottom End in one fell swish. We must have been every bit as terrifying to old people as they juggernauts hurtling down from the Bell to the Harrow be to me today. Yet PC Hudson is most connected in my mind with they 'WANTED!' posters, and always 'getting his man'. The changing world of post-war be such that his man were var' likely a foreigner, fleeing the law from miles away, trapped in the general migration limping through our Enstone.

Another change were marked in the women of the village. Used to doing the men's work while they were away, the womenfolk took on more and more now we was at peace. We even had women bellringers, women in the choir, and—biggest revolution of all—a Women's Institute. Most institutes in villages before the War had been clubs for working men. Women warn't supposed to club together on purpose. They'd congregate occasionally in the 'Bode of Love', the little kitchen at the back of the pub—by chance; and in the schoolroom to prepare the Club Feast—by request. But coming together on purpose, as a body, and calling themselves 'the WI'—well!

They women was the laughing-stock of the men in the village. Our Mam were one of the first to join. Our Dad couldn't understand it—reckoned 'that oak-barkin' done it'. There were a lot of talk amongst the old men in the pub about it; more was 'catchin' it' every month, 'fifty to sixty of 'em now at it.' Even we old bwoys 'ud tease Mam, pulling her leg every time she were putting on her best straw hat to go to the 'gossip-shop'. Our Mam 'ud sweep out regardless, little nose in the air, gathering up Lou Pearce and Granny Harris in *their* best hats on the way. They was only doing what we men going to the pub had been doing for years. We was awed too, hearing 'em opening out so strong with their special song, 'Jerusalem', on summer evenings in the schoolroom—'burning gold . . . clouds unfold!'—hear 'em chirruping up for themselves all over the village. Later they met in the new Parish Hall. They used to meet in the evenings in the summer and the afternoons in the winter. Our Enstone be a dark old hole in the winter. There be no street-lighting in the country in they days.

Even Miss Dillon took an interest in the Women's Institute. Miss Dillon and they others of high-born rank, who'd kept theyselves uppity on their high horse before the War, now seemed more natural, down-to-earth, walking about among the villagers and inclined to stop and speak. Miss Dillon and her friends, Miss Corbett and Miss Bruce, had faced the War together in the Ambulance Unit in Flanders, and seemed to need each other more than ever to face the Peace. Miss Dillon and Miss Corbett set up house together, and Miss Bruce settled nearby, though she were native to Scotland and Lord Elgin's granddaughter. Narn of they three high-born ladies married. It warn't only our Lottie's lot to lack escort after the Great Carnage.

A man 'ud have a job to match up to the industry of Miss Bruce, or 'Miss Brusque' as some called her. I never found her brusque, her always spake civil to me; it were her Scottish brogue that were brusque to our broad Oxfordsheer. But no man 'ud have come up to her keen standards and the house she later designed for herself in Dry Ground, near the Bicester–Banbury crossroads. Drives, hedges, farm buildings, stock, implements, everything kept up posher than posh.

Not only her own house were kept in order but other folks' affairs as well. If her spotted another's house in a sorry state or suspected a sick cottager's water-supply, her 'ud move hell and the Parish Council to get it put right. Her were generous too. It were her as drove away the final debt for the new Parish Hall. The whole village were kept on the right track with Miss Bruce in her helmet and goggles firmly handling the early twenties in her open racing Amilcar. It were a black rocket of a motor, with a spare wheel on the driver's door and the bonnet strapped down like a suitcase.

Motoring and mechanization grew rapidly after the War, though in the village itself the reign of the horse were exercised well into the 1930s. By 1918 we'd growed accustomed to the sight, sound and stink of convoys of Army trucks and military equipment churning through from the Midlands and the North. On the farms the lack of men during the War had driven some farmers to the tractor and the steam-plough, but these were still looked upon by the small farmer as outlandish measures for emergency or last resort.

Mr Lennox's Titan were the first tractor I drove. It were more like a traction-engine than a tractor. We was up in Green Ball cutting wheat, and short of manpower as usual during the War. We'd already scythed all round the outside of the crop by hand, and bound and set the sheaves against the hedge to give the monster room to turn. Mr Lennox had had a job to coax him to start, so we didn't want to run the risk of stopping him at dinner-time. He asked me to drive Titan while he sat on the binder behind. I were that fixed on cutting a close swathe, Titan's nose had crashed through the hedge before I—'WHOA!'

He rared back just short of crushing Lennox 'n' binder into one. I warn't what you'd call brilliant at tractoring. I mastered Titan in the finish, but I were always expecting him to have the same gumption as my old Blossom, who'd stop if she were getting too far ahead and turn to see if you was catching up.

Even the mighty steam-plough couldn't function without my horses on the coal-wagon and water-cart. The Oxford Steam-Plough Company were in existence before the War, travelling about the country with their own battalions of engines, troops and earth-moving equipment. A farmer 'ud hire a set of ploughs, two engines and five men with their equipment. The foreman and the under-foreman were the engine-drivers; the ploughman and scuffleman handled the various earth-working machinery, working to and fro across the field between the two engines; and the cook-bwoy did all the cooking and skivvying. They all lived on site with their caravan: the men sleeping on the four bunks, and the bwoy kipping on the floor.

Thee can imagine what a fearsome set and racket a full set of steam-tackle were for a horse to meet on a narrow road, with one mighty monster towing the caravan and the other towing the heavy earth-moving plough, scuffle, razer or dredger. They travelled under their own steam in transit, but on the site it were up to the farmer to feed 'em with steam-coal and water. I've done this foddering many a time, pumping water into the water-tank and fetching coal from the farm coal-house.

Coal were a terrible power for good in the land in them days. None of your little processed nuggets in paper bags from the coal-shop. The farmer 'ud buy it 'as dug' by the truckload from Charlbury Station. 'CANNOCK CHASE', 'MARRIOT'S', the names of the mines were painted proud, six foot high on the sides of the trucks. Some of the house-coal 'ud come in huge prehistoric boulders, heavier than a man could carry, and you'd have to heed not to 'bomb' it into the bed of the farm-wagon. . . . The steam-coal were special-hard, with a stinking-strong smoke—comed all the way from Wales.

The two 23-ton engines stood on opposite sides of the field with the plough threaded on a steel hawser between them. The hawser were wound on to a great winch-drum under the belly of each engine, one winding clockwise, the other anti-clockwise, hauling the plough back and forth over the field between 'em. The ploughman and scuffleman travelled bosun's-chair-style on the plough, the one steering her in the furrow, the other anchoring her tackle in the soil. The cook–bwoy were responsible for cooking and housekeeping in the van, for cleaning anything else he were asked, and for working his apprenticeship, learning every aspect of the job right up to engine-driver. The engine-driver used to signal on his hooter when he were ready for the other driver to start winding back. You could hear they hooters tooting all over the village when they was at work—and a smartish TOOT! for me if I were a laggard with the water.

Mr Lennox first hired a set when I were a bwoy-chap. We was going all-out on the harvest and hadn't the teams to spare for ploughing the follas. The weather was baking hot, ideal for getting the land turned over as soon as possible for killing the weeds. Warn't none of these weedkillers and pesticides they chucks about today, and we never dreamed of setting fire to the countryside.

Our horse-ploughs were single-furrow, the steam-plough did six furrows at a time. They Oxford ploughs was economical on coal, double-cylindered, using the same steam twice over, so I had to coal-up only twice a day: but they needed a terrible lot of water. I were bwoy–chap, working flat-out on the water-cart all by myself as usual. The ploughs was in Shilcott, the field furthest from the farm, nigher Taston than Fulwell; and the nighest source of water were Farmer Penson's farm pump at Taston. It were a fair old trek servicing both they engines back and forth across the field, and back and forth to Taston; even though Farmer Penson let me take the short-cut through his rickerd, I'd hardly got there when they'd start chivvying me, blasting me at long length on that old hooter. I were on the last lap of the day, longing for me tea and our Mam's roly-poly, when 'Brusher' Beckett came into the field waving a telegram.

Brusher were the yedsirag over all the steam-ploughs. Years ago he'd started work for Allen's up at Cowley as a cook–bwoy, and gained his nickname 'Brusher' 'cos he had a constant brush in his hand, cleaning and shining every tiff 'n' turn, burnishing all in his path through his apprenticeship right up to engine-driver. Now he were yedsirag over all the engine-drivers, with three of his sons as engine-drivers, and the youngest as foreman on our set.

'Government orders!' Brusher shouted, waving the telegram at his son. 'They wants another airfield!'

Aeroplanes was coming more and more into the War. The steam-plough was wanted down-country to level land for an airfield at a place I'd never heerd of, Biggin Hills.

'I've brought the engine-lamps,' Brusher said. 'Dost think thee can finish here and travel through the night?'

'Doubt it, but we'll have a go,' his son says, wiping his oily face on his oilier hankercher.

My stomach sank; there were a fair bit of ploughing to finish and I were famished. Still, they aeronauts was doing their stunt for us up aloft, it were only fair to do our stint for them down below. I were still pumping that night when Freddy Penson poked his nightcap out of his bedroom casement to holler, 'Goodnight, bwoy!'

By eleven o'clock it be too dark to carry on. Brusher sent me home and told me to be back with the water at first light to finish the peck.

'Thee had accident, Mont?' Mr Lennox were coming to meet me and my horses in the dark. 'Thee get awf home, laddie; I'll tend to thee horses and have 'em ready for 'ee at first light. Thee need na' worry about coal-cart in the morning, I'll tend to all that.'

Church clock were just striking midnight as I trudged up the dark Fulwell Lane under the black rustling trees to the ancient Hoar Stwun. I'd never been past they stwuns all by myself in the dark. There were scary tales of the old hoary king . . . THERE HE WERE! Wild grey locks, gwoostly whiskers!

'Wheer the hell hast *thee* been?'

It were our old Dad come to seek me with his lanthorn.

I dropped like a stwun into bed along of our Jim, fast asleep. He were still fast asleep when they hauled I out again just before daybreak. I were pumping yet another load of water as the sun rose. Farmer Penson poked his nightcap out of the bedroom casement, rubbing his eyes. 'Moy-hoy, bwoy! Thee been pumping all night?'

It certainly felt like it.

Water were the staff of life in they days. Pumps, troughs, streams, rivers, all they watering-places was of great importance to the traveller and the drovers of animals and machines. They steam-plough engines could carry only so much in their tanks and were glad to let down their pipes and suck up any surplus on their way cross-country. Old maps 'ud landmark all 'fluddes' and fords, just as all petrol pumps, very few and far between, was marked on some of they first motoring maps.

Hedges too was important landmarks. Old strip maps, showing the route from one important city to the next, showed all the roadside hedges. Old George Sheffield, who hoarded anything of interest to do with the history of our Enstone, once showed me the copy of a letter, written in 1787, giving directions for walking from our Enstone to the next village of Great Tew:

> When over the ford keep the hedge on your right hand thus, and turn to the right with that same hedge on your left hand till you come to a gate. When you come through the gate you will have a hedge on your left hand till you come to a little furze ground. Follow that road across that ground which will bring you to a great road directly athert. You will then have a hedge on your right hand which keep until you come down to the Mill. Cross the water and lean to the hedge on your left which will bring you to Great Tew town-end.

The only time Mr Lennox ever raged at me were when I were fourteen and thoughtlessly set fire to a pile of old thetch close to the hedge at Fulwell Farm. In they days twin hedges lined the road from the top of the village all the way up to the tree-belts, and from the bottom of the village all the way up to Ditchley Park. It were like walking up a posh drive to troop along the dusty road between 'em. Mr Pratley spent his life, like working on the Forth Bridge, cutting and layering they hedges. He warn't no bigger 'n six penn'orth of ha'pence, and his bandy legs 'ud never stop a pig in a passage, but such were the status of his job he were always *Mr* Pratley. I wonder what he'd think if he came back to earth today; narn a hedge left of his life's work, narn a beanstick, narn a besom. He were a man of few words and quaint sayings. 'Theer's a trick in every trade,' he were fond of saying, 'bar besom-making, and the biggest stick goes in the middle theer.'

We always swept out with a besom. The Co-Op delivery carriage were blazoned with a bunch of besoms as it plied its trade around the country villages, brushing the hedgerows from Chippy to Enstone three times a week, calling at every house in the village.

The Chipping Norton Co-Op were a high-class department store. Its Diamond Jubilee in 1926 were a tremendous celebration. Chippy were chock-a-block. Everybody in their best Co-Op suit and Sunday hat. A first Co-Op Sunday suit 'ud see a young man well into middle life; a second 'ud see him out, not exactly fitting but still respectable, at a ripe old age. Other rival tailors and drapers 'ud tote their wares around; Webb's from Chippy, Strong and Morris from Woodstock; their covered wagons chock-a-block with bolts of cloth and boxes of clothing tackle. They'd come and seek 'ee out in the pub, on th'allotment, and give 'ee a chance to fit or feel there and then. They lacked stock and horses during the War and for some time after; then they started spluttering back, some of 'em in old army motorized shops, poop-pooping their wares to their customers.

Carlo, the happy Italian, jaunted throughout the twenties in his pretty painted wagon with his name 'CARLO' singing up and down in coloured letters all along the side. It were a covered wagon with a chimney and a tin roof, yet it were opened up with a little awning on both sides. It housed his coal-stove on one side and his ice-box on the other. His gallant little cob 'ud tow it from Oxford to Chippy once a week; and Carlo 'ud serenade, 'Icy-cream!' from one balcony and 'Fishy-chips!' from the other. He'd start the fish a-sizzling just before he reached the village, tantalizing all us Enstone signors and signorinas to 'Come, buy!'

Friday night were 'Carlo night'. He'd cover your dinner-plate with fish for a tanner, or sell you an inch-thick wodge of ice-cream between two crisp wafers for a ha'penny. You'd get as much for a ha'penny then as you gets for ten bob today. He'd be all sold out, with his ashes all raked out into the ruts in some farm gateway by the time he returned from Chippy. You'd hear his gentle aria swell with the cob's plodding hoofs as they ascended the hill up through Enstone, and drifts of a more spirited finale 'ud tease back in snatches as he picked up speed past Jollys Ricks towards Oxford.

Our Enstone Hill be always a challenge to climb. Many of they early motors got stuck half-way, specially when it was wet. They was mostly belt-driven. Later, when they was chain-driven, they'd a better grip. But in the early days when they wet belts slipped, two or three of we mischievous old bwoys could easily hold one back while faking to push, then, suddenly releasing our grip, we'd leap on the back for a free ride as the roadster suddenly surged forward up the hill. Our weight on the back helped far better than pushing. The goggle-helmeted demon driver be too intent on killing time to risk stopping to shake us off, and we'd leap back off just as he were roaring away into the level. I had a ride *on* a motor years before I had a ride *in* a motor; from all the breakdowns and wrecks I see'd towed in by horses it were miles safer.

Another trick we used to play on they early motorists was to stop the flow of fuel to the headlamps of parked cars by pinching the rubber gas-pipe that ran along the side. This cut off the supply of carbide and put out the flame. Cor! That carbide did stink! The motorist had only to come out of the pub to smell out our crime. He'd be that wild!—and have to light 'em all over again with a match.

For the main cavalcade of folks through the village after the War, horse-power were still *horse*-power and the chief form of transport. Even the mail were only just beginning to rely on a red Ford Tin Lizzie. I well remember the mail-horses, and the mail-coach before the War. 'LONDON 69 mls' the old milestwun used to say outside Mr Adams's post office. Mr Adams kept the post office open till eight. Then, behind locked doors, it were 'Thump! Thump! Thump!' from within as he struggled to cork-mark all they letters by hand before the night coach came. Horses was changed every twenty miles. They collected the Enstone pwoost at nine o'clock at night, and delivered the return mail at five in the morning.

There was usually a team of two horses with a driver and a mailman. The driver 'ud never get down, always stayed with the horses. The mailman 'ud open the door, pick up and throw out the sacks of mail, and hardly have time to scrawf back on board before the coach were off again. It warn't built for passengers, only for mail with a flat roof and a metal rail all round the top. A few daring young chaps 'ud sometimes cadge a lift from the Bell back to Kiddington of a Saturday night if the coachman was willing; but he'd make 'em ride outside, clinging to the rail at their own risk. As he left the post office at nine o'clock, pronto, well before closing-time, there warn't much risk of 'em being too merry.

The ha'penny postcard set the pace for most transactions. The telephone were still beyond the ken of most ordinary folks. During the War the postcard were the vital link with morale at home and in the Forces. Regular 'field postcards' was issued free to the men to send home. On the farm a ha'penny postcard from the wagon-maker at Kiddington, 'begging to inform' us that the cart were mended, 'ud see me there in an hour to collect it.

The Ivings family was topping wagon-makers and wheelwrights. Their wagons 'ud run free with plenty of rattle. Wood against wood 'ud run hard, act like a brake, but the Ivings lined all moving parts with metal. They'd paint 'em Oxfordsheer yellow, with each letter of the owner's name blazoned big in blue and red at the front, and painted neat and small on the side. Every part were a workmanlike job, last for years; and their wheels 'ud shoulder tremendous loads on their wide four-inch fellies.

I once bowled a float wheel from Enstone to Kiddington to be mended. The postcard arrived next morning begging to inform me it were ready. I run to Kiddington straightaway, bowled it back, and were driving it on the float that same afternoon.

For most urgent business the telegraph machine still served at the post office. The post were carried and delivered seven days a week; and you could even send a pretty postcard 'for special delivery on Christmas Day'. At Christmas and holidays the post 'ud be that heavy they'd use a bigger coach with four horses in hand.

Even when in the early twenties the main mail were brought in the first GPO Ford red Tin Lizzie van, the horse 'ud still take over to the outlying districts. Half-past five every morning the post clan 'ud gather to sort the mail at Enstone Post Office. Harry Venvell 'ud hit the trail with his pony and little covered wagon to deliver to the Wychwoods; Eddy Paxford with his pony and GPO wagon 'ud trot off in the opposite direction to the Tews and on to Swerford; Walt Paxford on his GPO bike 'ud basket his lot to Cleveley, Gagingwell, Radford and Whiteway; and a troop of walking postmen 'ud scatter the rest about the nigher parish.

Ern Harling walked to deliver at Fulwell on his way to Ditchley, Dustfield, Norman's Grove, Shilcott and Henel. On his return trip he'd stand at the bottom of Fulwell and blow his GPO whistle, 'Bring out yer pwoost!' There warn't no pwoost-boxes out in the wilds. At the top by the farm pump-house he'd blow again, a signal to us on the farm it were time for nine o'clock lunch.

If you hadn't a stamp, Ern 'ud take your money and buy a penny red for your letter or a ha'penny green for your postcard. He warn't obliged to take an unstamped letter but, by law, he couldn't refuse a stamped one.

If Ern were ill a stop-gap postman 'ud take his place. With the shortage of men during the War the gap were sometimes more spread than stopped. Brocky Bishop done it once. We called him 'Brocky' because he were rough as a badger. He were a grandson living with Widow Taplin who garnered mice in her petticuts. When her got home from threshing, her 'ud call 'Pussies! Pussies!', lift up her skirts, and strew the floor with mice and chaff. Old Brocky must have been the GPO's last straw 'cos he were barely literate. I came out of the stable one dark winter's morn and nearly went ass over head over Brocky on his hands and knees in the snow, his cape spread in the light of a carbide lamp, playing Patience with the post.

Charley Hiatt were a stop-gap once for the Tews. He'd just come home from Australia after a spell in the Outback. He'd left the lot at the first homestead on the top of the pile, expecting the rest of the bush to come and collect their own; but the rest of the bush at Great Tew didn't think a lot to it.

The postmen 'ud return with their collected mail to the post office. 'Thump! Thump!' Mr Adams 'ud be at it again. 'Tip-tip-tap!' His hard-working daughter, Sarah, summoned by the telegraph bell, 'ud be at it, working that Morse handle round that old telegraph machine, shut away in her highly confidential cubby-hole.

Mr Adams 'ud cycle with his big wicker mail-basket to catch the midday train at Charlbury and bring back the next lot for the afternoon delivery. He were on that return trek when he brought the good news of the Armistice and, some weeks later, that the troops was arriving back.

Most of 'em walked home from Charlbury Station. The government couldn't afford to ship all the horses back. Some were shot, others were auctioned, twenty thousand Cavalry horses was sold into slavery in Egypt, fated, var' likely, to work long hours among the alien crops in temperatures above a hundred degrees Fahrenheit. But Colonel Ellington's old wounded war-horse were more lucky. He were a big brown hunter resigned to honourable retirement among Mrs Braybrooke's cows in Kitchen Piece with his campaign ribbons braided into his headstall, an elderly gentleman pensioner in a 'Home for Gentlewomen', content to accompany the 'ladies' on summer outings, grazing along the roadside verges.

Other horses was swung by crane, cradled under their bellies by a strong sling, and docked into waiting railway trucks for carting to auctions. 'Trooper' were one. Bought at auction by Mr Lennox, more out of pity than judgement, he were in a sorry state when we went to collect him from Charlbury Station. I were expecting to ride him back to the farm but I hadn't the heart; he were that ribbed and scarred, with a great Z and his army number branded on his rump and burned into his front hoof. I sent the saddle back with Mr Lennox and led him home to Fulwell. He'd need at least two months' care and some decent grub pushed into him before he were fit for farm-work. I were determined to gloss him up to the same good horseflesh as the rest of my chargers. The number on his hoof growed out in time but no matter how I fed, watered and groomed him, that old Z branded on his rump were a permanent memento of battle.

He had other permanent mementoes too I discovered when, ears pricked to the bugle call, he suddenly took off, plough and all, charging into battle after the Hunt. I were a keen follower of the Hunt in our local paper after that, making sure, if they was meeting anywhere in the vicinity of my ploughing, to harness Dozy Daisy in the front rank and Private Trooper behind as anchor man.

He be no good as anchor-man or thiller on a wagon; he 'udn't hold. We had the drag to act as a brake on the wagon, going downhill, and the scotch, an oak block bound in metal, to stop the wagon from running back; but the best brake of all on a wagon is the nighest horse, the thiller. Trooper had been so used to letting the extra strong brake on a gun-carriage do all the work. It were somewhat inconvenient, to say the least, to discover *that* half-way up Charlbury Hill with a wagon-load of cattlecake. Nearly had us all back down to the station in one '*Woa*!'

He warn't all that keen on canal-work neither. Though Fulwell be nigher to Enstone, it be in the parish of Spelsbury. Mr Lennox attended Spelsbury Church and did much for the church and the village. Spelsbury commemorated their dead after the War by building a memorial village hall. Mr Lennox sent me to the wharf near the Rock of Gibraltar pub beside the Banbury–Oxford Canal at Bletchington to draw a supply of cement from the barges to Spelsbury, for Dodger and Vic Lodge and Ken Cross to make into blocks to build the hall. I thought Trooper, after all he'd been through in the War, were the horse that 'ud most appreciate this leisurely clip-clop to a calm backwater deep in the peace of the Oxfordsheer countryside.

A small hoist dropped the first sack of cement from the barge into the back of the wagon. Trooper shot into the air, terrified— thought he were being shipped again to war. Nearly committed suicide hook, line and sinker on the barge. It took some time to convince him—and myself—the rest of his life were worth living and he were wanted on the farm. All in all he were a damned nuisance 'cos you never knowed when his past 'ud let you down. Yet I were very fond of the old soldier and he showed affection for me; he hadn't an atom of vice, just a lack of convenience. He were willing and valiant after that first fiasco, faced up to canal-work many more times, drawing more cement for the hall or coke for heating the church. Though he braved the canal-bank, outwardly calm at the smell of water and the sound of clanking chains behind him, there were always that tell-tale tremor of hoof, twitch of muscle, or nuzzle for reassurance that gived away his old fear.

In later years I never went into Spelsbury Memorial Hall without thinking with a smile of Trooper; nor studied the raftered roof and cross-beams, every cubic ton of which I had carted myself, without hearing the carter's astonished, 'Where's thee mate?' I had no mate except a willing horse, I'd loaded the lot from Charlbury Station all by my eighteen-year-old self.

Nowadays all they timbers be ceilinged o'er to conserve the heat, but for many years they was exposed. It takes a heck of a lot of timber to roof a dwelling, even more to roof a hall. At first I felt hard done by they station porters, who was supposed to help unload goods trucks, leaving me to struggle alone, lifting a forest of oak, while they struggled with each other to lift the tips and paltry packages of incoming passengers. But time and time again after the War, Spelsbury Memorial Hall and the stained-glass window in the church, and all the other memorial crosses, fountains, troughs, seats and tablets cropping up in all the villages around 'TO OUR GLORIOUS DEAD' made me realize how lucky I were to be gloriously alive. To have the strength to cart heavy oak instead of being wasted away under the sea like George Knight and Frank Benfield and all they other bwoy-sailors; to have sound lungs filled to the full with clean country air, not fouled with poisoned gas like our Jack; to have my two long legs to dance at the Thripenny Hop or go cross-country wenching on my bike, not take ages to hobble the few yards to the post office to collect my meagre compensation; or, worse still, wait for some kind soul to push me theer, penned and pensioned forever in a wheelchair.

In 1920 I were fully a man, with stamina and strength beyond my eighteen years. 'Where's thee mate?' were the question my lone feats be meriting, more and more, as a labourer. 'Where's thee mate?' were the question I were putting privately to meself, as I cast my roving blue eyes over the wenches, more and more, as a man.

— 10 —

'Here's to the Lass that
Queened on the Green!'

I CAN'T REMEMBER WHEN I first seen a girl naked; I see'd so many. Dozens of 'em, in the brook, down Hind Jones at Church Enstone. We bwoys was naked too. In they innocent days it were the natural way for kids to play in the brook when I were at school. Even if costumes for swimming in brooks was invented, none of we could have afforded 'em. I suppose over the years they gals made a private note of our surplus tackle, and we made a private note of their missing parts, but in the main they kept us hard at it, supplying the clats of mud from the bank for them to stop-gap the dam we was all building together. My first lesson in naked sex be co-operation.

As we matured, eleven, twelve, thirteen, covering up our burgeoning bumps and mixed feelings, co-operation turned more to competition. Competition amongst us bwoys to outdo each other in bodily strength and skill; competition among the gals, despite their long hindering skirts, to keep upsides with us; and competition between us all to reach Top Standard.

107

Top Standard be only an ancient wooden bench at the top end of the schoolroom. The one room housed the whole junior school: but that seat of honour held only three kids, and you was only allowed to polish its knots with your corduroy breeches or flannel drawers if you was bright enough. For the last two years I was at school, Chisel and me shared that bench with the first girl I proper-kissed, Gert Regan.

It were Gert's dad, Owen, as kept the Harrow, and her mother were the big raw-bwooned woman who often helped up at Heythrop Mansion. Their son Phil, Gert's adored big brother, were one of the skaters that were to lose his life in the Navy in the War. They was a generous, out-giving family and Gert were the same: a big-made gal but decent with it. Our meanders into first love along the brook at Cleveley was straight-furrowed enough compared with today's hanky-panky. We tickled trout as oft as we tickled each other, but her laughed a lot, and were nice and clean: keeping tryst as oft as could with her boots well brushed and her patches well ironed.

Ivy Titcomb and Hilda Ivings was worth kissing too. The trouble was, as they gals left school and budded into full bloom, if they had anything worthwhile to offer they went away and offered it elsewhere. There were nothing to hold 'em in our Enstone—'cept farm-labourers; and farm-labourers, often working seven days a week, had precious little time nor money for serious courting. There were still the Thripenny Hop once a week to the wind-up gramophone, crooning all the latest songs, 'Give me the moonlight, give me the gal'; there were plenty of moonlight over our Enstone acres, but 'How ya gonna keep 'em down on the farm?' after they'd been away to the munitions in the towns during the War and didn't want to come back.

In my late teens the most precious time I had off for wenching further afield be after evensong on a Sunday evening. In winter, if Mr Lennox's arthritis warn't too painful, he'd usually offer to rack up and bed down the horses for me. In summer I needn't trouble him, they was easy, out to pasture. We always walked round them together first thing on a Sunday to see they was all right. On a Sunday evening I could look quite the dandy, all togged up in me

Sunday suit with me silver watch looped across me weskut on the silver chain Uncle Frank from Oxford gived me for me sixteenth birthday; and me gaiters well polished, me dark hair brushed, and me new bowler-hat. Bought that hat for a penny. Adams Stores had a sale and flooded our Enstone with penny bowlers. I reckon now, looking back, they must have been a wash-out elsewhere, but in our Enstone us landlubbers was at last on the tide of fashion, splashing out our hard-earned pennies and revelling in it. Later, no end of they bowlers was pensioned off to working in the fields. Their hard curvy brims was ideal for guttering off the rain. I still has one I kept for best from my courting days. It be coming up to its diamond jubilee; sixty years of fun and funerals.

I had the bowler, I had the bike—and the moonlight—but where to find the gal? In winter the only place to go were the pub; and in they days you didn't meet nice girls in pubs. The other sort was all right, good for a laugh and a drink and for offering her all if thee took her fancy. The trouble was, if her fancy warn't all that 'ticular I warn't all that keen on taking it. I wanted more than animal antics, I see'd enough of they on the farm.

Summer was easier, with the longer evenings. In summer, gals was dotted about like daisies on village greens, bunched on a seat under the village elm, or blooming in twos and threes in the lush outfield, watching the tail-end of a cricket match. We foreigners 'ud pull up on our bikes within winking or aiming distance, picking the Daisy we fancied from the bunch by looping the pliant stem of a plantain into a catapult and pinging her bare neck with its soft rosy seedhead.

She were hardly ever there again the next chance I had to go. Either she didn't belong to that village anyway, or she were only briefly home from service, or the team were playing elsewhere, or 'Our Mont' let her down by being in demand back home. Winter were often back by the time Superman were free again to seek the queen of his dreams.

Her 'ud have to be on the tallish side; at six foot two I'd look daft with a pigmy. But I didn't want no Amazon. One race of giant Abbotts up the narrow stairs to bed at the Dovecote were enough for me. There were still us three big chaps at home, and Jim and me still fighting for our own space in the same old double bed. I longed for a gal to share my bed, a warm-giving gal I could love all round as close as possible on my level. She'd need to be a country gal, a village-green wench; I knowed no other trade to provide for her but farm-labouring. She'd need to know all about roly-polys and tommy-cloths. It 'ud be nice if she could put up with my singing and a walk round my horses with me on a Sunday. It 'ud be out of this world if she were like our Mam, comely and clean, good with her hands and helping people, caring for me and the childern. In short, poor wench, a ministering angel. I were looking for a halo in a haystack.

By the time I were an old man of twenty I almost give up. Then Les Oliffe, the carrier's son from Witney, married our Dora. Her were in a good post, working for Mrs Early of the blanket family at the time. They was wed at our Enstone Church, St Kenelm's, and looked so well suited and wrapt up in each other I felt quite left out. If a carrier from Witney could pick up a nice gal like my dear sister Dora, there must be another 'un around somewhere for Our Mont to cart off.

One fine Sabbath evening early in May I decided to go with my friends, Spiffer and Briss, for a spin on our bikes. In they day a 'bug' be slang for a waster, a no-good fellow; but a 'spiffer' be slang for just the opposite, the best, a good'un, a decent sort, and Spiffer Griffin from Tew be all of these.

Briss be a decent sport too. He hailed from Brissler, as Upper Cleveley was knowed in they days. Cleveley were a much bigger population then than now; and postcards was addressed Brissler as distinct from Lower Cleveley. Most of they hamlet towns of Enstone parish be more thriving communities with mills or pubs or chapels in the twenties and thirties. We used to chaunt:

> *Gagingwell for bacon,*
> *Radford be for beef,*
> *Enstone be a merry town*
> *But Cleveley is a thief.*

'Course, Cleveley chaps 'ud chant it quite a different way round!

Left: 'The boys back home,' 1915. From left to right: Jim, Gil, Mont and Fred.

Below: The Green, Neat Enstone. The entrance to 'down Alley' is between the two narrow houses on the left; Adams Stores is on the right.

The Green. Enstone.

Left: Fred, Mother, Jim and Dad. *Below left*: Horace Abbott, HMS AGINCOURT, 1913. *Below right*: Dora Abbott, 'out at service', 1913.

From left to right: Jack, Lottie and George, 1915.

George Abbott, in his 'high jackboots and white pantaloons'.

Left: 'Queen Henrietta's Waterworks,' Enstone, as restored by Sir Edward Henry Lee of Ditchley after falling into disrepair in the Civil War.

Below: Enstone House in 1905; the figure immediately to the left of the house is the postman, Jesse Bennett.

St Kenelm's Church Choir, circa 1900. From left to right, sitting: F. Hawtin, A. Huckin, F. Bennett, F. Hancock, T. Philipps, A. Hawtin, A. Capes, P. Huckin; middle row: C. Hawtin, G. Hewes, W. Hewes, H. Hewes, E. Griffin, B. Huckin; adults, standing: T. Hawtin, E. Capes, W. Niblett, E. Bennett, W.H. Knight, A. Reynolds, Revd J.E. Philipps, F. Reynolds, J. Beck, — Saunders, J. Harrison.

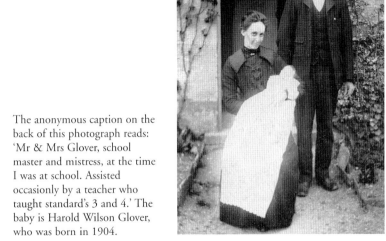

The anonymous caption on the back of this photograph reads: 'Mr & Mrs Glover, school master and mistress, at the time I was at school. Assisted occasionly by a teacher who taught standard's 3 and 4.' The baby is Harold Wilson Glover, who was born in 1904.

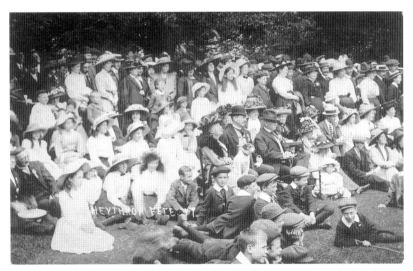

Heythrop Fete, 1912. Albert Brassey is sitting at the front, wearing a trilby hat; his wife is to his right, holding a dog.

'They swingboats were the nearest I ever got to heaven in my childhood.' Sideshows on Enstone Club Feast Day, in front of the Litchfield Arms. Stalls in the main road were discontinued in 1914.

Above: A band of oak-barkers in Heythrop Forest during the Great War. Mrs Abbott, Mont's mother, is second from the right in the front row.

Right: Mary Ann Abbott with her saw in Heythrop Forest.

'There were one little thatched cottage next to Old Man Turvey's at the bottom end of Fulwell.' Old Man Turvey, centre, with his dog. The large tree on the right is a walnut (see p.60).

The fire at Church Enstone; Arthur Simms's motorbike and side-car in foreground.

Mrs Sheffield: 'The first and last woman I ever knowed to catch the gracey-pig.'
Mont's brother Jim is the boy nearest the camera, on the left; Mr Glover is behind
him, holding a bell.

Lord and Lady Dillon at the opening of Enstone Parish Hall, 22 April 1922.

Above: Enstone Club Foresters, 1923. Standing, from left to right: Bert Ward, Bill Huckin, Mont Abbott, unidentified × 2, W. Simms, Percy Simms, Bill Newman, 'Little' George Sheffield, Alf Aries (in bowler hat), Ian Watts, unidentified × 3, George Frederick Sheffield, unidentified. 'Young' George Sheffield and Arthur Simms ('Smiler') are at the front, second and fourth from the left, respectively.

Left: The Reverend and Mrs Palmer, at the time of their silver wedding.

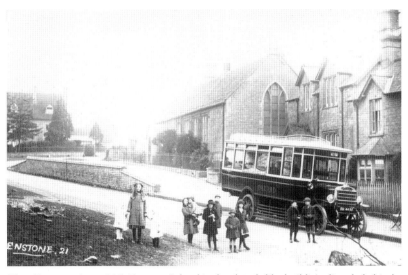

Neat Enstone, circa 1925. Enstone School is the church-like building directly behind the Daimler bus.

'They women was the laughing-stock of the men in the village'—Enstone Women's Institute, 1925. Mrs Abbott is standing in the centre of the second row from the back.

THE MEMBERS OF THE ENSTONE WOMENS INSTITUTE - 1925 -

'Little' Johnny Higley, shepherd and organ-blower, with his wife Susan.

Gil Abbott in his
Buckingham Palace livery.

Left: Mont outside Biddy's Bottom, Fulwell, summer 1984.

Below: Mont outside Manor Farm, Cleveley.

Mont at the lych-gate of St Kenelm's, Enstone, holding 'our Odd's' first grandson, 1977. 'You don't know what it meant to me. . . . It were like lifting the latch on all my days.'

Mont, aged 82, in his best wheelbarrow.

Mont, gardening at Rosa's—'I've been begging 'em to give I the sack for the last *fifteen* years.'

Mont at Marshall's Fountain, Church Enstone. 'Before the First World War, when most water were hard-won from the pump, it seemed . . . a tumbling torrent.'

'Old Mont.'

Briss bean't a thief; but Coggy was. He waxed too light-fingered for his own good as he growed older; joined the Army and died at an early age of something he'd picked up in India. Most of the old gang I used to go around with from schooldays had left the land after the War and joined the Army. The only way then for a poor country lad to see the world were 'at the King's expense'. Before the War they was offering you £150 and 150 acres of virgin land buckshee if you went to Canada to tame it. I can just remember Mr Glover assembling all us big lads to hear this fairy-godmother chap from the government offering us the New World. But, though he waft-wafted his wand about the map of Canada on the board in Enstone schoolroom, narn of we was charmed into taking it. Perhaps that's where poor old Coggy ought to've gone; nothing to pinch there, but he'd have been petrified of they wide open spaces. Coggy were all right to protect as a little chap when we was young, but I 'udn't have trusted him as a friend when I were twenty.

Chisel were the only pal I had still constant from schoolhood, but he were always of a more serious bent than me. His family hierarchy of parish clerks and master carpenters, going far back in Enstone history, was higher up the social measure. By the time we was twenty he had left the choir and the village and were doing well, apprenticed to a building firm in Oxford where my Uncle Charley were foreman.

'Let's bike to Oxford and fathom out old Chisel,' I says to Spiffer and Briss one calm, warm Sabbath evening in May 1922: and off us sets.

It were an evening sweet with the promise of summer, the fresh green foliage bursting forth from the hedges and trees as we cycled past Jollys Ricks, the pink tips of the sanfin blushing over the landscape between Kiddington and Woodstock, the window-boxes in Woodstock town chock-a-block with tulips and gilly-flowers; and, as we entered Oxford, the soft scent of they blossom-trees billowing over the garden walls of they posh houses along the Woodstock Road were rousing as any beanflower. There en't no lustier scent than a beanfield in bloom; 'tis just right for courting. But there bean't no village green in Oxford city. They city gals, transplanted to the country, was never much cop; wiltering for constant attention, they was no ministering angel.

I pulled up at the war memorial to get our bearings; perched back on me saddle, taking stock, looking round—*and there she were*. On a seat on a little patch of green among the trees behind the memorial. A slim steady-eyed gal, a nurse from the Infirmary across the way, with two other nurses sitting in attendance on either side of her. She were off-guard, gazing at me, completely unaware. I held her gaze. The second I winked she gave a fleeting smile and turned away.

They was all pleasant-looking gals and smart in their Radcliffe uniforms. There was a bubbly dark-haired'un, a shyer ginger-haired'un, and this taller brown-haired lass with a calm contained air that made her queen over the other two. They didn't want to talk to us at first, but we soon made 'em smile with our country banter, though the queen warn't so easily amused. Her warn't at all stuck-up, her had a country manner of speaking, in a warm voice with a warm smile, but the others seemed to look to her for a lead and she kept herself on a tighter rein. She were probably tired. They'd just come off duty, the chatty one told us, and were sitting on the green 'growing good and watching the outside world go by' before sauntering back to change at their lodgings.

'Wheer might that be?' I asked, quick as a wink. She were about to spill the beans, but the queen gave her a warning nudge, at the same time giving me a knowing look for trying. I could imagine no patient putting anything past her; yet there were a tenderness within. I'd fathomed it, first glimpse, when she were off-guard, yearning into space. No matter how firm her slim hand tugged that no-nonsense Radcliffe hat down on her brow at the front, there were little curly tendrils of hair escaping down her smooth neck from her coiled plait at the front.

I tried hard to make her laugh as much as the others, but the more I tried the less interest she showed. So I give up and asked her straight if she liked horses. They'd a war-pony at home and she missed him more than anything. I told her about Trooper. *That* sparked us off. Suddenly her eyes were laughing deep into mine, her smiling mouth asking for more. It were a moment worth all my longing, all my seeking. Her were the one for me.

She kept saying they must go and change, they wasn't supposed to hang about in uniform, but I kept her there chatting till the man with the pole came to light the lamp. She allowed us to walk them home. I longed to get close, to ask when I could see her again, but it were difficult with a bike to push, and she stayed in the middle of the other two, walking light and brisk. I couldn't even address her by name. The other two had readily given us theirn, Christian name and all: but she withheld her Christian name, teasing me she were christened only Nurse Carey, and the other two played up to her. Suddenly Briss and Spiffer were busy lighting their bike-lamps, the others were gone, and she were calling 'Goodnight!', hurrying away from me down the lit tunnel of blossom lining St Margaret's Road.

'NURSE!'

No dying patient could have pleaded more desperate.

Instinctively she turned and came back.

I were suddenly overwhelmed, tongue-tied. I blurted out the old schoolbwoy trick, 'Yer lace is undone.'

She laughed softly, her face lit golden under the blossom. 'Dost think I'd fall for *that*?'

'You coming, Kate?' the Irish gal called from the dusk beyond.

'See thee next week? . . . *Kate*?'

She never looked back.

The next Sunday evening I biked to Oxford by myself. The other two warn't all that keen. Briss had his eye on an Enstone gal, Winnie Snow from up the top of the street, and eventually married her. Spiffer ended up in Australia. They thought I were daft, expecting a gal like Nurse Carey to be sitting there on that seat waiting for the likes of a clathopper like me. If she en't, I thought to myself, I'll go and fathom out old Chisel. After all it's thanks to him being in Oxford that I met her in the first place.

Nobody on the seat at the memorial. I felt empty and deserted. All the week I'd saved every little bit of pocket-money I could earn, banking on her being there. I could hardly believe she had sat there only last Sunday, laughing and looking up at me. All the week I'd tried to recall the colour of her eyes; they warn't just blue, more blue-grey, flecked with violet, fringed with dark lashes. I were daft expecting her to turn up; and yet . . . there had been no scorn, no irritation when I'd tricked her back to me, just that soft warmth of her smile and her gentle tone in the lamplight, 'Dost think I'd fall for *that*?'

She were probably on duty. I turned back toward the Infirmary. It's impossible for people today, with all the wealth of free medical treatment available, to understand the special devotion we felt in them days in the villages around Oxford for our Infirmary. We even had 'Eggs Days' and 'Pound Days' at school when we took eggs or pennies or a pound of tea or sugar as gifts for the Infirmary. Kept up and run mainly on voluntary effort, it were firmly fixed in our minds from earliest years as the ultimate in the care of the suffering. 'He'll be all right now,' people 'ud say with comfort and confidence. 'He's in the Infirmary.'

You couldn't see so much of it then from the road. The entrance where the cars park now was all private, with high railings on top of the wall and the glimpse of a fountain pouring forth its bounty in the evening light. 'If only I were in there,' I yearned, 'with Nurse Carey on duty.' There warn't a nurse in sight, only a young lady under a wide-brimmed hat hurrying out of the side-chapel gate. Ladies weared their hats well down on their brow in they days. The lady were walking light and brisk, towards me, smiling at me from under her hat—'KATE!'

I think our first meeting were spent in Kate's favourite place, the Botanical Gardens; her loved plants and flowers. I can't remember; we was too wrapt up in finding out about each other to take stock of the world outside us. We was the same age, of similar country stock. Her dad were a market-gardener in the beautiful Vale of Evesham.

Our Enstone may not be all that spectac'lar from the main street, I told her, but I'd love to wander with her up the Green Lane and reach down the highest blackberries for her in due season; show her where the best mushrooms was in Lady Kerr; escort her along the brook and up Cling-Clang to Church Enstone; show her where I first went to school at Miss Vance's, and the fountain, and my place in the choir-stalls. I had to explain all the names of the villages that made up our Enstone.

She were guarded against telling me straight out the name of her village.

'It begins with a "P".'

'Paradise,' I guessed, being in the Vale of Evesham.

'Piddle,' she confessed. I roared with laughter. She were quite indignant.

'You should see it when all the orchards are in bloom. People come from miles in their wagonettes and charabancs just to feast their souls on the beautiful sight. It *is* Paradise.' From then on her beloved Piddle were always 'Paradise' between us.

Her Paradise choir used the same cathedral psalter as ourern. Her 'never absent, never late' Sunday School Bible were her most treasured possession. I showed her my pocket-watch. She begged me to show her the inscription. Her were thrilled. Time went so fast and were so precious. We had barely an hour to sit before we had to start walking back. She had to be up extra early the next morning 'cos they was having the chimney-sweep on their ward; and I had to bike back to Enstone.

Enstone be only fifteen miles from Oxford. A lad today 'ud hop into his motor, turn the magic key, and be home in no time. Biking were more of a problem in they days, but us got over it. The biggest hassle, apart from frequent punctures from they sharp 'arch'lls, be the struggle to keep your lamp alight. We had no rear lamp, only this little oil-lamp hanging on the handlebar. You had to fill it with paraffin and light it by opening the thick glass port-hole at the front. It had a knob for turning up the wick and a tin-flanged roof where a pesky wind 'ud blow down and fizzle out your flame. You could be summonsed if the bobby caught you riding without a lit lamp. The whole route were covered by the bobbies on the beat; and sometimes he were standing in the dark on point-duty. You'd have to watch out for unfamiliar bobbies springing out at you on the verges of Woodstock and Kiddington, but once you'd pedalled into the territory of our Enstone and he understood you was having trouble with your lamp on a blustery night, he'd var' like tell'ee, 'Ride on; thee'll meet narn other bobby on this beat tonight.'

All that summer I courted Kate with increasing urgency, only too aware how winter often parted country lovers. How lucky they are today, with their passion bolstered by motors and telephones. There *was* motors and phones, but not for the likes of we; and very little privacy. Every touch, every kiss had to be stolen in public; every moment for being together had to be snatched from the few precious hours a week we was both free from duties.

We made the most of those hours, told each other everything. She had two brothers, younger than her, still at home. Though she were their only daughter, her parents had encouraged her in her calling to be a nurse. They was much younger than th'Old Folks and managed their market-garden well between them, forcing early flowers as well as growing fruit. Like me, Kate had been plunged early into responsibility, starting nursing in the middle of the flu epidemic in 1918. She told me several of the nurses had died on the wards, and even the probationers had worked all hours with the number of cases being admitted, and the many that worsened into the dreaded pneumonia. Pneumonia were a killer in they days.

'We had it difficult on the farm too,' I told her. 'With the men away with flu the horses lacked exercise. I had to harness as many as I could in a single team, and different teams each day, to keep 'em in condition. But us got over it.' She laughed at my favourite saying, 'us got over it'. Soon she were saying it too, and us laughed together. How lucky we was, we both realized, to have 'got over' the War and the flu and found each other.

We shared our dreams—our dearest wish were to get married and love each other for ever after—and confided our nightmares. Hers were the constant one for market-gardeners: Jack Frost stealing stealthily over their orchard after a mild spring day and smiting with his black death all the young blossom full of promise and income.

'My worst nightmare,' I told her, 'ever since I were a little bwoy, is being thrown for dead, alive, down Ful'll well. Only t'en't Ful'll, it's somewhere unknown, somewhere I've never been in my life.' I'd never confessed that terror to anybody before. Not even to our

Mam when our Jim woke screaming for her 'cos I was strangling him in bed, trying to clamber out. In they days men was never supposed to vent their fears, never supposed to flinch, never supposed to cry, specially before a woman. Yet I felt I could tell Kate anything without loss of manliness. She understood men's fears. On duty in the ward in the middle of the night she knew how real, how terrifying such nightmares could be, with brave ex-soldiers nearly strangling her, screaming for their mam, and struggling to 'g-get out of this hell-hole'. The War had been over for four years but for some it were still shuddering on, a battle of nerves and hands so shaky and wasted that they couldn't bear the weight of a pen and Katy had to write their postcards.

She were a dab hand at letter-writing. I en't wrapt up in pen-scratting: but I sent little notes and tokens, a pressed flower, a four-leafed clover, whenever us couldn't meet. Anything I pwoosted into Mr Adams's pwoost-box by eight at night, she'd get first thing in the morning at Oxford. After working all day in the hayfield there warn't much time for penning an epistle. Sometimes, for fun, when I were resting in the field with the horses at dinner-time, I'd braid her a true 'carter's knot' or 'two-er'. It were the traditional token wore by carters at the old Hirings and shows and agricultural gatherings: two pliant stalks of wheat, worked into a loop, criss-cross, back and forth, over and under, with the two heads leading through the middle.

Every carter worth his calling knowed how to braid up a horse's mane and tail; braiding straws for tokens and string for halters comed to him quite natural. I prided myself on my even braiding when I were a young carter, weaving ribbons in with tails and horsehair in with tokens. A 'fiver' be the best masterpiece to show off your skill. For an heirloom you could add plumes and bells, but we made 'em plain for the horses in hot weather: five stalks braided to finish with five heads of wheat in a broad fan at the bottom. We'd tuck 'em up under the horses' head-runners and they'd dangle like giant earrings, fanning away the flies as the horses nodded along. But a 'fiver' be too bulky to send to Kate in a penny-ha'penny letter; that 'ud have to wait to grace the mantelpiece of our first home.

We was busting to be wed. Mr and Mrs Carey was willing as soon as I could provide a home. I warn't so worried now about providing for th'Old Folks, as long as I lived near enough to keep an eye on 'em. They was better off now with Dad's five bob a week from Lloyd George, and our Jim and Fred both bringing home their wages. Jim were a full man like me, winding up *his* school silver pocket-watch every night, and working on the Furland Farm up at Church Enstone. Fred were working as gardener's bwoy up at Heythrop Mansion. There were a great spasm of selling up farms and estates as the depression in farming began to sink in after the War. The Heythrop Estate had been partitioned off into farms and a sawmill. The Brasseys had sold out to the Jesuits. The mansion and remaining gardens were now a training college for priests. Our Fred were rolling in green pastures, bringing home more money at fourteen for culling daisies from lawns than I were at twenty, cultivating acres. What's more, with they Jesuits celebrating every other day as a saint's day, he had no end of paid holidays.

I were obviously in the wrong job, but I were happy working for my old boss, Mr Lennox, and there was one advantage in being a farm-labourer: the farmer usually helped you out when you wed, with a tied cottage. There were one little thatched cottage next to Old Man Turvey's at the bottom end of Fulwell that Mr Lennox kept to house the occasional piece-worker. It had its own chimney, and the luxury of a two-holer privy at the bottom of the garden. If I could bespeak that cottage, Katy and me could be wed. I knowed Mr Lennox 'ud do all in his power to help.

'I'm sorry, Mont; I'm retiring at Michaelmas.' Mr Lennox dropped the bombshell. 'The doctor says another winter here will finish me if I don't go to a warmer clime.'

I knowed his arthritis were very bad, and our Enstone be pretty exposed on the landscape, but farmers usually gived a year's notice.

'I'm afraid it's all come about sooner than I expected. Mr Hawes, the new tenant, is keen for you to stay on as carter, but he'll be bringing his own carter as well.'

'Can I keep my horses?'

'He's bringing his own horses. Ours'll have to be sold.'

It were with a heavy heart I tended my horses at Fulwell stable that night. Not only were I sad to think of letting them go, and of finishing for my old boss who had trusted me so much, but Katy and me had set our hopes and plans on that cottage. Stwun-built and solid, with piped water nearby, and a big patch of garden for Kate to raise the plants and cuttings her dad had promised her. In they days a wife didn't look to go out to work, but Kate had plans for selling plants and taking piece-workers as lodgers. I'd have been close to my work and near enough to keep an eye on th'Old Folks. I knowed Mr Lennox 'ud have been liberal where milk and firewood was concerned. Now it warn't his to give, the new carter 'ud need it, and I were to leave the Fulwell farm where I had worked all my bwoyhood years and learnt so much.

Mr Hawes himself came and asked me to stay on. He were a nice man, but I knowed in my bwoons it 'udn't answer to have two chaps as carter. I warn't a-feard of being out of work, despite the Depression. I could make far more money at piece-work than full-time farm-labouring. But it were only as a full-time farm-labourer I'd be entitled to a cottage. It 'ud have to be a farm near enough to keep an eye on th'Old Folks. Dad were over seventy now, and though he still took a pride in making a good pair of boots, he were beginning to be difficult and demanding for our ageing Mam to manage at times. Yet with Kate, when I'd wangled her home once or twice in Mr Lennox's pony'n'trap from Charlbury Station, he were docile as a lamb. He *were* a lamb, she reassured our Mam, compared with some of the old rams she had to wrestle with on the ward. I don't know what she advised our Mam as they sauntered close up the garden to view Mam's few flowers, but when they came back into the Dovecote I could see in Mam's eyes how proud she were of me to have captured the love of a gal like Kate.

They say one door in life doesn't close without another opening. I were sitting in the pub about a week before Fulwell farm sale, feeling very low and sorry for myself. Two of my old horses, Beauty and Jolly, had died that week. It were almost as if they knowed they was going to be sold. Beauty had just given up quietly and died in her sleep. I'd sat up all night with Jolly; the vet didn't expect him to last till morning. I kept on stroking him from time to time through the night. 'Thee a-gwinna live, Jolly? Or thee a-gwinna die?' The poor old chap just stood there, head bowed, patiently awaiting his fate. Towards dawn he suddenly reared up, his head travelling backwards all along the stable roof, and fell back on the floor bringing the hay-rack on the wall crashing down behind him. He and Prince had been a topping team. Now Prince were moping alone in their stall, and I were moping alone in the pub.

'Cheer up, Mont! I've come to offer you a job.' It were Ted Hunt from Church Enstone, a much younger farmer than Mr Lennox, and a very nice chap. 'Fred Ivings, my carter, is taking on the Furland Farm. His cottage at Church Enstone belongs to the Furland Farm but he's moving into the farmhouse and says I can rent the cottage for my new carter. If you can hold out till Lady Day you can have his job and that cottage as well.'

Kate and me was over the moon. The Church Enstone cottage be even nicer than Fulwell. It had a pretty outlook and were close to my childhood fountain, the church and the pub. It had its own privy, and a wash-house, and a proper stwun-built pigsty at the bottom of the long garden. In some ways it were even better than the Dovecote, standing more private, though I'd always think fond' of my old home down Alley.

Michaelmas Day and Lady Day were the traditional days for swapping over on the farm. Glad'n'sorry days, they was called. I were glad I were going to a happy future, but I were sorry to bid goodbye to my horses. It en't the young'uns you worries about so much as the old'uns, Prince, Boxer, Daisy, Trooper, the ones whose ways you've growed into, and they've growed into youern. Trooper came off luckiest at the sale. He were bought by Farmer Goodey of Lidstone, a quiet old soul who cared for his animals. Years before, I had once gone late at night to see him about something. His wife said he were in one of the barns. I were floundering about in the dark trying to find him. It be no good hollering the old fellow, he be deaf as a pwoost. At last I glimpsed a chink of lamplight in one of the pigsties. A strange scraping noise were coming from within. I peeked in. An old boar were having his dead tusk removed. Most people 'ud have knocked it out with hammer and chisel. Old Goodey were sitting in the straw in front of him with his back to me, gently filing it down with a rasp, and the old boar were sitting back on his haunches, rocking in rhythm, loving it. Trooper could look forward to spending the rest of his life in good hands.

I were looking forward to spending the rest of my life in Kate's good hands. I were determined that when I slipped that guinea gold ring on her slender finger I'd look my best in a decent wedding-suit. Up till then I'd had to put up with our Mam buying me ready-made tack. It were usually good hard-wearing stuff but, me being six foot two, it fitted only where it rubbed. The jacket were never long enough in the sleeves nor broad enough across the shoulders; and I had no say in the cut of the lapels nor the jib of the weskut. I dared meself to go to the best tailor in Chipping Norton, knowed for miles around for making hunting-tack for the nobs, and ask him straight out how much he'd charge to make a suit for the likes of Montague Archibald Abbott.

'G. HANNIS. BESPOKE TAILORING' it said over his double-windowed shop: though what Bespokes had to do with tailoring I couldn't fathom. It were a dark November evening. I'd looked in straight from work, worried he'd be closed, I hadn't had time to wash and brush up.

It were a small genteel establishment, stuffed with quality, from its thick mahogany counter to its new silent electric light. The sporty-looking tweed-suited proprietor and his quietly dressed lady assistant looked up in surprise as I stood at the opened door, not wanting to cart in all the mud on my working clobber.

'How much for a bespoke suit for the likes of me?'

They didn't take I serious at first. The lady shivered. The gent looked me up and down and var' near told me to hop it.

'*Serious*,' I says.

He pulled himself together, perfectly polite. 'It depends on the cloth, sir—and the amount,' he added, sizing up my workaday frame propping open his mahogany doorway. 'A good wool worsted for you, sir, woven at our local mill, would be £18.'

Eighteen quid! The most I'd ever earned in the heyday of farm labouring during the War had been twenty-five shillings a week. I were determined to earn that suit. I went mad, hiring myself out to every job and farmer in the district: whitewashing Owen's pigsties, digging Parson Palmer's garden, carting taters for Farmer Oliver, and biking out to Cornwell to plough for Farmer Dancer. I were even hired out by another farmer to plough some of my old acres at Fulwell for Farmer Hawes. Plough Sunday came early in January. It were traditional on that day for a plough to be brought and blessed in church; and on the following Monday all the farmers around 'ud give a day's ploughing to a new farmer, sending a man with a team and a plough to help him break his land. The new farmer had only the easy flearing to do after that.

I worked up at the sawmills at Heythrop. It were good money, but I couldn't stick the shiftless gang I were roped in with. The foreman were straightforward, but as soon as he were out of sight the other chaps 'ud sleer off for a smoke, despite the 'No Smoking', leaving me to stack on my own. Some of they trees they dealt with was twenty feet long. They was knowed locally in transport through Chipping Norton as 'Heythrop Giants'. There's a limit to the length of plank a chap can handle on his own, even with a gantry, and stuff was always 'missing'. We warn't exactly angels on the farm, but there were more skivers and twisters in that one bad gang than you'd meet on six farms.

One of the minor bosses deserved such labour. He were always flouting the 'No Smoking', and he were that foul-mouthed to the men you could hear him all over the timberyard. I en't saying I spouts pure English, but there's a limit to the amount of filth thee can take from a boss. 'I'm quitting, gaffer,' I told the foreman at the end of the week. He were genuinely sorry—even tempted me with another penny an hour. Much as I needed every penny, it warn't worth the misery.

I were next hired out by John Hawtin, with his two-horse team'n'cart, to work for the Council: carting stwun for the A34 and the water for the steamroller. It were quite like old times, working again with a team and on the water-cart. But that 'team' were hard work. They was the most ill-assorted pair in temperament and gait. They was both government surplus from the War, both mares, but one were a sober old thing with a long loping stride, the t'other were a mincing flibbertigibbet, stepping 'twice on a tanner'. It made for some fair old slops with the water-cart.

It were a miserable and dangerous job in the bitter wind, slithering on our frozen slops into the gutter down Great Rollright Cutting; but I were lucky that the weather kept open enough to work at all and I could keep earning. By the end of January I had the money.

Mr Hannis and his daughter was staggered when I insisted on paying for the suit before I were even measured. 'It's like this 'ere,' I says, plonking my bag of savings on the counter before them. 'If you was to get this bespoke suit together and I was to snuff it, slithering about on ice in this freezing wind for the Council, I'd like to will it to our old bwoy, Jim. He be the same B-size as me, give or take a few minor alterations.'

I were a walking wonder to they after that; and the next time I came for a fitting, the whole family, young George, old lady and all, came from round the back of the shop to have a gawp.

I can still remember the shared excitement of choosing my first tweed with Mr Hannis, flopping out all they quality cloths on the rich polished counter. It were to be the first of four best suits threading my life to him, and then to his son, over the next thirty years. They understood my needs and met my circumstances: giving me fittings out of working hours, and cutting my weskut to button high, with deep pockets, so that, years hence, when it were old and used for working out in the fields it were ideal for keeping out the cold and housing small tools.

I remember with fond appreciation, for comfort and good workmanship, each of they suits: but none of 'em gived me quite so much of a thrill as my first, my wedding-suit. Old Mr Hannis made it in three weeks; he felt beholden, he said, having been paid prior, to give me priority. I remember taking Dad with me for my final fitting. Dad studied it close.

'I'm buggered!' he gasped, looking up to Mr Hannis with great respect. 'Thee dost make posh!'

'Praise indeed,' accepted Mr Hannis.

They eyed me up and down, turned me right round, Mr Hannis rubbing his hands together with great satisfaction, and Dad pronouncing me 'a handsome frame, worth upholsterin'.'

I felt like a king. Only a few weeks to go before I'd be wearing my suit for real, standing beside my queen, getting wed. The wedding were all buttoned up at Piddle for Easter Monday. I read Kate's latest letter over and over again:

> Easter is a bit early where Dad's flowers are concerned; but we've always prided ourselves in the Vale on bringing forward the earliest blooms. Dad and Mam are determined, despite that old bogey, Jack Frost, that our little 'Paradise' church will look extra special for us this year. Dost mind travelling back in the cart to Enstone after the wedding with the new bed and mattress they have given us? I can fathom no other way of getting it home for our wedding-night. I am longing to hold you close, my own, my very dearest Mont.
>
> Your ever-loving Kate

I warn't intending to wait till our wedding-*night*. I'd already fathomed out a hidden corner of a field with an old barn to draw into on our way home. I couldn't wish for anything more grand for our brief honeymoon than holding close to my ever-loving Kate on our marriage-bed in a horse'n'cart with the spring countryside busting out all round us.

Jack Frost

Watch out! Watch out!
Jack Frost is about,
He's after our fingers and toes;
And all through the night
The gay little sprite
Is piercing where nobody knows,
Where nobody knows. . . .

ON THE LAST SATURDAY IN FEBRUARY I WERE going to bike to Chipping Norton to meet Kate off the early-afternoon train, and we was going to Simms's, the jewellers on the Horse Fair, to fit her wedding-ring. It were the first half-day she'd had since before Christmas. They were always overworked at the Infirmary at this time of the year. There were plenty of flu about, but not so dangerous as in 1918.

On Saturday, first thing in the morning, it seemed quite mild as I opened the door of the Dovecote and wended my way in the dark down to the privy. The bitter east wind of the last few weeks had

125

dropped, and snowdrops were lining the path in the light of the lantern. But by daylight the first few flakes of snow were floating past the kitchen window. By mid-morning the wind had got up and it were swirling the snow so fast I couldn't even see the Litchfield across the street. It were no good thinking of biking anywhere in this weather; and I knowed Kate 'ud have the sense not to start out from Oxford.

By three o'clock it were snowing so dense it were almost dark. I were battling up from helping Farmer Oliver with his animals when I bumped into another snowman staggering towards me.

'My motor's in a drift along the Oxford Road,' he gasped, waving vaguely over his shoulder. 'I've had to leave my wife in the snow on the side of the road, she's a cripple.'

It were obvious he were in no fit state to trudge back. I led him to the Litchfield—it were chock-a-block with folk who'd abandoned their motors—and set out to get help.

It were still snowing. Pokey Pearce were just coming out of the Alley with his lantern. I'd know his form anywhere, thin as a match with the wood scraped off, yet wiry as steel. He'd poke his nose in anywhere and flush anything out—bunkered hare, basking trout, bashful deer—'Come on, Pokey, you be just the chap,' I says. 'Theer's a crippled lady lying somewheer in the snow the other side of Bagnel. We can't leave her out in this; she'll be frez to d'yeth.'

He ferreted out Zicky Harris from down Alley, and fished out Eric Collett from the Bell. That made four of us, all Enstone lads, knowed the fields around almost by instinct from early years of playing fox'n'hounds. In good going Bagnel be, at most, fifteen minutes along the road, but the road be all blocked, and we was going to have to fight our way across the fields. By now it were really dark and the snow were still swirling in the lantern-light. We couldn't hurry 'cos we was sinking in up to our knees. It took us an hour and a half to find her. I be sorry for the poor soul; her had messed herself and were as much buried in shame as snow.

'We gotta find a stretcher of some sort, an old ge-at or hurdle,' I decided. Zicky stayed put with the patient and kept hollering to each of us in turn to give us a bearing as we trampled on the tops of hedges and plunged into drifts. Pokey unearthed a hurdle up by the 'sarts. It were no picnic striving back with our burden, trying to follow remembered walls and boundaries, lost over and over again in the driving snow; but us got over it. We was lucky to be in a bunch, one alone 'ud never have survived. It were nigh on ten o'clock when we handed our patient safely over to Mary and Mrs Peachey at the Litchfield.

Up till then it had been a good winter, bitterly cold but open; but that last week in February we copped the lot. Telegraph-wires came down, the post couldn't get through; we was completely cut off from the outside world for over a week. There were no council snow-machines, no salting, no gritting-lorries in they days; it were all shovel-work. You soon learned to shovel at a steady pace and throw with the wind. As fast as we cleared one lot, another lot flopped from the sky. After about a week it eased up enough for us to meet up with the Spelsbury shovellers to open the track through to Charlbury, and to clear another narrow track through Bagnel. Luckily all they motors be stuck in the one direction, coming from Oxford, so the horse-mail could at last get past.

I were looking out for a fresh letter from Kate, fixing another date to get the ring. Time were pressing on. In two weeks I'd be starting my new job as head carter for Mr Hunt, Fred Ivings 'ud be moving out of the cottage, and I'd be moving in with barely a week to get it all smart and ship-shape for my Kate before our great day. I hoped our wedding flowers be still surviving, and Mr and Mrs Carey hadn't copped the same severe weather in the Vale as we had suffered in our more open Enstone.

'Present for ye!' Our Jim chucked a small postal package to me at the kitchen table. Kate's writing be that blotched from being out in the arctic I could barely recognize it. They was all teasing me, hankering around to see what she'd sent. Part in fun I escaped up on to my bed to be with her close in private.

> My dear Montague,
>   It has taken me three terrible days to pluck up the courage to write—

'Montague?' . . . At first glance I couldn't take it in. Then I realized the letter warn't from Kate, it were from her mam; her writing were var' like my Kate's. I read that cruel letter over and over. I couldn't believe it were anything to do with me. Gradually the icy facts, one by one, pierced home.

My Kate had set out—like all they motorists caught at Bagnel—before the snow had reached Oxford. At Kingham Junction, where she had to change on to the single line to Chipping Norton, it had been blowing a blizzard for some time. The single-line train had been held up by a drift the other side of Hook Norton Viaduct. The next train back to Oxford didn't come for two hours. Kate must have been sickening for flu. By the time she'd spent two hours by a blazing fire in the waiting-room, had a slow cold journey back to Oxford, and trudged through that freezing blizzard from the station all the way back to the Infirmary, she were almost delirious. Pneumonia had set in. Because of the weather the Infirmary couldn't get in touch with her parents; later, they couldn't get in touch with me. Kate never regained consciousness.

> It was a nightmare bringing our dear daughter home in her coffin on the train through the huge drifts last Wednesday and burying her in the frozen ground of our little church here in Piddle. We all missed you very much. Father and I can't bear to look at the flowers in the glasshouse, they are still so beautiful and full of promise—

Poor Mr and Mrs Carey, Jack Frost had pierced the loveliest bloom of all. My poor Kate had been out in that terrible blizzard all alone, *and I never knowed.*

> She thought the world of you, Mont. I know she would have wanted you to have this. It were always by her bedside.

It were Kate's Sunday School Bible. 'Presented to Kate Carey, 1913. Never absent, never late.' I opened it at her marker. She had marked our favourite portion of Psalms, the one we'd specially chosen for our wedding service: 'I will lift up mine eyes unto the hills.'

Never no more 'ud my lovely Kate lift her laughing blue eyes to the hills. Never no more 'ud her eyes answer mine with overwhelming love and understanding. Never no more 'ud I hear her beloved voice, smell her sweet hair, hold her soft body close. I looked for the date of the letter. Already my Kate, my dear warm, ever-loving Kate had lain a week in the frozen ground of that little church in the Vale of Evesham. *And I never knowed.* My arms ached to cradle her close, to comfort her. I couldn't even write to her. I opened her marker. It were one of the earliest notes I sent her last summer, still enfolding the tiny wild blue heartsease flower found so abundant in our Enstone.

'*Sweetheart—*' The message ran with my tears. '*Dost find heartsease in Paradise?*'

12

New Bricks, New Tricks

'THEE CASSEN'T LIVE ALL ALONE in that cottage with nobody to look after 'ee.'

'I en't traipsing back to the Dovecote every time I finish work.'

I were determined, though I had lost Kate, to live in 'our' cottage. I knowed it'd be painful, after all we'd planned, all we'd dreamed, to move in there without her, but I had my new job to face and it made sense to live in the tied cottage near it. Mam was right, though; out at work all day, I'd have no time to look after it properly.

Mam couldn't look after two establishments. She were still sprightly at sixty-two, but Dad, at seventy-four, were demanding attention more and more. 'It makes far more sense,' Jim and Fred pointed out, 'for us all to give up paying rent for the Dovecote and live rent-free at Mont's place.' At least they looked upon it as 'Mont's place', and I'd be able to further my situation as man of the house. It did make sense; we old bwoys 'ud share the burden of the allotment, the garden, the house-keeping, and th'Old Folks.

But Mam were very reluctant to release the reins of the remnant of her family. (I were already master of me own pay-packet, after the tussle of saving for my wedding-suit.) And she and Dad was terrible stubborn about moving from their fond hearth down Alley.

We old bwoys kept on at 'em both:

'It makes sense, Dad; us'll all be nigher work—'

'Nigher choir, Mam—'

'Nigher pub, Dad—'

'And you and Mam en't getting any younger.'

'Us might as well shift, Mother,' Dad gave in at last. 'Us'll be nigher churchyard.'

It were to be nigher twenty years before they was both laid there, at rest.

It were hard that Easter Sunday, so soon after Kate died, to bear with courage the well-loved anthems of death and resurrection in the choir at St Kenelm's, with my heart in that other little patch of churchyard, decked with the best of our wedding-blooms in the Vale of Evesham.

It were harder still to bear the next day, our wedding-day, the whole family carting their clobber into our cherished 'Bode of Love' at Church Enstone: especially with the added distress of tearing our Dad and Mam from the arms of their weeping neighbours down Alley. Anybody 'ud have thought they was emigrating thousands of miles across the ocean 'stead of shifting a few hundred yards across Enstone Brook.

It were hardest of all to bear that night, my wedding-night, bedding down as usual along of our old bwoy, our Jim, in the old Abbott bed from the Dovecote. It were a particularly long bed, made specially for two of Dad's brothers when they was lanky young men, and me and Jim had grown into it over the years. Jim had hoped to be quit of me at last and have it all to himself when I were married, yet here we was, going through the usual bedtime ritual, sitting back to back on our own side of the bed, winding our precious Oxfordshire Education Committee school watch and placing it careful on our watchstand, before claiming our patch of mattress we had bagged when we was schoolbwoys.

Fred, younger and shorter than us at that time, had the little single room up the small flight of stairs to the attic. Our Fred, working cushier hours for the Jesuits up at Heythrop, could be let to lie abed in the morning: whereas Jim, a carter like me, were called at the same time, half-past four.

Lying there in the dark on my wedding-night I hated my sleeping brother, filling the room with his callous breathing behind me. I were racked with the torture of all the love I had lost, all that would have been. This was to have been our room, with Pinfold's little ash-grove framed perfectly in the window. *'The dear ones I long for again gathered here. . . .'*

'New bricks, new tricks,' we used to say with a knowing wink whenever a young couple moved into a new home of their own and a baby were on the way soon after. It were hard to accept that my loving Kate would never come back. Yet I had to accept it. It be no good clinging to the past. She'd expect her Mont to face up to life and 'get over it'. Thank God for work. There were still plenty of *that* to haul myself up for.

I well remember that first day at my new job. It were nigh on calamity one way and another. I were late for a start. The first and last time in my life I were ever late for work. All our lives our Mam had called us up in the morning by setting her alarm-clock. All through the move the day before she had looked to me for direction, to make decisions. It were natural under the circumstances; Katy and me had been in the cottage several times and knowed the layout, planning every nook'n'cranny to make the most of our few carefully garnered possessions. But it were a strange new experience for our Mam to look to me where best to place her familiar old chattels.

Whether she went to bed in this same frame of surrendering responsibility to me, or whether she and her clock were upset by the move, I shall never know. All I knows is, from that day forth I became more and more the master of the house and captain of my fate, and never no more needed anybody nor no alarm to wake me. Even in later years when I were a shepherd, snatching bouts of sleep all through the night at lambing-time, my own built-in alarm-clock 'ud always shift me to my feet at planned intervals. I en't boasting, I'm just stating a fact; I believe many sailors, nurses, and others who keep watch, tick in the same fashion.

Nobody savvied I were late for my new job that first morning. I worked double-quick to bait the horses, turn them out two at a time to drink at the trough over by the pump-house in the far corner of the yard, and traipse back, their winter moustaches dripping, to their cleaned-out mangers. Most of 'em growed a moustache while they was feeding indoors for the winter, but it soon wore off once they was out at pasture, grazing again, in the spring.

There were another near-calamity that morning when I dug my sheppick into the outside manger and a loud roar came from under the straw. An old roader were dossed down in there for the night. If he hadn't had his head in a bucket my sharp tines 'ud have pierced his jugular and I'd have started work not only late but a murderer. He must have had some near do's in his time—hence his head in a bucket. No debris was ever left in my mangers; not to thwart roaders, to stop rot. If you piles good food on top of old debris you courts mouldy hay and other troubles.

I felt at home having another old Jolly working in the yard that first day at Ted Hunt's. He warn't as big as my old Shire that had died at Lennox's; but he were the oldest working horse I ever knowed, thirty years, a family retainer from Ted Hunt's father's farm at Stwunsful. Nobody worked him, he were self-employed, drawing cartloads of mangold, turnips etcetera all by himself from the field to the yard. Nobody warned me he were set in his tracks, plodding into the yard in a slow purposeful sweep to a halt and then, without any command, backing the cart into the barn for somebody to unload him. I discovered just in time that first day that it paid to make sure the barn-doors was open for him; old Jolly 'ud have kept backing, barn and all.

The final close-calamity that day came at two o'clock. 'Farmer Oliver's barn be on fire!' The whole village turned out to help. We warn't worried about the livestock, we'd got 'em all out. We warn't worried about the barn, the thatch warn't worth saving; but we *was* worried about the thatch opposite. It were the Crown, our one and only pub.

133

In they days an only pub be in a ticklish situation. After the War, drink were on the uptake; the clarion call of Temperance were yet again sounding 'Damnation to drink! Down with the pub!' Just to keep the peace, some turncoats was clambering on the wagon, signing the pledge with some neighbours, and drinking secretly with the others. In such a small community any fire were 'all buckets to the brook!' When the fire in question were that 'den of the demon', the pub, true allegiance was bound to be brought out into the Square. It were full of helpful teetotallers.

My allegiance were unquenched. I dashed on my bike to Venvell's, the only known phone in the village in they days, and asked 'em to rally-up Chippy Fire Brigade. In they days the siren were worked by a long rope hanging down the front of Chippy Town Hall. We all knowed it'd be some time before they harnessed the horses to the engine, so we launched into the usual human chain of buckets to the brook and firkins to the fountain.

At one time it looked as if the Crown were doomed; we even set up a ladder on the roof. But by the time Arthur Simms arrived cheering on his motorbike and side-car to tell us that the engine were in sight, we'd got the whole fire under control. It were just as well, judging from their moth-eaten turnout. The hose were riddled with holes, water shooting in all directions—talk about Queen Henrietta's Waterworks! They turned up with the same unit ten years later when the carrier's house in the Square burned down. Since then, I'm glad to say, Chippy Brigade have plugged the gaps with a posh new set-up.

My days, during those early months of bereavement, were filled with all the bricks and tricks of my new surroundings and new job, yet I dreaded the nights with their nightmare wells of deep loneliness. I were just as much part of the close community at Church Enstone as I were down Alley, rescuing the perishing, fathoming sick animals, yet nothing seemed to salve my own festering wound of grief and loss.

It growed worse as the summer cropped on with the bitter-sweet memories of courtship brought back by the scent of the beanflower, the sight of the sanfin, the sound of the distant train on still evenings clattering on from Charlbury to the Vale of

Evesham. I were that low I couldn't even face the annual choir outing that year.

Even my horses no longer compensated me as they had done through bad times in the past. I were training most of my charges to leave me, it didn't pay to get too attached. Only old Jolly tugged constant at my affection. He be too old to be sold. I growed closer and closer to him that summer though I knowed his arthritis was getting worse, and he be doomed to the knacker's yard before long. He belonged more to my predecessor, young George, who had helped to raise him as a colt and had worked with him nigh on thirty years. Now I tended him as kind as I could. Most horses have a working 'best' of twelve or fourteen years, and some are still lissom at seventeen, but old Jolly were amazing, bowed and knobbly-kneed, still plodding on.

But not for long. When the morning came for old Jolly to be put down, George were judged best to fetch him in from the field; but George couldn't face it. Our Mont were begged to do the rotten job. We couldn't find him anywhere, the knacker and me. He'd been shut up in that field with a mighty hedge and gate. How he jumped it, arthritic as he were, we shall never know, nor how he jumped the wall into the stable-yard; but when we got back into the yard, there he were, standing patiently, back to the barn as usual, waiting for his invisible cart to be unloaded. T'en't much of a picnic standing holding a faithful animal when you know the humane killer is about to finish him off.

The loss of Jolly were felt by all, Ted's family and the workers. For all they years he'd been their friend and helpmate, and to me he were a real character. In contrast with the slaughter it were a beautiful hot summer's day. I carted Jolly's carcass to the kennels and then went back to the brook at Woodford to wash down his old cart, and swell the wooden wheels that had begun to shrink from their iron rims in the hot dry weather.

There were three of these public watering-places where you could back a cart off the road into the brook. One was at the bottom of Strong's Hill, in the dip between Road and Church Enstone, what they calls Stwunny-bridge; another at Cleveley, and this 'un at Woodford, where the course runs under an old stwun bridge. I can remember they women who lived in they roadside cottages at Woodford Bridge taking in washing and congregating to do it in the brook.

Nowhere in the whole wide world could have been more beautiful than that peaceful shady rill chuckling under the bridge on that hot June day in 1923, with the cool water swirling through the spokes of the wheels, the hum and scuttle of small insects and birds, the lush smell of the wet ferns and rosy campions, and the sunlight darting on the harness brasses and dappling the ancient mossy stwuns supporting the bridge; yet, cleaning old Jolly's tumbril, I were suddenly brought to the lowest edge of despair. What were the point of living? No matter how beautiful and rosy were the outside world there were always this maggot of death at the core.

'MONT!'

I jumped. Mrs Harrison, who lived in one of the roadside cottages, was leaning over the bridge. 'I've been seekin' thee all morn, our Mont. Canst come and take a look at this mangy stray dog? It's stinkin' rotten and floppin' its head about, half-dead.'

'If it's that bad, mam, I can do nothing for it. It wants shooting. I haven't a gun. Thee must seek elsewhere.' I'd had my overdose of death and decay. Somebody else could face up to putting the poor old thing out of its misery.

I thought no more about it until after I'd had my tea that evening and I see'd Mrs Harrison hurrying past our place with a basket of washing. 'How didst fare with the old dog?'

'I've got it here.' To my surprise she uncovered the basket. 'I'm taking it to Farmer Hunt, he says he'll shoot it.'

A black'n'white bag o' bwoons were slumped, shivering, in the bottom of the basket, with its eyes closed and a putrid mess of flesh around its twisted upper jaw. Despite the stench and the blood-caked mud I could see that it were a pup with handsome black 'n' white markings under the dirt of its cwoat: the sort of little Toby dog that ought to be prancing about at the circus, full of fun and frolic, leaping through hoops and landing on horseback.

'It seems a shame,' I says, 'that such a young thing. . . . Give it here.' I wrapped it in my old weskut and carried it into the wash-house. It be no good taking him into the cottage; Topsy, our Dad's old bitch, 'ud never let another dog anywhere near her master.

Gently I bathed his mouth. He were too far gone to even open an eye and take notice. It didn't take much skill to fathom out the worst that was wrong with it. Some of the putrid flesh I bathed away were on a bwoon that had wedged itself across the roof of his mouth. At first I thought it were *his* bwoon and his jaw were broken, it were wedged so fast and the jaw were so distorted, but it were a butcher's bwoon. Somebody had tried to pull it out, or maybe he had tugged at it himself, only to wedge it worse. A dog's mouth tapers towards the front, you has to push an obstruction back from the front. Goodness knows how long it had lodged there, driving him crazy, plaguing him to tear at his flesh, preventing him from eating and lapping, and poisoning his system. I got it out at last, but I reckoned I were too late; his eyes were shuttered, his head flopped, he were beyond interest in living. I tried spooning a little warm milk down the back of his throat, but it trickled back out. There were nothing more I could do. He'd probably be a goner by morning. At least he were freed from his worst discomfort. I wrapped him up in my old weskut and left him.

That night I had one of my old nightmares of falling down the well. I woke to the warm night, shivering, icy-cold, though our Jim were lying baking hot, fast asleep behind me. I tried to recall Kate's comforting words when I told her about my nightmares, but her voice were getting more and more difficult to recapture, her features more and more veiled, as the weeks passed by. Lying there in the dark I were very alone. I suddenly bethought me of that other lone bundle out in the wash-house.

He hadn't moved. At first I thought he were dead, but he were still warm. I knowed from experience that Nature, that great life-giving force the young are born with, were the greatest healer in young animals: but they has to be encouraged to make the effort, have the will to live. I tried to interest him again in warm milk but there was no co-operation, not even a swallow, hardly a breath.

'Between life and death there is but a breath.' I recalled Kate's voice from afar, telling me once about nursing back to life a badly injured child. 'Thee'll do anything, Mont,' her words came clearer and clearer. 'Talk to them, stroke them, all night if need be, just to keep them your side of life. Make them know "I'm here".'

'*I'm here.*' Her voice were so real, as if she were breathing right beside me, sitting on the wicker chair in the wash-house in the middle of the night. Suddenly I were overwhelmed with longing to conquer death. I found myself cradling Toby, sobbing, stroking his skinny body, willing him to 'cheat the old bugger, Toby. Thee's *got* to get over it. Thee's gwin to live. Thee en't a-gwin to give in.'

Us got over it. By the end of that summer I were constantly cussing him for being always under my boots, in and out of the horses' hoofs, missing death by the hair of a fetlock, leaping on my lap, licking me all over, and burying his nose in my weskut for a nap whenever I longed for a bit of peace and a quiet smoke. I had to put a little bell on his collar to know where he were and what tricks he were up to. You couldn't help laughing at him, and he'd sit there laughing back; I hadn't laughed for ages. He were just like that story-book Toby with a bell to drive the evil spirits away from his master. Strangely enough, he never barked, but he'd talk to you with a whimper. I reckon he must have had some circus blood in him, he were that neat and nimble on his pins. At first, while he were still weak and wantly, I'd take him up to the harvest field, and he'd sleep curled up in my old weskut under the hedge by my tucker-bag. As he growed stronger he'd walk a few bouts with me and the team. When he were tired he'd whimper, and I'd lift him up on to the wide rump of the nighest horse, and he'd curl up and rock to sleep there.

He were more at home on horseback than on the ground. One second he were poking with me in my tucker-bag, the next second he were enthroned, perched on the horse's back, viewing the landscape as if he owned the whole of Enstone. I couldn't make out how the little fellow had conquered such an Everest; they Shires was massive in height and bwoon. There warn't nobody else in the field the first time he done it, just me and the team of three. I soon discovered he could climb the horses' tails. We never clipped nor docked our horses' tails, they was always left to flow free unless they was specially braided up for a show. A horse uses his skin-muscles to tremor off the flies from the front of its body, but he needs his long tail to fend off the rest. Toby 'ud skim up and down they tails like a yo-yo. He'd trot all over they horses' backs, trooping his glossy black'n'white patches from end to end, horse to horse, eyes front, squatting with neat-packed balance on the spot of horseflesh he happened to be when he fancied a rest.

They giant horses was wonderful patient and gentle of him. He'd often sit in the shade under their huge bodies on a hot day, licking their feet in turn all round the coronet, cooling 'em off and savouring the salt. He'd play catch-tail, darting from between their hind-legs as they swished their long cascades to and fro. One swift flick of tail, one soft thud of hoof, 'ud soon warn the little varmint they'd had enough; and he'd sit, good as gold, hatching up the next mischief.

Toby were my first dog. He came into my life when I were in the pit of despair. Nothing nor nobody 'ud ever fill Kate's empty niche deep in my heart, but that little dog, bounding with love and life one minute, burrowing into my weskut and snuggling close to my chest the next, taught me to feel and laugh again, and began to heal the void wrought in me by Kate's death. I 'udn't say us got over it, but us began to sit up and take new notice. I were a dark-haired Samson of twenty-one. There were no end of girls and love and life yet—as everyone kept telling me—for our Mont.

13

'Side by Side'

Trav'lin' along,
Singin' a song
Side by side.

I JOINED THE NEW CHORAL SOCIETY for a start. We met weekly at first in the new Parish Hall, never dreaming we'd eventually make it via 'Killarney's lakes and fells' in Chippy Town Hall to 'Great God of Song' in the Albert Hall, and third among the winners. I were too keyed up to remember much about that famous outing, 'cept we went by courtesy of the Chippy Safety Saloon Bus Company, and the scorn I felt for London bobbies, pounding their beat in twos; ourern were man enough to plod alone in our Enstone.

For years we'd entered local church-choir festivals, travelling in wagonettes to meet up with other choirs, rehearsing together in the afternoon, having a slap-up tea, side by side, in the village pub across from the church, and giving of our choicest sacred songs and solos in the evening. Most churches had a handy pub along the way. The one at Brailes were reckoned to have first been built to refresh the ancient men that built the church; and many others must have been established for the same purpose.

The Choral Society were of a wider pull than the choir, with more popular songs; not the catchers-on we tapped our pots to in the pub, but more of a challenging hurdle, five bars high, with lots of lilt for the ladies. I loved to lean my tenor against the ladies; just harmony, not opera. I en't wrapt up in opera.

It were a new luxury for me to live so near my work and be free to join in more and more with village activities. I were lucky too to have th'Old Folks at home. After a year at Church Enstone they was now beginning to accept it as home, though Dad still clung to his daily pilgrimage all round old Enstone to down Alley and back: an airing he were to keep up for the rest of his life, almost daily, until he were ninety-two. He didn't walk, he went at a steady trot. His old heart were a remarkable old engine, chugging him on without a falter, changing down a gear to smaller steps up gradients. In his younger days he thought nothing of walking to Oxford to deliver in person his custom-made shoes. In later years I recall one or two of his old Oxford customers, faithful to their old boot-maker and their ancient bicycles, cycling from Oxford to seek him out at Church Enstone. One in particular, a high-born clergyman in a shallow black hat, upholding his dignity in a hammock-seat slung from the back to the handlebars. Other old customers Dad still stitched for and walked miles to deliver his work.

For years his constant companion on these marathons were Topsy, his faithful terrier-bitch, trotting equally purposeful close at heel. The trouble was, they two kept in the middle of the road, a great worry to us at home and an even greater nuisance to the increasing motor traffic. 'I were in our Enstone afore they charybongs,' he'd claim; 'they'll have to bide.' He was; and mercifully, they did.

Our Mam, once Mother's plaques were installed over the fireplace in the front room and Mother's caddy were given pride of place on the kitchen dresser, were also beginning to feel at home, though her felt quite lost sauntering down the long garden to the privy without sighting a single soul. It were also strange at first for her not to have us bwoys constantly clattering through her bedroom to the attic. It were the first time in their married life that her and Dad had a bedroom entirely to theyselves without cradles nor clathoppers.

She still missed the 'side by side' close companionship of all her neighbours down Alley, but she had to admit Church Enstone were 'a jump up in the world, all very spacious and private'. And soon there were new neighbours including Little George Sheffield who had called that very first morning after we moved in, and for every morning thereafter: 'Mother sent me to ask if I could fetch your jug of milk, Mrs Abbott, 'cos I'm just going acraws to fetch ourern from Farmer Warner's cowshed before I go to school.' Mrs Jennings and Mrs Paxford and the other ladies of the new-fangled revolutionary Women's Institute had called, 'to go with you on the outing' or 'to walk with you down to the WI meeting in the new Parish Hall'.

The new Parish Hall stirred up no end of community activities and outings. It were our pride and joy. It were nearly our bankruptcy too, but Miss Bruce stepped in at the last moment and paid off the final debt. It warn't easy in they lean years after the First World War, and in the even leaner years through the Depression, to scrape up pennies for parish projects. Our hall may not seem much of a corrugated-iron effort nowadays compared to all they posh community centres that have cropped up in other villages since the Second World War, but to us in the let-down twenties it were a wonderful lift-up from they tiny infants' chairs and narrow iron-shod desks which was all we had to meet on in the schoolroom.

It were opened with all due pomp and performance by Lord and Lady Dillon and our Enstone Pageant, complete with niggering minstrel. Pageants, Empire Exhibitions and Leagues of Nations was all the rage in them days.

Neighbours was all the rage too. All they years Mother lived and aged to the end of her days at Church Enstone, they Sheffield childern, in growing order, before they went to school of a morning, took on the task of fetching her milk. It warn't that our Mam were incapable of walking across to Farmer Warner's cowshed to fetch her own jug of milk; she were still in demand for the laying-out and the laying-in (more for the laying-out now they new-fangled contraceptives was getting more reliable). It were just one of the many ritual good deeds the young was brought up to do for the older members of the community. They 'Shuffels', as we used to call 'em, was brought up according.

It were 'half jug a ha'penny, full jug a penny' for fresh milk, straight from the cow at Farmer Warner's. He had a cow called Elsie, a topping good milker, for years. Today some other Elsie gazes at me over my garden wall from the posh herd in the field beyond, and I knows full well that the milk she yields this morning will travel miles and be at least five days old before I gets it on my doorstep in a bottle dubbed 'fresh milk'. Even then it won't be hers but some other Elsie's from miles away. That's nowadays for ye; all round the bull'n'bush to get back to the jug'n'Shuffels where we started.

There were an unbroke line of 'George Sheffields', ofttimes writ 'Shuffel' in old parish records going back to 1700. Old George were one of they ancient carters Mr Lennox had advised I to heed when I first started cartering. Young George, his son, were close on sixty, and had been Ted Hunt's father's carter for years. It were his job I had taken over as carter. Young George had moved over to become Ted's tractor-man. The new notice, 'WANTED. TRACTOR-MAN', cropping up more and more all over the countryside in the early twenties, were already the 'writing on the landscape' for me and my cart-horses. But I were just in time to teach Little George and his brothers to plough and reap with horses on Ted Hunt's farm, until they moved out of the doldrums of farming in the thirties to better jobs.

Mrs Sheffield were the first woman I ever saw on a tractor, complete with hat. It were exceptional in they days to see a woman out of doors, even in her own garden, without a hat. One of the first things our Mam were taught by the dangerous Women's Institute were to make a simple hat of natural straw, plaited round and down from a pointed crown with ribbons to tie under the chin. It were the traditional effort worn for centuries by women afield; it's always cropping up on wenches in old oil-paintings of harvesters and haymakers. But Mrs Sheffield's tractor-hat were a full-powered twenties' helmet affair with a small brim, well ramified with hatpins to weather the new openings to women afield after the Great War.

She were the first and last woman I ever knowed to catch the gracey-pig. Every year at Enstone Fete they'd launch a pig, covered in grease, on to the field. It were a free-for-all, whoever could catch it could keep it. Only the men was used to go in for it; no woman 'ud have the nerve. Everybody were flabbergasted when Mrs Sheffield donned an old cwoat, launched in with the Olympics and cropped up triumphant, complete with hat. They done away with the gracey-pig after that. Some said it were cruel to the pig, others it were cruel to the men, to be bested by a woman complete with hat.

To keep a pig in our new pigsty at Church Enstone were a big step up for Jim and me as men in the community, and a rise in our Abbott family fortune. To have a flitch or two of 'be-acon' hanging on your kitchen wall in them days were a sign of real wealth, 'better nor any of yer oil-pe-antings', us used to bwoast. We formed a mighty serious delegation, me and our Jim, to old Farmer Goodey's at Lidstone to choose our first weaner. Trooper hadn't forgotten me and came whinnying from the far side of the field to nuzzle me.

Choosing that first pig were the beginning of a growing 'side by side' partnership between me and our Jim. In later years when our joint fortunes had risen to raising a whole litter and Jim were Hon. Sec. of Enstone Club and the Cricket and Football, we was proud to donate, from time to time, a fattened pig for various fund-raising roasts.

I were lucky to have my long niche in the community and a good job. Ted Hunt were a decent 'Boss'; and when Boss came into the yard to give his orders first thing in the morning, Carter 'ud be there with his men and horses ready. Sometimes plans was cut and dried, so to spake, with teams and men ready-matched from the day before; but sometimes a change in the weather or the condition of the land 'ud mean splitting up teams of two into teams of three, specially for the heavier, wetter-lying fields. Then a brief conference 'ud take place, deciding which man were to stand down, lose his team for that day and work odd-job on the farm. There were no haggling; Carter and Boss sorted it out fair so's everybody accepted their lot, even if they warn't pleased. Ted himself were such a good sport; he'd drop out or make up the village cricket and football teams as asked, and he were addressed 'Boss' with respect. The men was addressed by their nicknames, 'Coffey', 'Dry-un', 'Tack', 'Cracker', 'Uncle', 'Buck', and my old friend 'Briss'. I were always 'Mont', 'cept on payday, when Ted 'ud always address me as 'Carter' and invite me round to the stable— not to be handed my wages with the rest of the men—but to accompany him further into his kitchen to receive my wages as we sat at his kitchen table, having a chat over the tankards of foaming beer Mrs Hunt 'ud bear in for us.

It were pleasant to see Mrs Hunt and her daughters. They'd never come up to my stable-yard unless they was invited or asked Carter first. A stable-yard with the entire, as we called the stallion, being brought round regularly to serve mares were not in them days deemed a safe nor seemly place for womenfolk and little lasses to wander at whim.

The peak of my job were the traditional walk 'side by side' with Boss all round the farm before church of a Sunday. Every field, Duckpuddle, Appletree, Hell-fire Corner, San Piece, Quar Piece and the rest 'ud all be inspected and plans discussed for the coming week. Ted 'ud sometimes joke, 'The Boss says I'm to have Thursday off, Mont, to go hunting'; and we'd plan how best to cover in his absence. He were so much a part of village life, he'd often know even before I asked. 'You'll be wanting Saturday off, Mont, to go on the choir outing.'

That year were the last we went in wagonettes to the station for the choir outing. We clip-clopped away from the village, about forty of us, in a fleet of wagonettes at four o'clock of a misty-cold summer's morn to catch the single-line train from Chippy to Banbury, and thence on the GWR excursion to the great Shrewsbury Flower Show. This were a daring departure from tradition for Parson Palmer, who had stuck faithfully for years to

Bournemouth-and-Beales-for-tea. Beales were a big department store with its own posh restaurant with potted palms, a pianist and pressed meats. Parson Palmer prided himself on his ordered-well-in-advance substantial 'meat tea'; and the one at Shrewsbury, with two big platters of cold bacon, looked as if it were going to be up to his usual Beales standard.

The only drawback was, each year, he'd drop on a different chap, man or bwoy, to say grace: a somewhat daunting task, even in the meatless privacy of your own family table, let alone in public at a bacon banquet miles away from our Enstone. This year he picked on Norman Nimlet, a timid lad who kept touching his cap to 'Mr Pelmer', and whose whole faith were bound up in Parson's broad feet leading him safely back to where they both lived, little Lidstone.

'Just say what you normally say before a meal at home, Norman,' Parson prompted.

'Me Dad always sez it, Mr Pelmer.'

'Just say what your dad would say.'

We bowed our heads.

'Go aisy on the be-acon; it's got to go all round.'

'AMEN!' us fervoured, and got tucked in.

Narn of we had ever see'd such a wodge of folks as was in that quarry-place at Shrewsbury. Parson Palmer had warned us to stick together and not to leave the ground. It were hardly possible to do otherwise. There were no way out but up, and no way in but down. Looking up at they multitudes streaming up and down from the town, I felt like Christian must have felt in *Pilgrim's Progress*. Moy-hoy! There just was some folks! Somehow timid Norman becomed separated in the throng but were miraculously discovered, beseeching utter strangers, 'Hast seen Mr Pelmer?'

A hot-air balloon race were floating over the tents, coloured tops spinning gracefully in space. And in the tents, moist and sweet, such produce! Such flowers! Dahlias big as dinner-plates. And in they pleasure-gardens, such gals! They wenches was a real eye-opener to me and our Jim. Arms, legs, bangles in sleeveless frocks and sheer stockings. We hardly knowed where to look at first, but as the band and the balloons sauntered on through the hot afternoon we got daring, cutting a dash, whistling with the music, bantering at our best. It were over a year since I'd lost my best gal. I still strove in my heart to cleave only unto her, but I were a tall dark-haired Romeo of twenty-two, and our Jim were a lusty eighteen-year-old, and they sunkissed gals was opening theyselves to us, bright as dahlias. Talk about the desires of the flesh! Our next outing we determined 'ud be on the Passion-Wagon.

Adams's Passion-Wagon were getting a reputation for matchmaking in the village. It were fundamentally a flat-bedded lorry with no sides. The make, I think, were a Rio. The Adams family used it to cart goods and supplies to and from their farm and their stores in Road Enstone, and Charlbury Station. It were a proper meccano job to convert it into a charabong for occasional village outings. First, the seats, long box pews, was bolted to the bed of the lorry. They pews went right across. The passengers loaded up from the open end, as in church, and latched their own little door across. Once you was cooped up in your pew you was stuck, so it paid to scrawf up next to somebody you fancied. There were no escape.

The roof were a rolled-back canvas effort strapped into a neat bundle across the rear. If it rained it took two chaps, one on either side, to unroll it. It were upheld like a calabash of a covered wagon, by long cane arches, channelled through seams in the canvas, held at either end in special sockets on the end of the pews. The front were held down by fastening the leather straps to the buckles mounted on the front mudguards. The windows was smoky cracked squares of yellow cellophane stitched to the roof at intervals—no good for viewing the scenery. Who wants scenery in a passion-wagon? They old windows 'ud wiffle-wuffle, whip-whack! in the wind, steamed up with singing and heavy breathing as the roysterers, side by side, went 'Rolling down to Rio'—or Bognor.

Jim and me, curious to try our luck afresh with the gals, booked to go on the next outing, whatever it might be. Our Jim even bought himself a daring new brand of trousers from Chippy Co-Op, 'guaranteed to raise the female passion'. They certainly raised our Mam's: 'Daft! They get baggy enough without paying to have 'em baggy in the first ple-ace!' It were the start of a fashion called 'Oxford bags'; the more daft and daring were to finish up wide as women's skirts around the ankles.

Unfortunately for us hot stallions the next outing turned out to be a tepid all-family outing to the zoo, 'starting early in case of accidents'. As the zoo were only Franky Grey's little private menagerie a few miles away, out by they stwun quarries near Kirtlington, they was allowing a heck of a lot of time for accidents. Probably expecting us all to land up on the rocks or turned into ''orses' 'ead 'andles' inside the lion, like 'Albert'.

It were women and childern first to board the wagon in the vast queue for potential disaster outside Worth's New Garage. Us called it Worth's New Garage, but it were still only a shed a step up the road from his other shed behind the Litchfield where Dicky Worth—like Mr Morris—had begun his climb in the motoring world by mending bicycles. It were also a step up in the world for Dicky, right on the main road next to the post office, with a long-necked petrol pump with a pretty glass 'SHELL' outside, and the Fortress, a Ford-8 taxi, inside.

Dicky often helped out the Adamses, and were driving the wagon for them on this occasion. Despite loading they pews to the gunnels it were obvious he warn't going to have room for us motley crew of chaps left to the gallant last. He told his young garage lad, Henry Hawtin, to get out the Ford and follow with the rest of us, he could 'do with a back-up party, *just in case*'—which sounded ominous for Jim's new bags and my best suit.

The Ford were built like one of today's iron skips, but with a saloon roof, left-hand drive, and a wind-out windscreen in a frame so heavy with chrome it took two chaps to wind out the handle. Seven of us piled in along of Henry: me and our old bwoy, Charlie Wakefield, Zicky and young Harris, and another young greenhorn nicknamed 'Rover' 'cos he'd never in his life been out of Enstone, let alone on a whole day's outing with a promise of accidents; and, last but not least, large Albert Panting who'd 'see'd enough of the world in the bloody trenches' but couldn't resist the odd lion 'cos he 'loved POW-er'.

It were obvious, powering along at speed, roughly in the

direction of Kirtlington, battling to back up with the out-of-sight wagon, that the Fortress had a bent of its own. Young Henry were having a job to hold her, having not long left school and only just learned to drive, as he informed us through clenched teeth and white knuckles; and in no time at all we was backing up the next telegraph-pwoost and sailing ass over head, to land upside down in the middle of the road—trapped—all of a yup—struggling and moaning, with young Rover bawling his head off.

'SHUT UP! THE LOT OF YER!' blasted Sergeant Panting. 'I've been in worser bloody 'OLES than this.' And heroically forcing his fat frame, ass-back'ards, through the fallen-out windscreen, led the Great Escape to the strangely peaceful outdoors. After that *Captain* Panting were chucking his rank about summat shocking, lining us all up on the verge, ordering me to report casualties. Miraculously, apart from surface cuts and bloody noses, nobody was seriously hurt: and my best bespoke suit hadn't a mark. Jim's new Co-Op trousers had come off the worst; they daft bags had caught on the gear-stick and ripped from ankle to bare loin, guaranteed more than ever 'to rouse the female passion'. Young Rover were wandering about in a daze, wringing his cap in his hands and wailing how we was ever going 'to get whum this far from our Enstone!' But as we was barely a mile out of the village we pointed him vaguely in the direction of Jollys Ricks, got fell in side by side beside him, under the command of *Marshal* Panting, and walked home. It were the shortest day's outing 'starting early in case of accidents' I ever had.

Henry Hawtin went on to become one of Worth's most trusted drivers. He worked for the well-known firm of Worth's Coaches all his life, and even when he was retired they'd still call on him when they was hard pushed.

That day's outing in 1924 were my first-ever ride in a motor-car, and, as life sadly turned out, my last ever chance to board the bandwagon of female passion. In the autumn of that year my dreaded nightmare came true. I fell thirty foot down a well.

⟜ 14 ⟞

Nightmare

HARVEST WERE LATE THAT YEAR. Whenever, years after, I see'd barley shooks standing out late, spoiled and forsaken in the fields, I were reminded of that October evening in 1924, and the waste wrought in me by fate.

Ted were working with us all day sorting out the cattle for winter: driving the littl'uns into Quar Piece, the middl'uns down Hind Jones, and the big'uns into the yard. We'd done a good day's threshing the day before and built a good straw-rick in the yard where the cattle could help theyselves to straw, treading in any debris they dropped to make their own deep litter that 'ud turn into muck and be fed back to the land. You had to keep a north eye on the rick, that they didn't rub or pull out the bottom too much and make it top-heavy, but in the natural run it worked well.

I'd warned Mam I'd be late for my tea; I'd decided to bring in some of my horses for the winter. I'd got two hundred acres left to drill and I wanted to harden my teams off so's they warn't too green. Winter were already in the air; cold and frosty in the mornings, and the nights fast drawing in. They used not to mess about with the clocks in they days.

'Hast var' near done, Mont?' Ted was hovering in the dusk in the stable-yard.

'Ar. I've baited the horses. I'll fill the trawf before I go home for my tay; then I'll come back and rack up with hay before I go home to roost.'

'I've got a meeting to go to at six o'clock; and I want to check those cattle have settled down in Hind Jones before it gets too dark.'

I looked at my watch. It were already ten to six.

'You go, Boss. I'll manage. Just got to pump up.'

''Night, Mont!'

He were gone, leaving the darkening yard to Toby and to me. Like his master, Toby be about whacked after chasing cattle all day, and longing for his tea; yet wherever I moved in the gathering gloom he followed, sitting patient, never taking his eyes off me.

The pumphouse were in the far corner of the stable-yard. It were a pump surrounded by an open stockade, shut off from the rest of the yard by a latched gate, with an extra bolt on the inside to stop the horses lifting the latch. The long spout of the pump went through the side of the stockade into the trough in the yard. To prime the pump you filled a bucket at the trough and tipped it into the top of the ram; this created an airlock for the wooden clack to suck up the water from the well thirty foot below. The well were solidly boarded over with a small trap-door in the ground at the front to give access to climb down and tend the clack. This clack were worn—the whole set-up had been there for donkey's years— and had been losing water of late; but if you sloshed a good weight of water in for a start, and pumped like mad, it worked. I were poised on this trap, just about to—*the trap went*! DOWN I dropped—boots slithering—back scraping—icy darkness rushing up—JOLT! A searing pain; I blacked out.

Freezing with cold, shuddering with shock, I came to my senses.

This time the dank sweating silence were no fancy nightmare. This time it were real.

'HELP!' I shouted with all my strength.

Weak as a whimper my cry dwindled back, stifled by the heavy pall of silence above. It be no use. Even if a cry did escape there be nobody up there. Ted be gone to his meeting. Young George be gone home to his tea, everybody in Enstone 'ud be gone home for their tea, and Mam warn't expecting me until late. I be in agony. I felt around. Loose stwuns plopped just below. I were just above the water, jammed between the shaft and the ram, saved by a narrow metal strut.

My sharp eyes be getting used to the dark. I could just make out my cap floating on the black gleam below, and the ram wavering up, up, up the long narrow shaft to a patch of pale twilight sky a bloody long way off. I had to turn my eyeballs right up in my head to see it. Dirt and stwuns showered on my face. Somebody were up there! The patch were blurring in and out. TOBY! He'd be going crazy, whimpering to be with me. More debris shied down. 'BUGGER AWF, TOBY!'

It be no use swearing at him, he 'udn't hear. Another stwun shied past. *He'd* be down next. I clamped my arms out to the sides of the shaft and braced myself for the agony of hoisting myself off that narrow strut. I knowed there be two other supports set at different angles somewhere up there if only I could summon the strength to spider up between the pipe and the sides. I must try. I *must* try. 'Playse God,' I remember praying as another load of rubble shied down, '*kayp Toby. . .*'

I come to, face down, on the muckle in the yard with Toby whimpering and licking my raw back. My shirt and jacket be in tatters. God alone knows how I bloody well made it. All I knows is, when Mr Milton the plumber what kept the hardware store on the corner in Charlbury came to mend the pump some days later, he 'udn't go down even a few feet to mend the clack, it be too dangerous. 'Rocks clawed out all the way down as if some massive wild animal's been caged up in theer!'

I don't know how I staggered home, my legs 'udn't come together, they was all over the shop. I can still see Mam's horrified face as this stinking raw bloody bundle of rags toppled in the door.

When I come to again I were all clayned up, trussed and aching on the sofa, with old Doc Croly peering at me. It seemed like the middle of the night.

'Well, bwoy,' he says, 'you've been sent for me often enough, now I've been sent for you. You're lucky to be alive, our Mont.'

I were indeed. *Very* lucky. I looked at all the dear homely faces gathered round, full of concern for me: Mam, Dad, our old bwoys Jim and Fred, and even Young George Shuffel. I began to cry. I couldn't stop.

'George! My horses! I never latched the pump'us dooer!'

'Doan't 'ee fret. I've see'd to all that, and done the racking-up.'

'My cap's down theer!' I were wailing, top notch.

'It can stop.'

And it did; from that day to this.

Ted were very upset over the job. The trap were solid enough and in a strong-looking frame. None of we realized it were relying on another underground timber that must have been rotting away for years. I still marvel that my limbs had such strength. My years of labouring, all that stairwork (no end of barns had flights of steps to lofts and granaries), humping sacks, churns, buckets; all they miles, cross-country running, bowling wheels to wagoners, legging it behind horses, handling teams of two, three, four heavy horses, must have given my muscles the will-power to haul my body through hell and wreak my own salvation.

Mercifully my back warn't permanently damaged, mainly bruised and flayed. Flesh heals quickly when you're young and fit. Within a fortnight I were well on the mend, though there were still summat 'down below' that I couldn't fathom out; but I supposed I'd be healed in time. I were all on me own the next time Dr Croly called. It were strange that he should call for nothing, and stranger still when he asked me, straight out, 'Do you plan to marry, Mont?'

'Course I do, doctor, God willin'; and have childern.'

Then he dropped the bombshell. I could never now have childern. When I fell on that metal strut I fell astride. I expect if a young chap done the same damage to himself today summat could be done, but in they days it warn't possible. It be still too personal—even after all these years—to go into medical details. Dr Croly made it quite clear; in that direction, I be no good at all no more as a man to any woman.

I were that destroyed. I never told a soul in my life till now; not even our Mam. There were only one I could have suffered to have shared such a shameful secret. Thank God her were at peace in the Vale of Evesham and never lived to have to bear the burden of it.

— 15 —

The Thirties—Jamborees, Jubilees, Crises

WITHIN A MONTH OF MY ACCIDENT my hair turned almost white. Doctor said it were shock and thought it might grow dark again, but it never did. I were almost as white at twenty-two as I be now at eighty-two. Yet I ne'er lost a squippet. I be almost as thick-thatched now as I were as a young man; but there's nothing so ageing on a young chap as a shock of white hair. No matter that my bright blue eyes and dark lashes were as good as ever, no matter what crises I conquered, what contests I won, our Mont, still only in his twenties, then thirties, became knowed more and more as Old Mont. And I've been Old Mont to all and sundry ever since.

I were only on the Club, drawing sick-benefit, for a fortnight. I were a fully paid-up member of the Ancient Order of Foresters Friendly Society. I were swore-in when I were sixteen. They does this swearing-in of new members once a month at their courtly meeting. Our Enstone Club were 'Court Victoria'.

I were the only lad waiting outside the schoolroom door on that day in August 1918. It were just after I'd been turned down by the Army for being so fit and precious. Suddenly the latch were lifted and the Sub-Chief Ranger challenged: 'Friend—I am authorized by our Worthy Chief Ranger to enquire your full name and place of residence.' They knowed me well enough, I'd lived in our Enstone nearly all me bloody life; but he had to say that 'cos it were scratched in the rulebook, and everything had to be conducted proper.

He stood aside, and there were the Chief Ranger, in his fine green-and-gold sash with that old fiery eye of the Almighty blazoned in silk, staring straight at you. He had his book open and charged me about original sin, pinching apples and suchlike, keeping on the straight'n'narrow, and above all loving your neighbour.

'Friend, we believe that no man liveth unto himself and we desire by association to provide against the common misfortunes of humanity and to encourage and aid every kindly effort to promote the well-being of the weak and distressed.'

Then you signed that you'd do your best to come up to their scratch, and they entrusted you with the secret sign and the secret password, and sent you outside the door to enter proper. They altered the password from time to time, so it be perfectly above board now to let on that my password in 1918, given according to the book 'in a low tone', were 'Worthy Chief'. With 'Worthy Chief', I lifted the latch into the Court Victoria, and were invited to 'take your place as a Member of this Court and share in its duties and responsibilities. With very great pleasure I welcome you into our midst, and in the name of the Court I give you now the right hand of fellowship.' And sick benefit of fourteen bob a week and £14 for my family if I snuffed it. For that I had to find a premium of 5*s* 10*d* a quarter. Though I knowed on that summer's day in 1918 that 'Worthy Chief' were only old Perce Welch and the Secretary were only old Walt Huckin, I were right proud to receive from them my membership trophy of Lincoln-green with a green silk tassel, and all the noble humanity they stood for.

After near-death in that old well six years later, it were a great comfort to know, thanks to the Club and despite the inflation of the twenties, my funeral were still—at £14—well provided for; but my sick-pay of fourteen bob instead of my usual wage of twenty-two were a bit of a worry. I were worried too that Ted were hard pushed to get in the last of a very late harvest. I warn't up to pitching the sheaves, but I could sit and do the driving home. Next day, two weeks after my accident, I were back at work driving my team, determined to prove myself in every other direction, more than ever, a man.

Despite the miseries of the hungry twenties and broke thirties, with hunger-marches again passing through from the north; and the [*Oxford*] *Times* chock-a-block with general strikes and co'lition governments, our Enstone managed pretty well to keep going. Our England were on the brevut too, winning world records for speed on land, sea and in the air; winning the Ashes, Wimbledon, the British Empire Games, and shining in the Olympics. Taking part, rather than boycotting, were the greater glory in them days.

Our local Olympics were the annual cross-country race held to raise funds for the Chipping Norton Football League. Hundreds of chaps, rich and poor, took part just for the fun or the glory of it. The year after my accident I were chosen again among the chaps to represent our Enstone. I didn't go a-purpose to win; I went to prove to myself I were still the sport I used to be, and because I enjoyed running. We knowed our Enstone 'ud never win; they two 'ticular Chads, whose Dad were some big nob out by Chadlington, always run away with it. They was pure athletes—been to posh schools and university, with proper paid coaching. The nobs was into athletics in a big way in the late twenties and thirties.

The race were usually run in the evening 'cos working chaps couldn't afford the time off work; but it were a full-bodied jamboree for everybody in the district, with bands playing, stalls selling, pubs open, and hundreds of folks out on the spree.

'The Year of the Mud' I were in my late shock-haired twenties. It had been raining for days, and even on the day of the race it had been wet: but it cleared off to give a fine mellow evening, fetching out the crowds all along the High Street and the Horse Fair to the Town Hall. Kick-off were outside the Town Hall as usual. They Persil-fresh Chads was already there, running on the spot, raring to go. They hadn't been clathopping, rounding up cattle all day, up to their backsides in mud.

We was OFF! Surging away after they two gods. Out of Chippy.

Up the Burford Road. Past the Tavern. 'Cross the allotments. Down the old Green Lane. That's where the trouble started, folks slithering, tripping each other up, all the way down to the River Glyme in the bottom. I kept clear. I warn't going to let a sea of mud sink me. I could see they two Mercuries winged with mud, slithering up the other side of the bank. By the time they was up to the Avenue I was within their panting distance. Soon I were going nicely in their muddy wake along to the Banbury crossroads. I had a job to keep up with their cleaner sprint all round and through Over Norton: but sailing down that last steep wooded dale on the far side of Chippy I found new energy. All three of us sped together, under the dappled light of they giant elms that used to line the wooded hill up to the Cottage Hospital, and burst through, level, into the golden warmth and roar of all they people lining the street in the sunset.

'Come on, Mont!' the cry went up from our Enstone.

'COME ON, MONT!' the crowd picked it up.

There were only inches between me and they Chads; but their training told at the finish. As one, we linked with each other, facing the cheers. Then we shook on it, runner to runner, thanking each other for the thrill of running our best. There were no trophy to covet: just the reward of a race well run, giving fun to all they folks, and for me a wonderful feeling of manly achievement.

Other jamborees held throughout the twenties and thirties were the camp meetings. These stemmed back to John Wesley, preaching all over the country in the open air and drawing to him all the poor and oppressed from all the villages around. I'd gone as a child with our Mam and Dad in the bad times before the War; and in the Depression of the thirties they was again very popular. On Sabbath evenings in the summer you'd see whole families setting out hours before to walk to Chawferd Green or Rollright, some such open space or prominence, linking up with other families on the way, until the narrow dusty roads were chock-a-block with a great gathering of the flock yearning to hear the Word.

It warn't entirely the Word of evangelism they was thirsting for, but word of lost friends and old workmates. The hiring-fairs had all died out by the thirties, but the farm-labourer and craftsman were having to seek work further and further afield; and the tied cottage meant uprooting your whole family from your old patch. At all the traditional jamborees, Witney Feast, Stow Fair, but above all at the camp meetings, you'd witness the different trades—dairymen, stwun-masons, carters, shepherds and the rest congregating together as if by instinct, swapping news and experience.

Mr Kirby from Barton were a topping preacher; perched up high on an old wagon with Barton Band, he'd 'Lead us, heavenly Father, lead us' into all the old Wesley, Sankey and Watts numbers. He'd always finish by inviting each of the crafts to sing their traditional National Anthem—the dairymen pouring forth 'Jerusalem the golden, with milk and honey blest', the stwun-masons rendering 'The Church's one foundation', the carters 'ploughing the fields and scattering', and the shepherds 'ud gather up the entire flock with 'All people that on earth do dwell'.

It were quite a moment, singing that at the finish, in that great company of farm-labourers, with the scent of honeysuckle in the nearby hedge, the distant clocks tolling time with each other, and the summer evening soft and peaceful, enfolding all round us the grazing stock and the rolling pastures.

Stow Fair were an entirely different kettle of jamboree. 1935, the year of the old King's Silver Jubilee, were about the last time I drove as carter to Stow. In the twenties I'd have met up with no end of other drovers along the road; but the General Strike of 1926 had diverted the carting of cattle from the railways to road and put paid to the regular job of droving stock for miles along the highways. They first cattle-lorries was a motley lot. Venvell's first were two converted Rolls-Royces. Later, during the General Strike, they bought a converted 'Long Anna' army truck from the Duke of Marlborough to transport cattle to Banbury Market. That market were founded alongside the railway, to ease the traffic of animals by rail. The year 1926 were an omen of things to come, they railway-wagons on strike, standing idle and empty, while every kind of motor-box trundled in with livestock.

In the Second World War the shortage of petrol for road vehicles revived for a brief spell the droving and the railway traffic; but the horse-boxes and cattle-trucks was already forming in shape and number before the War, and after the War they reigned more and more supreme over the railway.

Towards the end of the thirties the horse were all but finished for road haulage. Ted were turning away from breeding draught-horses to breeding sheep. My job as carter were veering more and more to shepherding; but we still had a few horses, and sometimes sold an odd one or two at Stow Fair. This meant getting up at four to tend my usual stock. If our horse's number comed early in the sale catalogue I'd have to groom and rib him up afore I set out at six to walk the fourteen miles to Stow. In 1935 our old mare comed well down the bidding order, and I'd have time to groom'n'rib her when we got there. I missed my old Toby that year. I'd lost him the year before with a heart attack. He ended as he began, curled up asleep on my old weskut. He had walked with me to Stow many a time, perched up on the horse's back. You was supposed to keep to the far side of the road when you was leading horses, and place yourself between the road and the horse. You could ride one and have another on the inside on a leading rein; but above two you was supposed to lead 'em in a string, overlapping each one on the inside. You was allowed up to six like that. We didn't often ride unless we knowed for sure somebody 'ud be at the fair to cart the harness home.

We used to walk cross-country to Stow: Lidstone, Stow Lane, Spelsbury Road, to Chippy, cutting across from the Beeches to come out by the old Brick Inn that used to be near Adlestrop railway bridge on the Cross Hands–Stow Road. In 1935 I'd picked up with a fellow drover by the time I got to the Brick Inn. It were kept by a mean old retired policeman, who warn't going to serve one drink at that unearthly hour of the morning. I pointed out, perfectly civil, we was bonafeedy travellers and he were bound by the law of the land to serve us providing we had walked at least five miles. *He* reckoned we hadn't a leg to stand on. *I* reckoned, seeing as me and my horse had already done double that, and my fellow drover with his string of six ponies had been picked up eight miles back, we had thirty-two legs to stand on. It warn't as if we was

160

expecting, with seven horses, the red carpet putting out to his taproom, we was quite willing to hang on to our bloodstock and consume refreshment off the premises. He gave in at last, not wanting a mount of droppings at his front door; but I were more knackered winkling one drink out of that dried-up copper than walking all they miles to Stow.

We had another drink off the premises of the Bell at the bottom of Stow, before they gyppoes and their fights got there, and before we tackled Mount Everest. Stow be on a heck of a bump and high on the wolds above sea-level. Whatever the weather elsewhere, it be always a top-coat colder at Stow. When we left Enstone it had been a muggy May morning; by the time we'd got to the top of the town and anchored in they two little paddocks at the top of the road to Slaughter, it were snowing. It were only a scant May shower, but it were straight from Siberia. I reckon the lie of the land at Stow favours Siberia. It wants tilting t'other way, in the burrow.

The steward gave me my catalogue number and I set to work to make my old gal look her best before that number were called. That 'ticular number I were decking out in 1935 be game enough, but her had the double drawback of the string-halt at the back and the dropped nose at the front. She be no good as thiller, to hold a heavy load, and she be too droopy to steal a beauty contest.

'Fit for nothing,' Ted had said when he decided to sell her.

'She's patient and willing,' I stuck up for her. 'She must fit *somewheer.*'

'She's a runt. Lucky if we get twenty quid for her.'

I got forty-five. The auctioneer were perched up on this ploomp beside the main thoroughfare. I couldn't believe his rising voice in my ears as I run my beribbed runt up and down the road showing off to the crowds our peculiar paces. She were a sport and went her best.

'SOLD!—to the gentleman in the kaydee!'

The kaydee, a wide-brimmed trilby favoured by judges and the Mafia in the movies, was just coming in from Hollywood (not that I ever see'd the movies, but I see'd the *News Chronicle*). This kaydee cut a dashing figure. He'd been very interested in the runt before the sale; I didn't gloss over her faults but I praised her

161

temperament. He were thrilled to bits to get her. I didn't like to ask what he wanted her for—once that hammer falled, that horse were his'un, warn't supposed to be no odds to you—but I wondered.

'She's for the pot,' he says.

My jaw dropped. He laughed. 'The *tar* pot.'

He were a hard-working road-maker and mender, rising rich in they days of the open road and merry motoring. He'd made enough profit to invest in another tar pot, but he lacked a good horse. There were no massive machines then to tar whole roads at one fell sweep. It were done by a patient willing horse pulling the tar pot, with two men tilting the handle to dribble out the tar. Our 'ticular Tar Baby—no sprinter, no looker—were just the job. I handed her over, expecting the usual bob-for-the-halter. By tradition the boss bought cord and webbing halters by the bunch, sixpence each, and the carter were entitled to a bob-for-the-halter from the buyer. A bob may not seem much of a tip now, but to me then it were six pints. Kaydee gave me a *whole quid*!

Warn't no sense getting drunk when you'd fourteen miles to walk home at the end of the day, but it were well worth looking down the other entries in the catalogue; you generally see'd the clue to somebody you hadn't met for a twelvemonth, and they'd have a halter or two to make merry. The square were chock-a-block with all the fun of the fair, and the streets was crowded with folks enjoying themselves. It were a day out for miles around, and so many comely country women and childern.

I like women and I love childern, but I'd learned by my thirties, especially at all these jamborees and jubilations, how far to enjoy their company and keep my distance. At times I must have seemed downright harsh and rude when a woman were getting too close for friendship: but there be no kindness in encouraging a woman up the primrose path if there be no flowering at the end of it. On the whole, life were less of a menace with me mates in the pub.

I won't say I didn't kick the verge with frustration on my way home, but in the main I were well content with my day's outing. I'd made me master a handsome profit and the runt were in good hands. Moy-hoy! Didn't that chap look smart! I'd still got half his quid in my pocket. I were going to save up and treat meself to a kaydee.

From then on the thirties was mounting crises, '36, '37, '38, all the way downhill to the Second World War. We'd hardly finished celebrating the King's Silver Jubilee in '35, with a jamboree for all ages and a new village seat under the old elm-tree, than the kids was charging round it singing:

> *Will ye come to Abyssinia? Will ye come?*
> *Bring yer own bread'n'butter and a gun.*
> *Mussolini will be there*
> *Shooting dum-dums in the air,*
> *Will ye come to Abyssinia? Will ye come?*

In 1936 our old bwoy, our Gil, were with the old Queen at Sandringham when the old King died. Gil had been in their service for years. He were most upset when he warn't allowed to follow on foot with the rest of the staff and estate-workers behind the coffin to Wolferton Station on that first stage of its long journey to Windsor.

'I need you to stay at the house, Abbott,' Queen Mary said. 'You're so good at coping with the phone.' Gil told us he done a lot of phoning when the King died. He said he'd never forget standing on his own in the window, watching that simple procession moving off from Sandringham on that clear frosty January morning through the pinewoods, with a lone piper playing the lament 'The flowers of the forest'.

Later that year they was all back in London at Buckingham Palace. It were a bit of an upheaval, with the old Queen waiting to move out to Marlborough House and the new King wondering whether to move in to the monarchy—not that *we* knowed anything about it. The new King were wanting our old bwoy to stop on for him at the Palace. Our Gil knowed all the procedure like the back of his wig, and he were quite monumental in his footman's livery, but our Gil declined. I reckon he considered himself a bit above the Prince of Wales. He told me in strictest confidence he were 'apt to drink and swear, and he had a *woman*!' I said he sounded just like any other bloke. But our Gil, being the nanny he were, didn't think 'there was any need for *that sort of thing*!'

That Bank Holiday, for the first time in my working life, I had no stock to tend and took the whole day off. I were all dressed up, best boots, best suit, new kaydee—at half-past four in the morning—and nowhere to go. I decided to walk to Charlbury Station and toss up on an excursion from there. According to the posters on the platform they was offering, among other temptations, Skegness, Mazzawattee, Andrews Liver Salts and Buckingham Palace. 'Just the tickut!' I says to myself. 'I'll go and see our old bwoy before they shifts to Marlborough House.'

Our Gil had often instructed me how to find him in London and which door to knock on. He said I'd be welcome at the Palace at any time, as long as he warn't in the middle of a state banquet. I done exactly what he told me, walked round to the back of the Palace as if I owned the place. Nobody took a blind bit of notice; they was far too busy changing the guard. I were just plucking up strength to yammer on this great door when the sharp end of a bayonet were thrust up in front of me nose, with a ferocious-looking sentry on the blunt end of it.

'Sorlroight,' I soothed him, 'I en't a-come to knock the place abaht-a-bit. I've just come to see our old bwoy.'

He thought I meant the King. Seems I were at the wrong door. Even when he escorted me to the right one I warn't allowed to set finger on it. *He* had to press the bell and announce me proper. 'Chap 'ere says he's come to see Mr Abbott.'

Our old bwoy were that chuffed to see me. He were bored stiff, buried in this glorified kiosk, chock-a-block with telephone sets. No wonder he were good at phoning, he had enough to practise on. Seems he were stuck there on duty for the duration of the Bank Holiday, on pain of death if he deserted his pwoost. There were even a WC, in case of emergency. He were that sorry he warn't available to show me round the premises.

'That's orlroight, Gil. I only come on spec. I warn't exactly expecting an audience with the Quayn.'

But I *had* an audience with the Queen!

We was having a nice chat when this young gal—her couldn't have been more than nine or ten, but growed-up with it—put her head round the door.

'Sorry, Abbott,' she said to our Gil when she saw me, 'didn't know you had company.'

It were Lilibet, our present Queen. Seems she were often at the Palace, stopping with her granny, specially when her mam and dad, the Duke and Duchess of York, was overseas, rounding up the Empire. She were in the kind habit of dropping in to have a chat with whoever was prisoned on duty in that there kiosk, specially when everybody else were out of doors enjoying the Bank Holiday. Our Gil introduced me as his brother Montague, from Enstone in Oxfordsheer.

'However did you get in?' She eyed my muddy boots with interest.

I told her I walked to Charlbury and tossed up from there. Her had never heerd of our Enstone. I told her all about Queen Henrietta's Waterworks—thought she might be interested, seeing as they was related. We had quite a chat. She wished me 'Safe journey, Montague, back to your Enstone.' Then, as she left, like a little queen: 'You must see that your brother takes some refreshment before he leaves, Abbott.'

Our Gil were worried about her dad, the Duke of York, but he 'udn't let on for why; just said if 'that Wally-woman' ever came to *his* door he'd *strangle her*. I'd never seen our Gil look so vicious. He really meant it. I'd no idea who he was talking about. We was all kept in the dark. Soon after, he cranked a handle and jabbered into one of these phones. After about a quarter of an hour, this ambassador chap from the nether regions appeared in his weskut bearing on a tin tray a meal fit for a king, a hunk of fresh bread and cheese and a bottle of beer. Moy-hoy! That were good!

The same ferocious-looking sentry were still on guard when I come out. I nodded at the great yup of Palace still standing behind him. 'Told yer I warn't a-going to knock it abaht!' I says.

And I come home.

Soon after, there were rumours that the new King might pack

the job in; and our Gil's Wally-woman were all in the papers, setting the childern singing round the village seat:

> *Who's this coming down the street?*
> *Mrs Simpson. Ain't she sweet?*
> *She's been married twice before,*
> *Now she's knocking on Edward's door.*

I only hoped, recalling Gil's threat, her had got the right door.

16

Nine Hundred'n' Ninety-Nine Ewes— And a Black'un

TAFFY HUGHES WERE THE OCKERDEST, inconsiderate, fly-off-the-handle gaffer I ever come across, yet I shepherded for him for thirty years.

He'd never send nobody to help me at market. It were bloody hard work, especially at Oxford Market, sorting all they sheep into different pens all by myself. When Venvell's let 'em down off the trucks I had to run 'em all in together to begin with, else have 'em gallivanting all over Oxfordsheer. Most auctioneers was used to seeing me battling on all by myself; they knowed and feared Taffy as a powerful customer. Once there were a young green auctioneer fresh from the city.

'You here all by yourself, shepherd?'

'Ar. Theer en't nobody else as I can see.'

'Who's your master?'

'Mr 'ughes.'

'I'll speak to him about this.'

'Thee'd be best awf if thee didn't!'

He did, and told Taffy what he thought of him: 'Grossly unfair, Mr 'ughes, sending only one man to sort a thousand sheep.'

'They en't a thousand sheep. They be precisely nine hundred'n' ninety-nine ewes and a black'un, and I'll thank you to know your own bloody business.'

As far as the auctioneer were concerned Taffy were the black'un, and he were listed heavily ever after in his little black book as 'Mr EWES'.

They sheep had to be graded, matched for size, weight, looks, into different pens. The auctioneers' bloke 'ud tell you how many he wanted in a bunch, twenties, twenty-fives, fives, and the odds. Sheep don't just go where you tells 'em, you know! It took me and my dogs a couple of hours to sort that lot, running to and fro. Sometimes we was still at it when the auctioneer had started selling. In the War the government bought the pick of the flock at a set price to feed the Forces; the rest, including the black'uns, was sold on the open market.

We knowed in '37 that war were coming; they started speeding up the building of aerodromes. They stwun-folks from London had been paying Ted a royalty to cart off the stwuns from Quar Piece. It were to be only enough for one little drome at Moreton-in-Marsh. I don't know whose daft idea was that to put a drome on a marsh, but they *did*. The marsh were often fog-bound, so they needed 'a bit more stwun' for a back-up drome at Enstone. Enstone warn't quite big enough for some of the new planes, so they needed 'a bit more' for a back-up drome at Chippy. Ted were fed up with 'em carting off more and more of his farm; made 'em buy the lot, and bought himself another farm at Bloxham.

The stwun-folks was only interested in the stwun and sold the farm back to the Ditchley Estate. Ditchley, having sold most of their tenanted farms after the First World War, were now buying them back again ready for the Second. Taffy stepped into the tenancy of Ted's farm. He were on the up and up; besides owning and tenanting farms elsewhere, he now tenanted the Ditchley farms, Church Enstone, Cleveley and Fulwell, three in a line, from Gagingwell to Charlbury Green Lane, about thirteen hundred acres.

They used to call Taffy a land-robber. A land-robber takes all from a farm and clears off, giving nothing back. Taffy were a

Welshman but he warn't no thief. He were a very successful stwuny-hearted business-farmer.

We'd knowed each other ever since we was bwoys before the First World War. He used to come round with his dad, Mr Hughes the vet, from Woodstock wearing his little 'Burford Johnny', the Burford grammar schoolboy cap, like a daft pimple on a haystack compared to the large flat labourer's cap I wore as a bwoy-chap at Lennox's. Taffy were eighteen months younger than me. His dad were one of the nicest, calmest men I ever knowed with animals, yet his only son were nervous and blundering; and it didn't help when his dad 'ud plead, 'Why can't you be like Mont, sensible with animals?' Taff 'ud glower at me with his good eye—the other had been damaged by a cricket ball—yet he'd keep tagging around after me like a lost child, parking himself beside me at ockerd intervals while I be trying to do my work.

When he left school he said he wanted to farm. His dad begged Natty Parsons at Radford to take him on and teach him to farm. There be good 'Farmer Parsons' at Radford for centuries. 'I've got three sons of my own,' Natty said. 'I don't need a fool like him.'

He were farmed out for a year on a farm at Rollright; then he started up on his own on a smallholding at Glympton, hawking his home-grown greengroceries around the district. He did very well with new taters. It were the days when men was already forsaking their allotments to garner higher wages in the motor industry, and before the days of imports from Morocco, Spain and the Canary Islands. Soon he had several hundred acres under taters. After a few years he were set over the Major's farm and dairy herd at Glympton. By the time he were set over the tenancy of Ted's farm at Church Enstone at the beginning of the Second World War he owned or tenanted six farms.

By then I were doing more shepherding than carting, besides helping with all the other seasonal work on the farm. Before Ted quit we'd built some topping good foddering ricks. Taff had bought 'em, but they wanted thatching. Taffy begged me to stay on and work for him, shepherd his new flock when they arrived and, in the meantime, thatch they ricks. I agreed, and Tom Jennings agreed to 'feed' me, doing the yelming while I capped 'em. Taffy was all over us, promising to draw us a good supply of thatching straw straightaway and the water to soften it.

We waited and waited. One; two; three; four hours. No thatching straw, no water.

'I'm awf!' said Tom. 'He promised all and he's drawed nothing. I en't workin' for that sort of bugger.'

'I en't neither,' I says. But it seemed a shame, after we'd built such good ricks, to let 'em spoil. I set to on me own and thatched 'em. I didn't thatch 'em with proper wheat-straw—Taffy never drawed me none—I drawed it out the ricks as I went along, whether it were oat or barley. I just pegged it, overlapping, so the rain 'ud run off. Ye never see'd such a mish-mash of thatching in your life. I were glad Ted warn't there to scorn.

'What the hell's *that*?' Taffy thundered two days later, throwing his new-gaffer weight around the rickerd, shaking his fist at my makeshift effort.

'That,' I says, 'is thetching with straw the gaffer don't draw! T'en't the best I can do, but it's the best under youer promises. I think thee'll find it'll kayp out the wet. I've finished for thee, gaffer. I'll have my wages, playse, and bid thee good-day.'

He took on alarming, just like a kid, stamping his feet, throwing his arms about, almost blubbing. 'You can't leave me, Mont! You can't leave me without a bloody shepherd. What am I going to do with all those bloody evacuees?' (A load of nervy sheep were *en route* from the Kent coast, being evacuated by the War Agricultural Committee to our safer Oxfordsheer pastures.) Taffy were a big chap, almost as tall as me, but stockier. I felt sorry for him, having all they acres, yet behaving childish like that.

'Orlroight,' I gives in; 'but only for the sake of they bombed-out ship. The minute they'm requisitioned, I'm awf.'

'You'll have nowhere to live!' He were the gloating tyrant again.

'I'll find somewheers, doan't thee worry.'

Only our Jim and me were left at home. Our Fred had volunteered for the Navy. Dad had died after a month of we old bwoys struggling to stop him getting out of bed—at ninety-two— 'to go and HOVE my allotment!' He be fit up to that last month. He talked a bit wayward at the end, couldn't place our Mam, his Mary

Ann, but he knowed we old bwoys. Thomas Hawtin made Dad's coffin in his old workshop adjoining the churchyard at Church Enstone. The old pump be still there in the yard. Thomas made Dad's coffin of polished elm with brass furniture (real brass, none of your plastic), pillow-lined with wadding, he dug the grave (extra deep so Mam could join Dad one day), tolled the bell, paid the vicar—all, in 1940, for the princely sum of £7. I still have the receipt.

Our Mam went to pieces after Dad had gone: cooking taters for him in the kettle, making roly-polys at all hours for her bwoys coming in from the fields, washing sandwiches to get rid of the germs, and hoarding enough Parish's Food to feed the parish. Poor Mam! Her had struggled to be provider and nursemaid to so many for so long it were no wonder, at eighty, her could no longer be held responsible.

Jim and me tried to cope, popping home from work at all hours to check on her, never knowing what state she and the house 'ud be in when we come in tired and hungry from working on the land. We stuck it for twelve months. The neighbours tried to help, but in the end it were too much for all of us. Mrs Jennings and Mrs Paxford tried to keep her interested in talk about the WI; Mam had been so keen on the WI. Mrs Paxford called one evening.

'I'm sorry, Mrs Paxford,' I says. 'I'd offer thee a cup of tay, but theer en't a cup'n'sarcer in the place. Mam's smashed the lot.'

Mrs Paxford went straight home and came back with four odd cups and saucers. 'They'm not Wedgwood, Mont,' she says, 'but they'll hold a cup of tay.'

I've still got two of Mrs Paxford's cups and saucers—survived daily use for forty-five years. I reckon they'll rank same as Wedgwood at the finish!

Our Dora took her to live with her at Witney. Mam only stopped two nights—kept running away—couldn't place our Dora—'udn't let her do nothing for her—kept asking when our Horace were coming to fetch her home.

Our Horace worked at Chippy. He were supervisor at the workhouse. Our Mam in her right senses had a mortal dread of ending up in the workhouse ever since ought-eight when our

Horace, the breadwinner of thirteen, had saved us all from it. I felt awful the day we took her there, even though her knowed nothing about it, happily telling total strangers she be 'going to live with our Horace'. Her seven old bwoys each had to pay half-a-crown a week for her keep. The gals wasn't expected to contribute; there were none of this sex equality in they days. Our Horace and his wife and childern were very good to her. I used to go and see her every week, but her never knowed me again. Her lingered on till she died at eighty-four, then Thomas did for her what she had helped him many a time to do for others, prepared her for burial with dignity and respect, and borne her home to our Enstone to lie at rest with our Dad up in the churchyard. '

By then the War had been on for four years, and I were shepherding well and truly for Taffy Hughes. The call-up were extended to men of fifty years but our Jim and me was exempt, being on the land. Everybody was 'digging for victory', scratching old England on the back, and her were giving of her utmost, with grand lawns ploughed up for crops, every spare patch turned over for allotments, and cottage gardens ablaze with cabbages and taters.

In 1940 we'd moved to Twiggs, a tied cottage on one of Taffy's farms at Cleveley, still in the folds of our Enstone. We'd a chock-a-block garden, a sty full of piglets, our own privy, and the electric light. The electric light were bequested to us by kind courtesy of the previous tenants, London evacuees, who'd had the electric in the slums for years and couldn't bear to come down in the world without it in the wilds of Oxfordsheer. It were only light, not power. They'd been allowed to milk the supply that the Ditchley Estate had laid on to the Cleveley Farm cowsheds in anticipation of the milking-machine revolution in worlds to come. Only me, Jim and the cows had the electric light. Freddy Claridge, Taffy's cowman who lived next door to we, still plodded on with candles; and he'd potter up to the cowsheds on dark winter mornings—as he had always done—to do his milking by lantern-light, often forgetting he'd got that little magic Bakelite switch just inside the barn door.

Our Jim were working up on the Ditchley Estate, tractoring,

building and filling in all the other odd jobs they lacked men for; keeping Enstone Cricket and Football Clubs alive by coaching the youngsters, keeping the affairs of the Foresters Club straight by doing the scratching, cycling all over the parish, dishing out due payments to sick members, and doing his regular shifts for the Royal Observer Corps.

I were still Old Mont, not only in the village but in the sheep world far and wide; fitting in with most folks, falling out with others. There were a bit of a rumpus in the village about I not joining the Home Guard. After Dunkirk everybody were expecting the Germans to invade us. Milestwuns and signpwoosts disappeared, village names were blotted off shops. Whole tree-trunks were mounted on wheels and stationed at every junction to be wheeled across the lanes to impede the enemy's progress, and the Home Guard were formed 'to guard valuable property in case of invasion and to form night patrols on the look-out for German parachutists or enemy airmen whose planes have been shot down'.

Dickie Worth were the stalwart Captain Mainwaring of Enstone parish. He kept coming up to me in the fields when I were in the middle of shepherding, up to me eyes in sheep's feet, gums, udders.

'I don't want to fall out with you, Mont. I know you be a good chap at heart; but I have to be completely impartial in my line of duty. It's my duty to enlist every able-bodied man. You're more able-bodied than most. You must join.'

'Dickie,' I says, 'I'll gladly go gallivantin' around these lanes every weekend with yer Home Guard, guardin' whichever valuable pub ye decided to finish up at, if one of yer men'll take on guardin' my spindly little evacuees, pennin' and foldin' 'em every day, rarin' 'em fit and clayn to fayd they chaps in the Forces, lambin' 'em on night patrols all on his own with one little candle in a lantern while they Jerry bombers, throbbin' with bombs, saunters over his yed.'

Dickie 'udn't budge. 'I'm very sorry, Mont. Orders is orders. It is my duty to conscript you into serving your country. I shall have to report you to higher quarters.'

'You go ahead, Dickie,' I says, plodding on with inspecting my flock. 'You've got your duty to do and I've got mine.'

There's a lot to shepherding. Some folks thinks you only looks over the bloody gate. Besides the annual rituals of lambing, tailing, dipping, shearing, there's the daily tending of feet, cwoats, udders, mouths. A sheep arn't got no front teeth at the top, nor has a cow, nor a nanny-goat; they has to chew their cud. A horse has a top and a bottom set, he can eat up and down, whereas a sheep has to crop only up'ards all the time. Her grows two broad teeth, one on either side of her narrow front teeth, in her first year, another two the second year; by her third year her has six broad teeth altogether and her's then what we calls 'full-mouthed'. In a bad year a ewe might lose all her teeth and become a gummy, or she might be 'lost a quarter' of her milking bag—a ewe has only two 'quarters', a cow four. She can't feed herself proper, so she can't feed her lambs: so you culls her out, gives her easy grub in a trough and sends her to market.

In they days a good shepherd 'ud pen his flock on a different strip of field each day. It used all to be done with hurdles before the wire-netting were invented, nowadays the electric fence answers. My folding-bar were extra long, a heavy iron rod, specially tempered and blacksmith-made for me. It were a traditional tool for the job, with a sharp toe to make a hole in the ground for the stake or the hurdle to stand in, and a cupped eye to hammer it home. That folding-bar were as much as a strong woman could lift with two hands, yet in my prime I could wield it one-handed. The hurdles were tied together or the wire-netting was tied to the stakes to form a temporary fence. This meant you could limit and monitor their grub, watching what went in one end and what came out t'other; and they only soiled one strip of field. The next day you penned again, heeling in the old holes so the sheep didn't break their legs, moving 'em on continuous to fresh pasture. I never reckoned in one week to pen my sheep where they could 'hear the church bells twice the same', but it took some wangling with a thousand sheep.

I always had two sheep-dogs to help me, the training of the young'un overlapping from the old. But you mustn't let 'em follow the old'un for too long, else they lose their initiative. If you buys a good strain of pup it's bred in him from the start. I started 'em on the whistles from the very beginning. Take him with you, put him on the ground outside the wire and hold him, let him watch the old'un at work.

My training warn't a bit like the telly programme 'One man and his dog'. There were hardly any long-distance rounding up; it were all close work. I trained 'em to guard the fresh strip of feed and not let the sheep on to it until I were ready to let 'em run on, to keep the main flock quiet so's they didn't huddle and break my wire, to stop the ones I'd already culled from getting back in with the rest. All my dogs I trained myself. You has only that first year to lay the pattern between you for ever after. They was all my mates. I had to stop taking them to help me at market; crowds 'ud gather to marvel, and hindered us so I had to make more use of a cops instead. A cops is a plied noose of three cords used to hackle an animal or hasp a hurdle. I could put a ewe's head and front foot in a cops and her 'ud lie quiet.

Ted were my old'un when Glen were a pup. I remember how pleased I were with Glen that very first day, how I'd wondered as I'd taken him up Dead King's Ride to Ditchley 'sarts where my sheep was penned, whether he'd be a good'un. He'd have a job to live up to my old Ted. I never let him in the wire that first day, but he kept wanting to get through to help old Ted. I could see he were keen. When I let him in the wire I had to be sharp with him. If I blew 'Stop!' at Ted, Glen 'ud look to see what Ted be doing, and *he'd* sit too. It comed natural. Glen turned out a topping dog.

I were up in the field with my sheep one evening making a cops for a hurdle when my dogs give a low growl and my flock gives 'eyes right' to this posh recruiting officer, all braid and buttons on his great-cwoat, picking his way in his cherry-blossomed shoes across yesterday's Brussels stems. I shouldn't think from the look on his face he'd ever been near a sheep in his life. It were a miserable wet evening, and the rank combination of wet feet, wet Brussels and wet dung did nothing to improve his uniform nor his temper. He snapped out this proclamation: 'Montague Archibald Abbott, Parish of Enstone in the County of Oxfordshire, of fit and able body,' and all the ceteras.

I told him the same as I told Dickie; if he'd tend my sheep I'd tend his Home Guard. Up there in they fields, with the whole of

Enstone spread out before me, there warn't much that escaped my eagle blue eyes. I were guarding 'valuable property' to feed our lads in the Forces, I were on frequent night patrols with my lambing, and 'if any bloody Nazi lands anywheers near my sheep, me and my dogs 'ud put paid to him quicker'n any of your Home Guard!'

It warn't up to him finally, he said, it were up to Oxford. He agreed 'an army marches on its stomach', and were very interested to know what happened to the valuable meat if one of my sheep 'accidentally' got bumped off. I soon tumbled to what he were hinting at. I told him to 'Bugger awf! I en't guardin' my sheep night and day from Jerry for some bloody dishonest field marshal to scawf on the black markut!'

I'd cooked my mutton with him. I'd probably end up in Oxford Castle clapped in irons for the duration of the War.

The next Saturday I happened to meet Dickie Worth outside the pub. 'Your dispensation paper's come through, Mont; now your exemption's all above board.' He held out his hand. 'No hard feelings?'

I shook it. 'The trouble is, Dickie,' I says, 'the Lord made thee a bloody good patriot—and he made me a bloody good shupperd!'

There were tremendous air activity over our Enstone during the War, with Jerry's lot on a direct route to the towns of the north-west, and our hedgerows bristling with secret signal-pwoosts to guide our lads taking off and coming home on the dromes all round us. When fog shrouded Moreton-in-Marsh, they planes 'fled' from our Enstone. They RAF chaps, the originals of that famous radio programme after the War, 'Much Binding in the Marsh', 'ud have to hang around the Crown awaiting orders, plotting their course, and hatching their jokes for their present morale and our future entertainment. We was lucky not to be hit. The few bombs we caught landed in open fields. The nighest were in Green Ball but nobody knowed he were there 'cos he didn't go off. I *think* he's gone by now. . . .

Our Gil were evacuated with Queen Mary during the War. When War broke out the Marlborough House lot had to draw straws to decide who were to be called up. Our Gil lost or won—according to your politics—and were posted with the rest of the

Queen's retinue of sixty-two and their gas-masks to Badminton, c/o the Duke of Beaufort. The old Queen always referred to her staff as 'my people'; the old Duke must have thought half the nation were come to stop.

In 1943 there were great rejoicing in our Enstone when our Fred, home on leave from the Navy, married Mrs Huckin. Huckin be an old Enstone name. For generations there be few village councils or clubs without a Huckin serving on board. During the War there were *fourteen* Mrs Huckins in our Enstone. Fred's Mrs Huckin be knowed to everybody as Clara. Clara's husband had been killed before the War by a rolling tree-trunk he were helping to load on to a train at Bloxham Station. It were one of they 'Heythrop Giants', straight, strong and tremendously long that were transported intact by horse and rail for ships' masts. Clara were left with two small childern to bring up on very little money and a lot of courage. When our Clara married our Fred so great were the celebration, Clara's little house couldn't contain it, and we all had to overflow with our ration of utility beer across the street to her friend's larger premises.

Only Jim and me were left at home unmarried. Next door to we at Twiggs were Mr and Mrs Claridge and their seven unmarried daughters. When we first moved from Church Enstone in 1940 somebody said to me, 'Thee and Jim'll be puttin' the broom out with all they gals next doo-er.' ('Puttin' the broom out' were an old country saying, meaning a chap were touting for a wife.) Before I could answer, somebody else chipped in, 'They young Claridge girls won't spake to you two crusty old bachelors.'

I be thirty-eight and Jim be thirty-four. I knowed my broom be past it, the bristles be all gone; but I'd never thought of Jim being left out. He'd had plenty of gals, but none of 'em was much cop. There were one he thought of marrying—kept company with her for quite a while, even got his boots under her table. I 'udn't say they was close; her were a terrible prude, always 'kept her hand on her ha'penny'—if thee knows what *that* means. Nobody wants to marry a gal who offers her quarter to all and sundry, but thee wants a bit of give'n'take.

All they Claridge gals spake to we; none of 'em was uppity.

When, after the War, Mabel, Joan and Lois went air-hostessing and dietician to Australia, they wrote to us for years. When Sheila and Freda died we did what we could. Ruth was a nurse and always come round for a chat whenever her come home. Olive were only little during the War. After the War, we was madly goaded by the Coronation to lash out on a Bush television set, all box and very little screen. Olive used to cadge permission, after her homework and before her bedtime, to come in and 'watch for the fashions'. As the main fashion in they early days were lack of picture, they was always fobbing you off with this set-piece of a chap fashioning a flower-pot. It warn't as if, for Olive's sake, it were a variety of pots. He were always throwing this same old pot on this same old potter's wheel. He were at it every tiff'n'turn for years after the War. Never did discover what happened to him and his pot in the finish.

The trouble with they early television sets was you ended up nearly every night with your kitchen full of folks. Some of 'em you'd never see'd before—until the light went up. The village school-teacher, a sporty young chap, 'ud invite himself when the rugby were on. They was sometimes short of a camera or two to cover the whole ground, and every time it didn't stretch he'd leap up demented, lunging himself behind the television to see where the ball had got to. We had to give up standing for the National Anthem when the pictures was finished, it just warn't squeezable in Twiggs' little kitchen with all they watchers-on.

All through the war years I fell in and out with old Taff. I were nigh to quitting him many a time, he were that tyrannical, but I got his measure over the years. You hast to stand up to a chap like Taffy, don't let him bully you. It helped that I were his size. I stood real close, took the full force of his spetter straight in me eye without a flinch. No matter how togged-up he were in the eyes of the business and racing world, pulling up at my field gate soon after the War in his posh motor on his way to the races, he knowed in his heart of hearts *I* never see'd him as the mightly landed racehorse owner, J.H. HUGHES, I see'd him as little Burford Johnny, bwoy to bwoy before the First World War, man to man after the Second.

I *thought* I'd got his measure, but in the bad winter of '47 he sank below zero in *my* little black book. It were the worst winter in living memory, not for frost, but for snow. Fathoms of it. It started in January and went on till April. Thee could stumble along the tops of where the hedgerows used to be, touching the telegraph wires where the telegraph wires used to be. I lost count of how many sheep me and my dogs dug out. Sheep won't back into the wind like a bullock or a horse, they go with the wind and let the snow drift up over 'em. They huddles up together and sometimes they'm suffocated. You has to look for a little hole on the top of the snow, dig out sensible so the thrown snow forms a gully behind you, and lead 'em out along it. The hole is made by several sheep putting their heads together and breathing out warm air that melts the snow above. Sometimes if the ground be frozen on top you can tunnel through, but you have to be careful if the top collapses, else you'll be buried with the sheep. My old dog Ted worked like a Trojan digging out they holes. We was up in Exercise Ground and the drifts was ten feet deep. 'Come on, Ted,' I says. I be buggered up and all for having a rest, but he 'udn't give in, scratting at these holes. His old heart never recovered from the strain of it. He were fourteen, and never so lissom after '47.

In they days we was running a flock of Dorset Horns. Dorset ewes are good milkers. They make wonderful mothers, though not so prolific as the Jacob. I heerd tell of a Jacob ewe as reared twenty-one lambs in nine years, including a run of triplets and a set of quads. The Dorset ewe 'ud be more prolific if her had the chance; she comes into season twice a year, even when she's still suckling. We used to lamb in the November. The lambs 'ud run with their mothers all winter. By Easter they was as big as their mothers, and we'd send 'em to market, uncut, undocked, as 'unblemished lamb'.

I never reckoned to send anything blemished to market. Zicky Harris once delivered a load of my sheep to some stately mansion.

'Who shepherded these sheep?' asks His Lordship.

'Some old chap they calls Mont,' says Zicky.

'Well I never! Five hundred sheep, and not a single lame one.'

'Naw,' says Zicky, 'he doan't reckon to go in for lame'uns.'

I didn't reckon to go in for tups on the loose nor broken fences neither. Some farmers with Dorsets were careless with their tups and feckless with their fences, and 'ud sell their 'wild' pregnant ewes to Taffy for Old Mont to lamb. I were fed up with that lark in '47. I'd been lambing almost continuous, first with my own in November, then with other folks' random mistakes in all that snow. When I warn't lambing I were digging out. When I warn't digging out I were yomping hay to racks and feed to troughs.

About three o'clock in the afternoon were your lowest ebb working out in the fields in the snow. That's when the cold really catches hold on you. Any faint hope of a wintry sun breaking through or the air warming up is gone; your belly's empty, your eyes and nose too frez to run; your face too stiff, your soul too raw, for salving with a song.

Yet worse than the snow were the thaw. All they streams and underground gissles couldn't take all that snow with more snow, sleet and rain on the top. All that water with nowhere to go came bubbling up mud. The fields was moving with mud, loosening gate-pwoosts, marooning flocks, caking caked boots and layers of muddy cwoats. I rescued a horse. It were almost out of sight in a quagmire of mud. They all said I ought to have a medal. I reckon they Jesuits deserved it more; the horse and me 'ud both have been a goner if they hadn't put a rope round us and had a tug-of-war against the mud at the finish.

All that winter and spring, Jim and me never see'd the fire in the kitchen at Twiggs for muddy cwoats. We doffed 'em at night, dripping and cold, and donned 'em in the morn, damp and warm. All our lives we used to warm togs before the fire before putting 'em on. There were no such things as airing-cupboards for the likes of we. It were the ever-running saga of life on the land, drying your cwoats.

Eight years before, I'd had my appendix out. I'd been sick and weak every tiff'n'turn for weeks, and Ted had taken me to old Doc Croly. I laid on his old couch and he scrat and done me about.

'Doctor,' I pleads, 'I don't want to go on the Box.'

'My boy, if you don't go *on* the Box you'll soon be *in* a box.'

The surgeon chappy said it were the longest elongated appendix he had ever seen. When the gate fell on it in '47, it couldn't miss the scar. It were ruptured top and bottom. It felt as if half me insides was hanging out. It were uncomfortable, to say the least, but I were trussed up and could just manage to keep going with my flock while I waited for the Radcliffe to fit me in for an operation. At least I'd finished lambing. It were getting on for the end of March. I were just setting off home from work in the dusk one evening when this truck full of sheep draws up from the gate.

'Loads of tegs for yer,' the driver says. 'Crawsbreds.'

'Thee must be mistaken.'

'See for yerself.' He held the ticket in the sleet falling past the beam of the headlight, 'J.H. HUGHES.'

'He never told me. I'm wet through. I'm awf home.'

'They've been in here five hours.'

I never reckoned to take out my spite on animals. 'Thee'd best let 'em into this field. T'en't their fault; I'll give 'em some grub.'

Taffy came up next morning, full of himself and his bargain lot. Told me he'd bought 'em over the phone as a mixed bunch, and what did I think of them?

'I'll tell thee what I thinks of 'em. Twelve of 'em be very pregnunt, that's what!'

'Don't be so daft!' he snapped.

'Use yer eyes. Even if I was blind I'd still know by their holler; a pregnunt yaw bleats different.'

'Talk sense!'

'You asks yer butties at that posh Vet'n'ry Dinner yer goin' to tonight. See if I'm roight. And another thing,' I says calmly, 'thee'd best get somebody daft to come out in all this mud and lamb 'em, 'cos Old Mont en't a-gwin to be here. They've sent me summons from the Radcliffe. I'm to turn up for me operation on Monday.'

He took on as usual, ranting and raving.

On Sunday, I'm getting all ready for the Radcliffe, ironing me pyjamas extra-special, when Taffy draws up outside the cottage in his posh motor. 'I've been to the Radcliffe. They've put it off for a month. With a bit of luck you'll have lambed all those ewes by then.'

I never spake word. I couldn't think of one black enough for a black'un like him. There were nothing a labourer like me could do about it in they days. I had no posh motor to drive myself to the Radcliffe. I had no phone—never used a phone in my life—and anyway who in a big infirmary like the Radcliffe 'ud speak with the likes of me?

I stuck it for two more weeks, the sleet, the mud, and the rupture. I were okay as long as I didn't slip into one of they muddy crevasses and jar myself. Despite the grey skies and sodden landscape, spring were sneaking in: quickening the hedgerows, greening up the mud. I knowed the sly mudholes to avoid, specially the worst, the Severn Bore, disguised as innocent new grass down the middle of Bagnel Hill.

It were Black Friday, pouring with rain—as if we hadn't had enough!—and I were in pain bending to my lambing. I were soaked through. I had my shepherd's hut, but my work were mostly out than in. I hadn't seen a soul to spake to all day. I could hear a happy band of tater-sorters working under cover, singing in the barn across the fields. Taffy hadn't been near me for a fortnight, not even to see how the lambing was going on, not even to bring me my pay-packet; sending old Twistle, Mr Entwistle, the foreman, instead. One good point about Taffy; he always paid on time. It warn't lack of money that finished me that Friday, it were lack of appreciation and human worth. 'Tell Taffy I'm quit,' I says to old Twiss when he brought my wages. 'Theer's one yaw left to lamb. I've got the fold ready. He can get on with it.'

I were going up with my wheelbarrow to collect my tack from me shepherd's hut when Taff came slithering to meet me, all flustered. 'That ewe's started. She's in difficulty.'

'Thee'd best get down in the mud and help her,' I says, catching a glimpse of Persil-white cuff under his racing-mac, and smart grey flannel over his point-to-point wellingtons. Ranting and raving he stomped off across the field. 'Don't go empty-handed!' I shouted after him. 'Take a hundredweight of fayd for the others while yer about it!'

Snorting and swearing like a great bull under the weight of the sack, he were charging straight for the Severn Bore. I were about to warn him.

'Naw,' I says to myself. 'Why should I? He can taste a bit of his own medicine.' He had mouthfuls of it, nosefuls of it, caked on his cuffs and wodged down his wellingtons.

'Wish I'd never bought the bloody sheep! Wish I'd never seen this bloody farm!' He were beside himself with temper, chucking the feed everywhere but in the trough. He disappeared into the lambing-pen and came out howling, 'I can't do it.'

'I'll go and relieve the old gal,' I says, 'but I en't a-doin' it to please *thee*. And theer's two more bags of fayd for thee to fetch!'

I lambed the old gal and came back into my hut to wash my hands. He were slumped on the straw, his head sunk on his muddy chest. 'Let's talk,' he bleats.

'Thee can talk till thee's blue in the face,' I says, loading my crook and my folding-bar on top of my barrow. 'I don't want yer bloody job. I've been workin' me guts out for thee for seven years, humpin' sacks of fayd, rolls of wire, piles of hurdles. Thee tells other folks, "If everybody made me as much profit as Old Mont I'd be a millionaire"—but thee never tells *me*. "Don't be daft," thee snaps, then finds out I be roight—but thee never admits thee's in the wrong. All they folks doing taterin' in the dry; and me stuck out 'ere all on me own in the pourin' rain. And thee knows now,' I says, nodding at his muddy toggery, 'what manner of ground it be in this field, and how heavy they sacks be. A little appreciation, a bit of consideration, 'udn't come amiss. Instead, thee piles on the lambin' and buggers up me operation!' I were almost in tears. I were cold and in pain. For all his bulk, all his power, he were just like a naughty kid sitting there snivelling, taking every lash of me tongue. Daft as I was, I were beginning to feel sorry for him. Nobody really liked him. They liked to do business with him; he were always straightforward where money was concerned. He were a bachelor like me—'cept *he* could afford a string of housekeepers, coming in one day and walking straight out the next. Yet there be a bwoyhood bond between us. I wavered. . . . It be no good. If I give in, he'd be just as bad all over again. I pushed off quick with my tackle in my barrow and abandoned him.

My barrow were a good'un. He were a token of appreciation from Ted Barrett for saving his old horse in 1930. Ted used to get that dickery if he'd got anything middling: and he thought the world of this horse. I stopped up all night, drenching him every two hours and walking him gently round, trying to get him to pass water. I led him to the trough but he 'udn't drink, just drooped his old head. I used a catheter, and still he 'udn't oblige. Time were running out if nothing else was; dawn were breaking, and I'd got me own horses to breakfast at five o'clock.

'If thee's gonna die, thee might as well die in comfort,' I says, spreading him a nice clean bed of straw—and he stalled all over it. Ted were overjoyed. I reckon he'd have give me the crown jewels if I'd wanted. Offered I this fistful of ten-bob notes.

'I'd rather have the barrer,' I says, nodding at the home-made wheelbarrow standing nearby.

'We en't got narn if thee has that 'un,' he says; 'but I'll get Wilf Oliver to make thee another just like him.'

'I got a wheel,' he says, 'all it lacks is a barrer.'

Seventeen years I'd had that barrow. I'd treated him to a pneumatic tyre in '33—cost a guinea from Ambrose's Agricultural Hardware Stores in Chippy. It had never needed pumping up; and as I wheeled him on the last lap home along the muddy lane to Twiggs in the spring of '47, carrying all my shepherding tackle, he were still going strong.

'I be unemployed,' I suddenly realized as I trundled up the garden path. 'All me qualifications for a job on the land be in this barrer and in the strength of me arms.'

I put my precious crook and my folding-bar behind the kitchen door, took off my wet cwoat, chucked it with all the others off the guard on to the floor, stoked up a roaring fire, lit my pipe, and set down to take stock of my position in the job market.

I could swap the land for Morris Motors. Half the male population of our Enstone was being shifted night and morning by buses to the factories in Oxford, bearing home the fatted pay-packet. 'NAW!' My whole being cried out against it. It'd be the death of me. I couldn't sacrifice the beauteous countryside, the open air, wind, sun—even *mud*—to be prisoned in a pay-packet. But I be forty-five, old-fashioned in my ways, getting left behind on the land. There were a tremendous leap forward, during and after the War, in animal medicine and farm mechanization. Dozens of old remedies was now contained in one little injection. The need for all my proud old labouring skills was vanishing fast.

I'd reaped my last swathe—teaching they land-girls in the War, before the 'Sunshine Harvester' binder cut the rest of the crop, to reap the outer field as our ancestors had done for centuries, with a hooked stick and a sickle. You hooked the bundle of corn towards you, cut it with the sickle, drawed it towards you into a sheaf, made a bond of twisted straw, tied it round the sheaf with a neat Oxfordsheer knot, and stood it against the hedge. All sheaves were once made like that, whole swathes, whole fields, whole landscapes, culled by hand. The binder cut and tied its own sheaves, throwing 'em out with rounded fronts that butted up close, and flat backs that channelled off the rain when you built 'em into a rick.

I'd built my last rick. I'd learned my rick-building when I were at Lennox's. Hay, beans, peas, straw, sanfin was ricked loose, there were no knocking it about into bales. Later the beans, peas, grasses was threshed for seed or protein feed; and the hay and straw was cut from the rick and tied into trusses and boltons. Some was dispatched by rail. I've filled many a truck with straw at Charlbury Station. It were the porter's job to sheet 'em up and make sure not a wisp stuck out to touch the gauges. They iron arches spanning the track made sure the load 'ud fit under all the railway bridges along the route. Hay-tying for trusses and boltons were a full-time job; and the hay-tyer's childern 'ud work hard before school and straight after, wetting and twisting the hay or straw into a stock of bonds for their dad. Neat and tidy they trusses and boltons had to be when they was delivered. There were hell to pay at posh stables like Miss Bruce's if a knot were less than a work of art, or as much as a wisp of straw were shed.

I'd yelmed my last thatch. After that first fiasco in 1940 I'd thatched all Taffy's ricks thereafter. I were pretty high up one day in the War, thatching a rick along the Gagingwell Road, watched by a very attentive pilot-officer. He didn't speak, just watched, fascinated, every yelm, every stalch, every spray, every risky shift of the long ladder. 'Want a turn?' I hollered down.

'No thanks!' he shuddered. He were terrified of heights, only felt safe cubbed in a Wellington bomber at thirty thousand feet.

I'd threshed my last rick. Threshing were a dirty old job, but it brought out the best of the old life on the land—team-work. Keeping pace with the relentless tug-tug-tug-tug of that ancient stationary steam-engine that drove the huge threshing-machine, I taught the land-girl on the outside of the corn-rick to throw the sheaf, just right, to the gal in the middle, who'd throw it, just right, to the gal on the bond-cutting. I taught the gal on the bond-cutting to hold it by the knot, so it didn't slip through into the straw to choke the cattle; and to feed the sheaves into the drum at a steady rate—a back-aching job—knowing if she fed too greedy the drum 'ud belch WOOFF, the belt might come off, and she'd let us all down by holding up the whole operation.

The corn were sieved into three categories, down four chutes. The top grade were fed down two chutes into alternate sacks. If it were a heavy crop two men 'ud have to be on this job, to keep bumping the sacks to fill 'em nice and even, without pucker. As soon as your sack were full you'd switch the clack to channel the grain into the other chap's sack—lift off your full sack—put an empty one on the hooks in its stead—and sack-cart it across to be weighed. There were set weights made of iron, guaranteed to give you a weight-lifter's muscles. Wheat ($2\frac{1}{4}$ hundredweight), oats ($1\frac{1}{2}$ hundredweight) and barley (2 hundredweight); so in a good year of top quality your sack may not hold the same quantity as in a poor year, but it were always the regulation weight. There were a hod of grain nearby to scoop out or to make up weight, allowing four pounds for the Hudson sack. You had to work steady to tie up your sack—pleating they thick tops were very sore on the fingers— take it to the barn on the sack cart, and get back to the chute in time to cope with your next sack.

Meanwhile the brave lass—it were usually the lightweight of the team—on chaff'n'cavings 'ud be raking out all the husks and rubbish from under the throbbing machine with a big wooden rake, on to a six-foot-square canvas sheet, bundling it up and carting it off to be burnt. It warn't the hardest job, but it were the most unpleasant, and the tired dillen 'ud finish up black as a coalman, eyes, nose, mouth, ears choked with dust.

Two stalwart land-girls was catching the straw on their pitchforks as it flopped off the belts at the far end, and carrying it across to the chap building the straw-rick. At the beginning of the War, before we had enough Lainchbury elevators, it were very hard for they gals when the rick were getting high to bear their loaded pitchfork in one hand and climb the ladder with the other. Then it were up to us men, as oft us could, between sacks, to lend a hand.

Now, in 1947, reaping, ricking, thatching, threshing were disappearing fast into the maw of the new combined harvesters that had landed like locusts, one or two, there and there, during the War, but swarming soon after, crawling across the countryside shovelling up acres and chuting out grain, ready-cut, carried, threshed, into trailers. Taffy, shrewd business-farmer as he was, had one of the first. The old black'un farmed so many acres I'd have to emigrate miles from Enstone to escape his employ.

We'd have to move from Twiggs too. It were a tied cottage. I looked round the homely kitchen with Mam's caddy on the dresser and Mam's plaques over the mantelpiece—and the cwoats on the floor. Despite one or two drawbacks, me and Jim was very content at Twiggs. Neither of us 'ud want to move from our Enstone. Jim were wrapt up more than ever in the sports teams and the Club, always scratching correspondence, fixtures, accounts, reports, umpiring football and cricket.

It had been a very bad winter with my rupture and all, but deep down I were very content shepherding. *If only old Taff*—! It were a wonderful independent satisfying job; and I were proud when all they farmers 'ud form a welcoming party round my pens at market 'to see what goodies old Mont's brought.' *If only old Taff*—! I were even happy lambing—it were always a miracle to see first they little black hoofs, then that little black nose—but I'd had too much of it that year. *If only old*—!

I turned round. Taff were standing in the doorway, his face still tear-stained with mud. 'Stop on, Mont,' he pleaded. 'We'll have no more lambing. I'll buy ewe-lambs for fattening; and you can have the old horse and cart from Ful'll to hump your feed and your hurdles.'

I were won over, but it 'udn't do to show it. 'I'll think about it,' I says, distant-like, 'after me operation.'

Me operation went well, apart from one old frost of a sister, sitting doing the scratching at the desk when I went in.

'Good day,' says I, being amicable.

'Name?' she says, sharp as an icicle, without looking up.

'Just scratch "Old Mont".'

'Don't be familiar with *me*, my man! *Name?*'

I let her have it, distant-like: 'MON-TEE-GUE, ARCH-EE-BALD, ABBOTT.' Her thought I were having her on.

She gave I this nightshirt-affair and told me to go to the bathroom to put it on. I didn't think a lot to it as a garment. There warn't enough of it; it were up to me knees and flapping open all down the front, showing me unmentionables as I walked back down the ward.

'You dirty old man! Go back to that bathroom at once and put that gown on properly!' How was I to know 'properly' was back to front? Never weared a frock in me life.

Everybody were nice and called me 'Mont'—'cept old Crosspatch. Her thawed out a bit in the end. Seems I went up in her estimation by insisting on going down to the lavatory an hour after I came round from me operation, to save her nurses from perching me up on one of they bedpans. I warn't having no woman manhandling me. I prefers me own pedestal.

They all, including the surgeon and her, came to say goodbye. I thanked 'em all for me operation.

'I hope we shall see you again one day, Mr Mont,' she says.

'I hope not, sister,' I says.

And I come home.

I were utterly lost in hospital without my sheep. I could understand the retired ancient shepherd, Levi Hathaway, begging me to let him 'walk amongst 'em, Mont'. Old Taff came one day when Levi was with me with the flock.

'What's that old fellow doing up here?'

'He's doing no harm—just wants to walk amongst 'em.'

'Never heard of anything so daft!'

I even missed old Taff in hospital. I knowed he'd never change, it 'ud always be 'Don't-be-so-daft' and no appreciation; but better the Black'un thee knows than the devil thee don't.

Taff were true to his word. I had no more lambing; and there was the old horse'n'cart waiting for me when I got back. It were no cop at all. I piled twelve hurdles on the cart and the bugger 'udn't budge. I usually managed to carry six myself. I sent him back. Years later, Taff got around to buying me a little second-hand tractor. It were a little grey Ferguson, and I fixed an old potato-riddle behind my seat for my dogs to travel on.

We sold our old Dorset flock in '47. From then on I had 'flying flocks', they came and they went. We had various breeds, mostly first cross, a Border Leicester ram on a Cheviot ewe. They was easy to sell for breeding; you'd got the narrow nose and long ears, more streamlined for easier lambing.

I've lambed most breeds in my time. They little bull-headed Southdowns be the worst. You needed a vet, a midwife and two nursemaids to lamb one of they; they be so tight behind. Yet they make good wool and the poshest mutton. They'd weigh as much as a bigger breed. They'd go eight, nine, ten stwun, but I reckon it were all in their head. They Oxford Downs and Hampshire Downs was much bigger; it were as much as a chap 'ud manage, to handle one of they. I preferred the old Oxford. She were easier for breeding, narrower in the nose than the Hampshire, with longer looser wool, and more clean-shaven. The old Hampshire were like a granddad, with a beard and mutton-chop whiskers meeting over his nose.

The crossbreds I fattened for Taffy be much smaller than the old Cotswolds I'd shepherded for Ted Hunt. They Cotswolds looked the size of young donkeys when they be grazing, and so fat on their rump it were like slapping a whole quartern of dough. Two fleeces from Ted's Cotswolds 'ud weigh twice as heavy as two from Taffy's crossbreds; but the Cotswold wool was coarse, more suited to rugs and upholstery than to fine gents' and ladies' clothing.

One of the finest sights I ever saw in the old droving days were the Sheep Fair at Stow. Six main roads meet at Stow—just imagine the thousands of sheep pouring into the fair from the surrounding countryside.

Taff 'ud go up to Scotland for the 'September doubles'. They'd sell the single lambs first, then the doubles. He'd usually buy crossbreds, nine hundred to a thousand, five or six quid apiece, and they'd easily double their value and weight down here. Even our shortest grass was better than their thin stuff. At first they was transported by rail. The farmers 'ud charter a whole train of trucks, dropping off the different lots at different destinations. Moy-hoy! They wild Scottish sheep 'ud shift when you got 'em out of the trucks at Charlbury Station. They'd been shut up in they trucks for hours, and when they see'd the promised land of our lush Oxfordsheer pastures after they stingy highlands they'd go mad.

The furthest I ever drove sheep were six miles. Took five of us to keep they Scottish hordes on the straight and narrow—and they warn't used to motors. There warn't so many motors then, but every time the odd one appeared they Highland-flinged 'emselves over the hedge. They be fiercely clannish. We dreaded meeting another flock. My mad lot once met another mad lot head-on in the narrow road. All was racket and rumpus. 'Let 'em into this field, the lot of 'em!' I shouts. 'Before we has the Massacree of Glencoe, we'll all have a bite and a bit of quiet.'

Within half an hour they'd ganged up separate and we was able to drive out each flock all of a piece. I had to pen 'em stingy at first so they didn't gorge and blow theyselves. They didn't like being penned after roaming wild, but they soon got used to it.

My dogs warn't trained for droving but for penning, sorting, guarding. I've had Welsh and Scottish dogs in my time: Luke, Ted, Ben, Glen, all my dogs served me well. The Welsh had a coarser cwoat, the Scots more silky and soft. A good sheep-dog is broad between the brows so he can see far and wide, with a good 'bump' of brain, and a clean mouth, all pink, no black, no overshot jaw. He should keep his tail down. A dog that cocks his tail when he be working en't much cop—frightens the stock. My dogs were trained to work mostly to whistles. I had two: a metal Acme with a heavy note, and one I carved from the thrown horn of a Dorset sheep, with a light note, very clear. They hung from a ring in my lapel.

This left my hands free to signal and use my crook. The pitch, length and number of blasts covered a multitude of stealthy manœuvres throughout the year and the annual campaigns of dipping and shearing.

I always sheared stood up. I used to tie two bales of straw together and sit the sheep with her dock between the bales. She didn't mind once she were there and you was holding her quiet, but she didn't want being hustled about. Twin sheep 'ud always fuss if one were being sheared before the other. I first sheared with Shepherd Akers when I were a bwoy. I managed with hand-shears until the machine came in. I've still got the last pair I bought, forty years ago, ten-and-a-tanner.

I used to shear three tons of wool on average, from nine hundred to a thousand ewes. I used to take my wool to Shilson's, the staplers at Charlbury. They staplers know by touch if the clip be good or if the wool were ever sheared off a dead'un. Only the top-quality wool was baled straightaway. Arthur Prew were one of the examiners at Shilson's. He'd come and inspect my wool on the lorry. I'd be that proud if it be put into one of they long baling bags that the bwoy 'ud have to get inside and tread down.

One year I were even more proud when Arthur said, 'Your wool always comes in so clean, Mont. Who ties it?' That year I'd learned a backward chap to do it. It had been hard work. It be all right if he kept going, but if he stopped to sneeze, he forgot, and I had to stop and show him, fleece by fleece, the whole simple operation all over again. He were that proud when I told him of Arthur's praise. It went to his head; he told me later he were thinking of applying to Oxford to learn to read and write.

When Shilson's closed down I had to take my wool by lorry to Pearce's of Thame. I didn't know anybody there. It were all up-to-date, with a queue of lorries and a modern baler.

'What sort of wool is it?' the foreman asked.

'Cheviot–Border Leicester, first clip.'

'I've never had your wool before. You'll have to wait.'

I suddenly see'd Arthur working there. 'Thee ask Arthur, foreman; he'll tell thee if thee wants to know aught about my wool.'

'All right, shepherd,' he says, coming back from Arthur. 'We'll have your lot off straightaway.'

When they'd unloaded it, 'Thanks, shepherd,' he said, 'ten't often we get a load of wool in like that.' He gave I thirty bob and the lorry-driver ten.

Shepherds used to get a bonus, so much a tail for lambing, so much a head for shearing. In the old days us bwoy–chaps 'ud be sent to go with the shepherds to the staplers, to bring 'em home tight. By the end of the fifties the contract-shearers were beginning to come round with their machines, and the fleeces was baled and taken away by lorry.

By then the big cattle-trucks was coming in, and Taffy 'ud send his new-bought flocks from Scotland down by road. Bell's, a big firm in Scotland, were the first truck I see'd three tiers high with sheep. Took 'em umpteen hours in they days to come down from Scotland: warn't no motorway. They'd run in convoy through the night and I'd be in the field by two or three o'clock in the morning to welcome them. There were far less dead'uns than by the old train, they travelled quicker and were delivered straight into the pen. You had to watch for chest infection the first few days. After over-heating, penned in they trucks, they tended to catch a chill when they was turned out into the open and they'd cough, 'Awf! Awf!' I used to light sulphur all along the length of the pen, so they fumes blowed all over 'em. It were the next best thing to having 'em all round a basin of Friar's Balsam with a towel over their head.

Venvell's always done our transport from the Enstone end. I always travelled with my stock to market. I never branded or tagged my sheep. Once, I were just off home after selling 'em when the constable came up. 'There's trouble, Mont. One of your sheep has got in with another lot, same breed: would you know it?'

'Course I 'ud.'

'There's *hundreds* of 'em, all unbranded.'

I stood quite still among the alien flock and held up my crook. None of 'em took a blind bit of notice, jostling with each other and bleating, upset. I see'd her at last, standing quite still, looking at me as if to say, 'Yes, master?'

'*I know my sheep and am known of mine*'—I reckon Jesus got it about right.

Taffy 'ud never provide my transport home from market. I'd have to start walking or cadge a lift. I once asked one of Venvell's drivers if by any chance he were going back to Enstone. 'I'm going right now,' he says. 'Hop in!' He forgot to mention he had a load in the back and were going via Baldock. I kept wondering when we was going to turn for our Enstone. I warn't bargaining for a trip to the Far East.

Shrewsbury Flower Show's the furthest I've ever been north of the border of Oxfordsheer; and the Sunday School outings to Weston, the furthest west. I've been to Bournemouth with the choir many a time, and once to Worthing for a holiday.

It were the only holiday I ever had: 1959 I think it were. We used to sell off our fatted flock by the end of August and buy the new stock at the beginning of September. Taffy, true to form, said I'd have to have my holidays 'in between'. Our George had just retired from being an inspector in the Mounted Police. He'd had a serious stomach operation and had taken a house for several months to convalesce. He'd done a smart bit of bouncing, riding in all that ceremonial steel clobber when he were in the Life Guards. When they'm riding with the Queen's carriage in that flashy cuirass they mustn't bump the saddle, the edge of the metal 'ud thump like the back of an axe, they has to keep up in the stirrups having their guts shook about. They chaps in the front of the carriage en't a-wearing the steel, so they can bump the saddle with the rhythm of the horse.

Our George invited me to spend a week at the seaside with him and his wife. Their son were growed up by then. I en't wrapt up in the seaside. I reckon it's a dirty old place: all they seagulls picking up rubbish at one end and floppeting it about at the other. I grant that salt-water may be beneficial to the body, but when thee considers what else gets chuck into it at the seaside, thee'd be better off chucking a load of salt into your bathtub. I be used to rising early—couldn't rest even on holiday after four o'clock. I be only fifty-seven, in me prime, I be spun out of things to interest by half-past six or so. By the time I'd gone down to the quay and watched they old fishermen a-gutting they fish, and they old seagulls a-slawping they guts up and flopping 'em down, I'd see'd enough: and it warn't even breakfast-time.

George were kind enough. He had aged a lot, and spent his time sitting by the fire doing tapestry. After soldiering all his youth *under* canvas, he were stitching his old age *over* canvas. His missus be all right, but her kept cherruping about 'folks, supposed to be on holiday, getting up at the crack of dawn'; and I were feeling more and more like an Enstone fish out of water. Two days is plenty for a week's holiday.

'George,' I says, 'I think I'll be awf. Is theer any job ye'd like done before I go?' He'd had a load of logs delivered, but they was far too big for their fireplace, and it were too much for his missus to handle. I left 'em with a huge stack of handy blocks. Thanked 'em both for having me.

And I come home.

By the end of the fifties Taffy had farms all over the place, most of 'em within droving distance. The rule of the old droving days used to be 'engines stop for horses; everything stops for cattle and sheep'. The lorry-drivers was most understanding; they'd straddle the road with their vehicles, holding the traffic in check. But as traffic increased into the sixties it were no longer fair to hold up the busy A34 from Enstone to Great or Little Rollright with a thousand sheep, and we was calling in Venvell's for any distance over a mile on the road. This meant planning your grub more carefully, making the most of a field of turnip-tops or lattermath, keeping a close eye that the new tack suited 'em, that they didn't gorge too rich and get blown. If ye see'd one standing still, lifting her old nose up and up gasping for air, you got her out quick and kept her on the move. I've knifed one or two in my time, saved their lives by letting out the gas and stitching 'em up; but prevention is better than cure. I were watching all the time what went in one end and what came out t'other: supplementing with additional feed when needed. In the old days, when we used to break up all our own beans and cattlecake, we knowed what was in it. By the sixties the protein feed come ready-packed, and there were some expensive mistakes if you gave 'em too much concentration. They'd start scouring and snuff it. You still had to keep thinking.

Sometimes I never see'd a soul all day. I'd sing to keep meself company, and have a word with my dogs from time to time. Old Taff left me to it. He'd come round once in a while to discuss my next destination, and what equipment I'd need there. He'd sail past in his Jag at other times and never stop to have a word. He'd sometimes come and nose at my flock on a Sunday when I warn't there. I always knowed when he'd been, a cops tied different, a tell-tale wire bent lower than I left it—because he were too lazy to go in the proper gate—and the sheep slightly on edge and restless.

I were often left stranded after hours, waiting for transport to fetch me home. Taff used to curse at sending his foreman. It were a lot easier when he bought me the little tractor and I could cart myself back and forth over short distances.

Taff never grumbled about calling out the vet. He knowed if something were beyond me, it were serious. I done most of my own vetting where foot-rot, maggots and broken limbs was concerned. The first time I had a sheep with a broken leg Taffy insisted on calling out Mr Kearney, the vet from Woodstock. I'd assisted Mr Kearney with all kinds of stock over the years. We once operated on a cow and got a whole bucketful of wire out of her stomach.

'You've assisted me with so many operations over the years, Mont, surely you could have coped with this break yourself.' It were a straight break, her had stamped her foot ockerd at one of my dogs. He made it clear that I were losing him business, calling him all the way out to Rollright to mend a simple break for a set fee, when he could be in the surgery tending a queue of pampered budgies, dogs and cats. I done all me own setting after that.

There were wonderful new ointments and injections for some of the old incurable diseases. Old Taff didn't believe me when I told him to 'get the vet, I'd got "New Forest".'

'Don't be so daft! I'm not telling the vet *that*, there's no such thing.'

'What's *that* then?'

I showed him my old manual, *The Husbandry of Sheep*, what old Shepherd Levi Hathaway gave me. 'Listerelosis, sometimes known as New Forest.'

'Thee tell Mr Kearney I've got New Forest. *He* won't say I'm daft. If we don't get that old gal's eyes attended to, that skin'll grow all over her eyesight, she'll be blinded for life, and the flies'll carry it to all the rest of my flock.'

I once suspected one sheep had pulpy kidney. It were the first and last time I ever tried to use the phone. I were up in the field out by Whiteway just opposite Stewart's old stone quarry. I ran across to Jesse Stewart in the little office.

'I reckon I need the vet quick, Jesse. Can thee phone old Taff?'

'What's his number?'

'No idea. Never used the phone in my life.'

'Don't worry, Mont, I'll look it up for you.' He handed me the phone. Taff sounded all jabberwocky, jabber-jabber-jabber. I handed it back. 'Can't make head nor tail of him, Jesse. Tell him I've got pulpy kidney.'

'DON'T BE SO DAFT!' I heerd him, plain as plain, without the phone, 'PULPY KIDNEY DIED OUT YEARS AGO!'

By eight o'clock that same morning Mr Earle, the other vet from Woodstock, diagnosed I be right. By ten o'clock a fresh batch of serum were travelling from London on the train to Oxford. By midday it had been picked up from Oxford and brought out to Whiteway where me and my dogs was at the ready with the filing pen to send through a thousand sheep for Mr Earle and his assistants to inject. Half-way through the operation Taffy turned up to watch. I be too busy to bother to say 'I told thee so.'

'Well done, Mont,' Mr Earle says at the end of the day. 'You've saved your boss a fortune.'

The boss never said a word.

Old Taff were envious of any knowledge he hadn't got. He once tried to teach me to sort taters from a clamp. I'd sorted more taters than he'd had posh dinners, but I let him get on with it. I could do with the entertainment. He over-riddled 'em so rough, he cut the whole tub of chats ass over head and ended up in the clamp with his trousers caught in the riddle.

It used to puzzle me, with all his grammar-school education and his thousands of pounds, he could only count sheep one at a time, stabbing the air with his forefinger. He'd lose count, flare up, flinging his arms out and upsetting my sheep. Thanks to old Shepherd Hathaway, I always stood quite still, holding up my crook, dividing 'em off in tens in my head. Thanks to old Shepherd Akers, I could measure whole acres, standing quite still, with my crook or my forearm held up in front of me. I could tell within a foot how many rolls of wire I'd need to pen a field, and exactly where to drop each roll to save over-walking. Thanks to my old schoolteachers I could reckon in my head—given so many acres and so many sheep penned on so much each day, how long 'ud the keep last?

Every new pasture or lattermath, every new location, called for husbandry and common sense. You was always learning with sheep. Penning wide for a dry day on the tops of Brussels sprouts; penning narrow for a wet day near the bottom of the same stalks. The combination of wet and pulpy stems 'ud sometimes prove too rich for 'em. I mustn't supplement with hay when they were getting to the end of a seed lattermath. Taffy growed pedigree grass crops—rye, fescue, timothy, coltsfoot, Italian rye-grass on a three-year rotation for Twyford Seeds. It 'udn't do to lapse it back with seeds from bastard hay.

Each location brought its own hazards: bogs, gaps, walls, water. At Long Hanborough the farm were a mill, totally surrounded by a river. It were just like the Wild West, the old homestead stockaded by water, the only access a crude bridge of sleepers with no rails, and every time the farmer's wife fancied a fish for her old man's supper her 'ud rally on the pioneer bridge and shoot one with her rifle. Getting my flock across that bridge all in one piece—despite the antics of the farmer's wife—were a hazardous feat, one way and another, but they sheep trusted me to lead 'em to green pastures beside the still waters.

Every farm, every field had its special lie of land and outlook. My favourite field of all be San Piece at Church Enstone, especially on a Monday morn in spring with bright sun and a warm breeze. Even in the sixties there be still many women at home without a washing-machine, without a spin-dryer, without a twirly-whirly washing-line. To look down on the whole of Road Enstone with Church Enstone clustered up on the hill, to see the sun on the warm stwun of the church, glancing off the higgledy-piggledy roofs of the houses, to see the blossom tossing and the gillies nodding in the back gardens and all they long lines of washing flapping in the breeze, were as if the whole of our Enstone were a-clean and blowing. And at the end of a fine day, all the washing safely gathered in, to see the smoke from one chimney then another rising into the fading afternoon as the women stoked up their ranges, cooking for their menfolk and childern coming home for their tea. . . .

San Piece were on the opposite side of the brook from Miss Bruce's property. She always took an interest in my flock and often came across the brook to have a look at 'em. She were most appreciative of the advice and healing I had given her over the years for her own horses, hounds and cattle. She'd invite my flock across the stream to feed for nothing on her turnip-tops just to keep her ground in good heart; and she'd come across to have a chat, sometimes calling me 'Mont' and sometimes 'Shepherd'.

In the winter of '63 I'd saved one of her horses that had fallen through a frozen pond; '63 were far colder than the snows of '47. It were supposed to be the coldest winter since 1881, when there were a fifteen-foot snowdrift at Oxford Circus in the middle of London. In '63 we had thirty-two days solid when temperatures in most places didn't rise above three degrees centigrade. Rivers became skating-rinks, the sea froze, babies died of the cold, and birds froze in the hedgerows. The greater spotted woodpecker that throve in hordes in Ditchley Woods was almost wiped out in '63, and was only just coming back in 1984. In '63 Miss Bruce had to call me to send my dogs to see off the deer that were fighting her cattle for food. She sent out hot drinks for me, and hot kettles to melt my troughs.

By 1966 her were getting a bit wandery. The police had picked her up several times at night walking miles away from home. Her were getting unpredictable in her behaviour. She invited me one afternoon to come in and have a drink. I didn't like to thwart her;

her be still aristocrat. But I warn't used to drinking in the middle of the day. I felt uncomfortable, stuck among the valuable knick-knacks in her front room in my old shepherding gear, drinking her whisky from a crystal glass. I were wanting to get back to my flock. She set me next to a posh silver ornament with polished ram's horns 'so you'll feel at home'. She called it a mull. It were part of the grandeur of her Scottish childhood.

She asked me several times about my ram's bell. I'd told her over and over again I hadn't got no ram no more, but it didn't sink in. She kept asking after 'Old Nod', a poem about a shepherd what old Glover had learned us in Top Standard and I'd written out for her many years ago. She told me about the police picking her up the night before. "'I'm perfectly safe, officer. . . ." It wasn't even midnight. . . . I fancied a walk, Mont, that's all.'

The evening before she died she called me to her across the brook. 'Shepherd,' she says, her eyes shining with a strange light. 'Last night I had a vision. The same vision I once saw in Scotland when I was a child. I saw a new heaven and a new earth and you and your flocks were the flocks of "Old Nod" shimmering in glory of crimson and gold.'

'I knowed exactly what you see'd, mam. Last evening, after the storm, the sun came out and we had a glorious sunset. That shimmerin' halo were the low rays of the settin' sun slantin' through the beads of rain on their wool, chargin' their fleeces with—'

Her warn't listening, chanting 'Old Nod' in a wayward voice:

> *Their fleeces charged with gold,*
> *To where the sun's last beam leans low*
> *On Nod the shepherd's fold.*

'You'd best be getting home, mam.' I led her up towards the house, up the bank.

> *His are the quiet steeps of dreamland,*
> *The waters of no-more-pain,*
> *His ram's bell rings 'neath an arch of stars,*
> *'Rest, rest, and rest again.'*

The next morning her were found in her nightgown, her hair spread out all round her, face downwards in the brook. They said it were suicide. I reckon her just fancied a walk, as she had done so often in the past, to look at my sheep. In the old days suicides warn't admitted through the lych-gate on to the hallowed ground of the church. Our St Kenelm's warn't like that. Our Enstone, mindful of all Miss Bruce had done for the village, flocked to her funeral and were only too grateful to gather her into the fold.

I've see'd some spectacular storms in my time. Our Enstone usually escapes the worst of the lightning, being on an open hill, and having the nearby well-wooded areas of Wychwood, Ditchley, Blenheim and the Tews to attract the bolts. I've been struck only once. I were mucking out with a fork and stood sheltering just inside the stable. There were an almighty bang and flash, and the fork shot clean out of my hands right across the yard. I remember Jack Harrison, grandfather of our Odd from down Alley, used always to sit and face the road at his front door playing the cornet whenever there was a thunderstorm. It were believed that music, like church bells, kept evil spirits at bay. He'd done it ever since his house were struck by a thunderbolt in the nineties. The old men in the pub 'ud talk of the 'Great Storm of 1843' when hailstones fell 'as big as crickut balls'. I loved to listen, but I never believed 'em until I read in George Sheffield's old book an eye-witness account of the storm:

> The most remarkable phenomena of this storm were the immense size of the hailstones and the great roar of their approach. The average size of the circumference was six inches, though some were seven and eight. . . . Individually they were icy meteors, beautifully faceted, and formed of several crusts; the nucleus of soft snow, the next of crystals radiating outwards, the next of veins of ice running round the circumference, and an outer crust formed of smaller stones stuck together.
>
> The great roar had been caused by the rapid rotation of the hailstones in the course of their formation and fall. The tremendous height of their descent can be gauged from the fact that the roar of their approach was heard distinctly for five or ten minutes before the first stones struck, and yet there was not a breath of wind.

> Great was the devastation of the earth after that terrible bombardment. . . . Where but half an hour before all had been smiling, and hopeful, and promising, nothing was to be seen but desolation and dismay. The smaller animals and birds lay killed in abundance and many larger animals, cattle and horses (some with their ploughs and implements still attached) had injured themselves in stampeding about the hills.

I reckon our Earth in the making must have been var' like that storm, for when I once see'd oolite stwun under the microscope it were formed close to they hailstones.

Some years after Miss Bruce died, I were sheltering with Taffy from a sudden thunderstorm. He were strangely subdued, sitting on a bale of straw, talking of his bwoyhood and going on call-outs with his dad. He suddenly asked me what I thought of marriage. I said it were fine if a chap could find the right partner. He asked me why I'd never married. I didn't tell him about the 'well-job', but I told him about Kate and our courtship. I were sixty-seven; I hadn't spoken about it for years. Taff were the last person I'd have thought to tell. It all came tumbling out, the disappointment when we couldn't have the cottage at Fulwell, the joy when Ted offered us the one at Church Enstone, the bitter ending in the snow. He were silent. I couldn't see his face; he had his back to me, sitting quite still, looking out at the brilliant landscape. The storm were over as sudden as it had come. The sun were racing across the sparkling fresh-washed fields, rolling back the shadows. I thought of Miss Bruce.

'And I see'd a new heaven and a new earth,' I says aloud.

I waited for 'Don't be so daft!'

Without a word, he got up and blundered off.

'I reckon summat's up with old Taff,' I said to Tom Davies when he come with my wages. 'He's losing his bite.'

'He's losing his *sight*.'

My world stood still. Every furrow of the new-ploughed field in the distance, every shooker of the dry-stwun wall nearby, every sheep dotted clear all over the field, every wisp of the silky cwoats of the dogs at my feet. I were blessed with wonderful eyesight; out in all weathers, washed by the rain, focusing up and down, nigh and far, I've never needed glasses for distance nor for reading. Even in my sixties my eyes be still as blue and clear as when I were a lad. Only the night before I'd been reading about a clever surgeon in London who were grafting good eyes on to bad.

'Mine be two good'uns, Tom. Tell him he can have one of mine. I don't need both, I'd manage.'

Taffy replied without thanks, back to his usual form, 'Tell him not to be so daft.' He'd broached my offer to the specialist, Tom said, but in Taffy's case it 'udn't work.

Tom drove blind Taffy round on the day he retired. 'If you've got any sense you'll retire too, Mont,' Taffy said, as he felt for my hand to give me my last wages. 'I've spoken to the Ditchley agent; you and Jim'll have to get out of Twiggs, they want to modernize it. They'll find you other accommodation at a peppercorn rent. No work, your pension, and a peppercorn rent—you'll be a millionaire.' His sightless eyes were just off-course on a level with my old cwoat. 'What would you have if you *were* a millionaire, Mont?'

I thought about it. 'Ye can kayp yer yacht and yer proyvit jet, all I wants as a millionaire is one of they airin'-cupboards.'

I retired when Taffy retired. I were sixty-eight. I'd laboured on the land, seven days a week, for fifty-five years.

Taffy's funeral were a big affair at Woodstock. I'd shepherded for him for thirty years. I couldn't begin to count how many sheep I had reared and taken to market. When we came out of the church, Tom and the other foremen were invited in with the nobs to the posh Bear nearby. I waited for him out on the street. Mr Brookes, the agent, came out.

'You're invited in with the best, Mont; Mr Hughes's sister wants to meet you.' The place were packed. The old gal were about done by the time she got to me, but her face lit up. 'So *you're* Mont! He used to talk so much about you. He thought the world of you.'

I thought to myself, 'He'd a bloody funny way of showing it.' But I 'udn't dream of saying it to *her*. Her were the nicest gentle-lady thee could ever wish to meet.

As I were coming out, I bumped into the well-known auctioneer who as a young beginner all they years ago had tried to teach 'MR EWES' his business. He could cross the black'un off now.

17

Lifting the Latch

OUR NEW COTTAGE WERE THE ONE that Katy and me first had our eye on at Fulwell. The old two-holer privy be still there at the end of the overgrowed garden, very handy if me and Jim was took in emergency. But the thatched roof be now tiled, the warm kitchen had a brand new range, there were a real bathroom, and—standing in the corner, with its doors wide open, warm and willing—a brand new AIRING-CUPBOARD. I don't know if it was Taff as wangled it, but I be very pleased.

The only thing our millionaire's abode lacked were a name. Jim offered to scratch one if I'd invent one. I were sitting in the warm kitchen toying with 'Home on the Range' when the Ditchley agent called to see if we be settled in satisfactory.

'Warm enough for you?' he says.

'Warm as a biddy's bottom,' I says.

And it's been 'BIDDY'S BOTTOM' ever since.

When Jim and me first comed here fifteen years ago, in the olden days, Biddy's Bottom sported only a latch on the front door. Many a cottage had only a latch. As the wolf said to Red Riding Hood, 'Lift up the latch and walk in!'

When I first went to school, the schoolroom door had only a latch: too high to reach if thee be only a 'little varmint' just out of petticuts, but easy as pie when you was a big bwoy leaving Miss Vance's with the rest of your mates for the big school.

Our St Kenelm's church had only a latch, a big handsome ring-latch, fit to enter the House of the Lord. It had a big handsome lock too, but the heavy iron key were hardly ever used.

The pub too had a latch. In the old days going to the pub were knowed as 'lifting the latch'. Thee only needed a penny for a pint of fore-ale to lift it. A chap as was stwuny-broke "adn't the rattle to even lift the latch'.

Nowadays, to our shame, Biddy's Bottom has a lock; the big school has several; the church is only open at a set time; and, more often than not, the pub has a burglar alarm.

Home, school, church, pub: these have been the main openings in my life. Mam and Dad done well to provide in hard times a good home for their long lanky Abbott childern, and to send each of us out into the world well fortified in body and bringing-up, to survive our three-score-year-and-ten and beyond.

Hardly a day of my old age passes but I bless my schoolteachers, who taught me to read, so I can enjoy the company of books and newspapers, to reckon and plot so I can budget my pension and plan my produce, and even to sew. Yet, apart from a few golden scholarship kids, we be only a rough bunch of clathoppers and stocking-menders. (In they days, whenever a new baby come into the world, it warn't 'Is it a bwoy or a gal?' but 'Is it a clathopper or a stocking-mender?') Only yesterday as I sewed on my braces' button, I could hear Ma Glover's voice chanting in my bwoyhood ear'ole—

> *Three good stitches at the bole*
> *Up and in to every hole.*
> *Leave some slack to make a stem,*
> *Up and in, and round agen.*
> *Twist it down from the head,*
> *Fasten fast, and cut yer thread.*

Our old school boss, Glover, made us keep a needle and thread always in our desks. If ever there were as much as five minutes' slack between salvaging the Empire or rocking a tree-trunk, between furrows of mental arithmetic, spelling, drill, dictation, spouting poetry, practising pot-hooks and chanting tables, 'We'll have a go at threading the needle!' he'd suddenly announce. 'See if the boys can beat the girls today. Needles up! Threads ready!' Bullseye! I'd get him, first time, but it warn't often we paddle-fisted clathoppers beat they destined stocking-menders.

Every morn he bound us as a Christian school, 'hands together, eyes closed', for a prayer and a hymn; and again at the end of the day 'to support us . . . till the shades lengthen and the evening comes'. I grant it were a very enclosed world, but he opened the gate as wide as he could for each child. There must be many a dedicated teacher ploughing a lone furrow in today's field of education. Plod on! There'll be an unknown Mont to bless thee at the end.

As I've told thee before, Glover were very keen on us clathoppers having a smattering of horticulture. One day soon after we be settled into Biddy's Bottom and got the garden planted, I heard a knock on the door.

'Lift up the latch and walk in!'

'I've come to ask you a great favour, Mont.' It were Rosa, Tom Davies's wife. Tom had been Taffy's foreman out at Hanborough when I were shepherding out there. It were too far to travel on my tractor and Tom 'ud ferry me home to Twiggs in the jeep. He'd often bring little Smiler for a ride. The little gal were only about three when I first knowed her. Her real name were Victoria, but she were such a sunny little mite. She'd smile and sit on my lap, not a bit afeard of Old Mont nor my two sheepdogs with their sharp teeth and lolling tongues panting on her eye-level. I became very fond of her over the years, and it had brought a real interest into my life, watching her grow up. Rosa had come to tell me that they'd moved into the big farmhouse by Twiggs at Cleveley. 'Will you come and work for us, mornings only, as gardener–handyman? You know us well, and Smiler loves you dearly; you've only to lift the latch and you're one of the family.'

I were only sixty-eight, fit and well apart from a bit of hearing trouble, and I had my tools and my wheelbarrow. 'I'll give thee a week's trial,' I says. And I've been begging 'em to give I the sack for the last *fifteen* years.

I be over eighty now. I be very happy down at Rosa's. I pleases meself what I does, she leaves me to my own 'vices unless her wants any job done 'ticular. When I fancies a rest I sits in my old wheelbarrow. It be fifty years old now. I've creoso'd him over the years, but it be the same pneumatic wheel.

It be a lovely old manor farmhouse, very homely out the back, with only a little latch between me and a cup of coffee in Rosa's kitchen; and very aristocratic out front, with a giant keyhole carved out of the Cotswold stwun over the front porch. I think it be some kind of fire-insurance symbol from another century. I grows me posh dahlias out front, and me prize parsnips out back. I be aiming at no limit this year, using my folding-bar to drive a long straight channel for each parsnip-seed to have right of way as far as possible. One of 'em's a corker; I reckon he be but a chain off Australia.

Smiler's in Australia, working her way across the oceans on they big cruise-liners. I've watched that gal grow up; watched her sail over gymkhanas and sweat over A-levels. Her warn't afraid of hard work nor getting up in the morning. I've choked her off a time or two over the years, even made her cry when she's done something silly with her pony or thoughtless with they horses. Her warn't never one to bear a grudge, her always come back to me smiling. That gal's always showed respect for me; and now pretty postcards come to 'Montague Abbott, Esq., Biddy's Bottom' from all over the world 'with lots of love from Smiler'.

Biddy's Bottom suited our old bwoy and me well. He kept the house as he done the scratching, neat and tidy. I done the washing and cooking. I 'udn't say I were Mrs Beeton, but I has a bash.

'Take over, son,' Mam used to say, sitting back weary from rolling out a roly-poly or beating a cake, specially in her declining years, and I'd carry on, glad she were still there to learn me. When she first went, I tried hard to cope with the washing after work. One dark night our wash-house at Church Enstone were like a witches' den. I be out of me depth with the copper, billows of suds, clouds of steam. . . . 'Anybody in there?' Our Dora's voice penetrated from the outer atmosphere. 'Whatever are you brewing, our Mont?'

'The washing, gal.'

From then on Big Sister took our washing, trailing backwards and forwards from her home at Witney every week, until illness and old age overtook her; and I fathomed the innards of a washing-machine.

All through the seventies I were still lifting the latch almost every Saturday night, singing in the pubs around our Enstone. It had started by chance, singing an old song to some Americans in the War. By the fifties it had snowballed to every Saturday night. I done it for the fun of it and to please they that asked me. In the swinging sixties, unbeknown to me, Banbury Jack and Chris Leslie, two topping musicians, brought three chaps, Bee . . . Gee . . . somebody or other, to hear me sing in Tew pub.

'Come with us, Mont,' they says.

'For why?'

'Grow your hair, sing, make lots of money!'

'Not bloody likely. I've growed my hair short ever since Gardener Capes first pruned it outside his hovel before the First World War, and I en't a-goin' to change it for thee. 'Sides, our old Dad learned me to sing for pleasure, not money.'

You don't reckon to give folk pleasure by charging 'em for it, do you? How we used to sing for pleasure in the pub before jukeboxes, posh carpets, lounges and other improvements spoiled everything. Thee could tell a man's trade by the song he sung—'*Slap-dab-slap with the whitewash brush, Painting all day long*'—and where he hailed from—'*Down in Lankyshire-O!*' Each of us had our well-known party-piece. When Zicky were driving for Venvell's he once got in a tiz, lost, at Immingham Dock. From then on the chorus 'ud be 'Come on, Zicky, let's have "Immazaz"!'

> *I'm going back to Immazaz—*
> *I'm as 'as the pub next dooer!*

'Come on, Seven Bees, give us yer "Bugler" song!' Seven Bees were so called because he were always a-swearing he'd been the Best Bloody Bugle-Blower in Banbury Borough Band.

'Come on, Mont!—"ROLY POLY"!'

We was mostly unaccompanied, apart from the tapping of tankards on the taproom bench or the clatter of hobnail boots on the stwun-flagged floor.

Once upon a time pubs was all ever-open, and plenty of 'em: six in Neat Enstone alone.

> *The Harrow to harrow*
> *The Plough to plow*
> *The Swan to swim*
> *The Bell to ring*
> *The Litchfield Arms*
> *And the Talbot Inn.*

There warn't a lot of drunkenness; we hadn't got the rattle. Most chaps gived their weekly wages to their womenfolk and she'd dish 'ee out with a shilling for the week. Best beer, Hitchman's, Hall's, Hooky, be tuppence a pint, but you could get 'Witney Straight-through' for a penny. There were no such windfalls as overtime money; they used to sack thee if thee went moonlighting.

Most of us on the land scrombled by with a bit of extra 'pocket-money', as tips was called. Tanner-a-day for journey money, delivering loads, carting heavy sacks up granary steps; flogging sheep's wool and horsehair you'd collected off the fences, or the straw you'd used to line a load of taters; halters, harvest, lambs' tails, fleeces, all brought a set bonus, vital in they days of low wages. In all my years on the land I never brought home more than ten pounds a week in my regular pay-packet.

In '76 me and our old bwoy, Jim, had Asian flu. Jim had been middling for some time. He were first broken by no longer being capable of doing the scratching for the Clubs. When they young professionals took over his books they said they 'udn't have kept 'em any better even with their exams and all. Early one Saturday morning—we both still got up at the crack of dawn, we was so used to it—he were sat at the kitchen table with his head on his arms when I went with Luke, my little terrier, along the woods for his walk. I didn't feel like taking him, I felt anyhow, but he were on the brevut, begging so soulful, paws together, head on one side, as he always did first thing in the morning before breakfast.

When I got back Mollie Harris and Ginger, her husband, were standing in our kitchen. I'd knowed Mollie for years, ever since the Second World War when her were spokeswoman for all they women tater-picking at Hanborough. 'Whatever have you been up to, Mont?'

I looked down at my cwoat. It were filthy with mud. 'I must have fallen. . . .' I were all at sea. 'Wheer's our old bwoy?'

'We've put him to bed.' Mollie's voice were very far away. 'And *you* ought to be in bed, by the looks of you.'

'Shall I make thee some breakfast?'

'Breakfast!' says Mollie. 'It's nearly tea-time.'

I must have been laid out in they woods all that time. I can't remember 'em putting I to bed. I recall one moment in the darkness Jim were still there; the next he were gone. I woke up when it were light, in hospital. Our Horace and Fred were sitting by my bed. They told me it were the Chipping Norton Cottage Hospital, and I'd been there a whole week. 'Wheer's our old bwoy?' I says.

'He's gone, Mont,' Horace says. 'His funeral were yesterday.'

'We're sorry, Mont,' Fred says. 'We had to go ahead.'

He'd died along of me that Saturday night in the old Abbott bed.

'Us'll have to get over it,' I says.

Friends rallied round, and still rally. Mollie, Rosa, they young Shuffels now retired, Horace's bwoy from Chippy, and many others. Nancy, my next-door neighbour, be very good to me, checks to see I be still alive each morning and nags me if I go out in the cold without me cwoat. Nancy were widowed very young and brought up her littl'un all on her lone. I were invited to littl'un's wedding at Spelsbury. Her looked a real treat in her wedding-tackle.

Our Odd and his wife invited me to the christening of their first grandchild. It be quite a moment, after months of forced absence, to set once again in my place in they empty choir-stalls at St Kenelm's and lift the latch on so many memories.

They old grids be still in the floor where us bwoys used to play before choir-practice with torn paper, seeing whose 'ud float the highest in the heat rising from Thomas's faithful boiler. The brass plaque be still polished on the organ, dedicated to Mr Knight who were organist and 'a ready helper in every good work' for eighteen years.

If I closed my eyes I could see, looking back, little Johnny Higley, who were organ-blower for close on fifty years. He'd been badly hurt as a child and walked as if he were squat. He were a happy old man and very civil. When he warn't tending the organ he were tending Gregory's sheep, grazing 'em along the verges and shovelling their dung over the hedgerow to fertilize the fields. He weared posh shiny patent-leather gaiters on Sundays, winter and summer, so big for him he had to stand to blow the organ 'cos if he sat they comed up to his chin like a wicket-keeper. He were always clean and respectable, in a little bowler-hat and a cloth jacket. I 'udn't vouch for his breeches—you couldn't tell for gaiters. It must have been quite a strain for him, drawing up the handle. Our St Kenelm's be a biggish organ; her draws a hundred and fifty foot.

They choir-stalls be still as uncomfortable as ever, with small arches carved in the back, very useful for poking contraband to the chap behind you, specially when we was surpliced together, thirty-two strong. Old Stump, our Odd's grampy, who used to play the cornet in the thunderstorm, were leading bass and always poked us younger chaps through they arches if we was getting out of order. He could remember *his* grampy telling him of the string-band that played in the gallery that used to be at the west end. The old band-leader used to play the bass viol. It were a violin, but he were obliged for reverence in church to bow it like a double bass; played on the shoulder as a fiddle, it were linked with dancing and the devil. It were very hard work playing some of they old instruments. Whenever Psalm 119 with its umpteen verses cropped up, it were 'Awf with yer jackuts, bwoys! We be in for a sweater!'

Joan Ogles once assaulted me through they arched choir-stalls. Her were with the sopranos in front. I were a young man with the tenors behind. I warn't exactly behind her, but I got carried along on the fervour of 'Bless ye the Lord, praise Him and magnify Him forever' when I felt her hand a-poking me in my private parts. I asked her afterwards what her thought she were a-playing at in the middle of the psalm. She didn't realize it were me behind her. She'd offered her snuff-box to the chap before, and were fishing for it back. I en't wrapt up in snuff. I told her to change to Nippits, they tiny cough-sweets, then I might be tempted in the future.

Jesus's feet were still ascending into the lost clouds of old stained glass in the Lady Chapel. 'Old Wisdom,' one of our Enstone benefactors, 'WHO DECEASED THE XXIII OF APRELL AND WHOS BODY RESTETH HERE IN HOPE OF A JOYFUL RESARECTION ANNO DOMINI 1633' were still crouching, very unrestful, in his niche. And the marble folds and cherubs of the 'Beefe Charity' be still up on the wall: 'Benjamin Marten . . . Gave by his Last Will 120 pounds to Buy Lands, the Income whereof He Order'd to be Laid out on Meat to be Diftributed to Twenty Poor Parishioners of Enfton, Five of whom are to be Inhabitants of Radford.' They'd be hard pushed to find a poor'un in Radford today; they be all nobs. I never dreamt all they years I spent in my youth gazing at that plaque that one day I'd have my Christmas joint 'with compliments from Benjamin Marten'. I be a bit upset at first to be deemed 'poor', and worried too, now I lives in Fulwell, that I bean't rightly Enstone parishioner. 'Let not your heart be troubled, Mont,' they trustees says. 'You *are* Enstone.' It be a very kind compliment.

After the christening, Sally, our Odd's daughter, wanted me to have my photo tooked, standing at the lych-gate holding the baby. Sally, me gal, you don't know what it meant to me, holding your little mite at that old gate. I thought of all they old folk who had passed through that gate before and guided my life, and all they babies I had 'fetched the doctor for', including your old dad. It were like lifting the latch on all my days.

Biddy's Bottom be getting shambly since our old bwoy en't around. It's all I can do to keep myself clean, do the washing, and cook me bit of grub. I be gathering dust and losing old friends. I be the last of the family since our Gil died last year. I reckon he had the cushiest life of the lot. When Queen Mary died at eighty-five in 1953 she left money to all 'my people', according to their years of service. I don't know how long our old bwoy had served, but it were enough to keep him in bacca money to the end of his days.

Gil were always on at me to have the phone, specially now I lives alone. It 'ud only gather more dust. I en't never used the phone since that one time when I couldn't fathom old Taff. When I fell down that old well I banged my left ear, and now my hearing's beyond it.

I en't never been to the pictures. I went once but I never see'd nowt. It were a buckshee propaganda picture put on by the government during the Great War. I drove a wagonette chock-a-block with Enstone folk. When we got to the Oddfellows Hall in Chippy where it were being showed, there were nowhere left to graze my horses. It be too long to leave 'em standing all that time. I stopped with 'em and took 'em cropping along the verge.

I en't never had no holiday, 'cept when I were out of my depth at Worthing. I don't hanker after flitting abroad and colour telly. I en't never fled in an aeroplane. Don't want to. Too far to drop. What you've never had you never miss.

'You've had a hard life, Mont,' folk says.

Looking back on my careering on the land, carter, shepherd, gardener, I be well content. I 'udn't say I've enjoyed every minute of it—t'en't much of a picnic, eating your lunch in the burrow of a barbed-wire fence—but ploughing, penning, planting, I've scratched old England on the back and her's given me wealth untold.

Rosa still fetches me every morning—her still won't give I the sack—and sometimes her drives me right round the world, my world. Hanborough, Glympton, Whiteway Bottom, Peewit Corner, Rollright Stwuns, Neat Enstone, Church Enstone, San Piece. . . . Our Enstone, our Oxfordsheer, this England, take a lot of beating. *'Blessed is the man that stoppeth where he be.'*

I en't been so well lately. Doctor says I could pop off any day. They asks me if I've made a will. I got nothing to will, 'cept this old pocket-watch, my shepherd's crook, my folding-bar, my wheelbarrow. They'm like me now, out of date, antique, ought to be in a museum.

They asks me what I'd like put on my tombstwun when I snuffs it.

'For why? I en't nobody famous, to sign awf with a flourish.'

'People might ask, "Who were you?"'

'Just scratch . . .

OLD MONT
ENSTONE
OXON
ENGLAND

. . . I reckon that 'ud answer.'

Biddy's Bottom, 1985

THE PUBLICATION *of Mont's life story brought him many new friends and an extra lease of life. Before he died on 18 February 1989, he had made a special pilgrimage to Woodstock to present his precious watch, folding-bar and shepherd's crook to the County Museum. The inscription he suggested for his tombstone was not allowed; but a simple headstone has been erected by public subscription on his grave at Church Enstone. It reads:*

MONTAGUE ABBOTT

'OLD MONT'

CARTER & SHEPHERD

in

ENSTONE

1902–1989.

Glossary

'adlands headlands, the strip of land left unploughed at the ends of a field, where the plough turns

anyhow all at sea, light-headed

'arch'lls Hartshill stone chippings

ashup ash heap

athert athwart

bacca tobacco

barnum showman

baulk to make a ridge between two furrows, drawing up soil on either side of a row of potatoes to encourage growth

black-jack-tack Friar's Balsam

bolton parcel of straw cut from the rick

Box, the parish relief (originally from the church poor-box)

brashy full of loose broken rock

brevut to forage

bum-the-barrel-bum children's game like leapfrog, leaping over several backs at once

butties chums

bwoons bones

Chad a native of Chadlington, Oxfordshire

chats small poor-quality potatoes

Chawferd Chalford, near Enstone

Chippy Chipping Norton, Oxfordshire

choked off told off

clayper to cake with clay

click clique (i.e. group)

clod twopenny piece

cloze to encase in leather

clozier someone whose job was to cut the uppers of shoes

cub to coop up

cull to select

curve to cut a measure of straw or hay from a rick

cwoat coat

dickery panicky

diddycoys not true gypsies; tramps

dillen the weakest of a litter

dish to escape from

docks tail

drag iron shoe that acts as a brake on a cart

duss to dare

farming out shovelling muck from sty, shed or stable into a wheelbarrow and tipping it on the muck-heap

flearing cross-ploughing

follas land left fallow immediately following harvest

fox'n'hounds chasing game (see p.34)

frit frightened

fromard right-handed

frost-nail-holes specially shaped nail-holes in horseshoes, designed to accommodate iron 'frost-nails', which clipped on over the shoes, to give extra grip in icy weather

fudge tool with a small wheel used to score leather to define the line for stitching

geo-tack plough harness

gissle field pond fed by an underground spring

grinserd verge

grockle to sing deep in the throat

grommet to sing tunelessly and out of time

GWR Great Western Railway

hames the curved pieces of wood or metal on the collar of a horse, to which the traces are attached

hirings large annual fairs where farmworkers stood for hire

hold to take the strain of a stationary load

holey-holey game in which children cast pebbles from a set distance into a hole in the ground

Hooky Hook Norton, Oxfordshire

hotch a hop, skip and heave

Hudson sack popular brand of close-woven sack

JCB make of mechanical digger

jillies mayblossom

kaydee wide-brimmed trilby

keach to ladle or pour

larrup beer

lattermath the latter mowing, or the crops then reaped

mafficking wild behaviour (originally as displayed by mobs celebrating news of the Relief of Mafeking)

meg halfpenny piece

middling unwell

mind to remember

ockerd awkward

peck point; apex of triangle remaining at the finish of cultivating an irregularly shaped field

pickèd piece triangular patch of grass or pasture

ploomp platform

quiff knack

rack up to fill the racks with hay in the stables

rattle metal or money

razer a grader for levelling land

rib to deck or braid with ribbons

rickerd rickyard

sanfin pink-flowered herb used for fodder (sanfoin)

'sarts assarts, forest land cleared and converted to arable

scort to shamble

scour to have diarrhoea

scratching official writing, records etc.

scrawf to scramble nimbly (especially as applied to a scrawny individual)

scuffleman one who uses a scuffle[r], or horse-hoe

shellboard part of the plough that turns aside the earth as it is cut

sheppick instrument similar to a pitchfork, but with the two tines set wider, and with a shorter handle

shooker stone set on its end with others, like teeth, to cap a dry-stone wall

shut to get rid of

siccy sycamore tree

skeets long-handled scoop or shovel

sleer to slink or steal away

slinkit a wooded hollow between two fields

spajit sparrow

spare rule older child used to keep order; a monitor

spetter spit and venom

spike workhouse

spray forked hazel-stick used to pin thatch

spun out spent up

squippet tiny piece

stalch row of *yelms* up a rick

stall to urinate

Stan' Harcourt Stanton Harcourt, Oxfordshire

string-halt a muscular disorder of a horse's hind legs

stwun stone

Stwunsful Stonesfield, Oxfordshire

Super police superintendent

Terriers Territorial Army

thiller the shaft horse in a team of horses

tilth cultivated land

tine spike

tollert toll-bench, wages table

tommy-cloth cloth in which one's lunch etc. is carried

tomp to drag or be dragged

tup male sheep

t'ward to turn left-handed

wantly feeble

yedsirag head man, foreman

yelm bundle of straw prepared for thatching

yet, yut (e-at, e-ut) to eat

yomp to hump a heavy load on one's back

yummery (y-humoury) moody

yup heap

People and Places

The following notes are designed to give additional information about some of the people and places of Enstone, and its immediate neighbourhood, that feature in *Lifting the Latch*. I am indebted to the archive of the Enstone Local History Circle and to all those who have helped me with their recollections of Mont Abbott and the people in the book.

Graham Binns, Cleveley, June 2002

ACOCK, NANCY, née Eden (now Hampton). Mont Abbott's next-door neighbour at Fulwell; in Mont's later years she would look in to see him before she went to work. She remembers his fine tenor voice, and how he used to sing at the Falkland Arms in Great Tew on Sunday nights: 'He always had a buttonhole. When he went out, he was just like a film star!' Nancy Acock worked for the Ditchley Foundation for 32 years; and her father, William Thomas Eden, was foreman at the Ditchley Model Farm.

ADAMS, JOHN (Johnny). Schoolmaster at Enstone from 1875 to 1891. He took over the post office on the death of the previous postmaster, Mr Kibble, whose daughter he had married. In his day, five postmen were employed at Enstone.

ADAMS STORES. Founded by James Joseph Adams, who lived to be 100. His son, J.A. Adams, took over the shop after returning from the Boer War.

AKERS, THOMAS HENRY ('old Spurgeon'). Shepherd, born in Cleveley in 1875. He married Jane Huckins of Fulwell in 1896.

ARIES, ALBIN (Alf). Groom, who lived with his wife Ellen (née Huckin) at 3 Chapel Lane, Enstone. He died in 1957, aged 84.

BARRETT, EDWARD (Ted) (1893–1975). Farmer, originally from Stonesfield, who leased Manor Farm, Enstone. The wheelbarrow that he gave as a reward to Mont (cf. Chapter 16) was subsequently left to 'Smiler'. It was stolen, while in her possession, from the stables at Manor Farm, Cleveley.

BEALE, ALBERT ('Diddy'). Farm-labourer, born in 1903. He was the son of Richard Beale (d.1918), and had a sister, Alice.

BECK, ALBERT ERNEST (1906–1978). Farm-labourer, who lived at Cleveley Cottage. His wife Isabel died in December 1992, aged 82.

BECKETT, 'BRUSHER'. Steam-plough team foreman. He died in 1975, aged 72.

BENFIELD, FRANK. Born 1898; in October 1910 he received a silver watch for six years' perfect school attendance. Frank Benfield died on active service in the Royal Navy during the Great War, though his name does not feature on the war memorial plaque in St Kenelm's Church.

BENFIELD, JOE. Stonemason on the Ditchley Estate. He lived at Gagingwell.

BENNETT, EDWARD (Ted). Born 1861, the son of Richard Bennett; he enrolled at Enstone School in 1873, and afterwards worked as painter and decorator on the Heythrop Estate for 56 years. He was lead tenor at St Kenelm's Church, and at local feasts used to play the fiddle and make up songs about Enstone characters.

BENNETT, FRANK. Petty officer in the Royal Navy. Son of Thomas Bennett of Church Enstone.

BENNETT, WINIFRED. Born at Heythrop Lodge in 1893, the daughter of Edward Bennett. She later lived at The Copse, Enstone. She began work as a schoolteacher (or 'monitress') at the Infants School at the age of 12, and stayed for 10 years, teaching the girls how to knit, while Miss Vance taught them how to sew. Winnie Bennett became honorary secretary of the Enstone Local History Circle on its foundation in 1949, and established its archive.

BISHOP, PHILIP ('Brocky'). Cowman for J.J. Adams at Manor Farm (by Adams Stores). He lived with his grandmother, Patience Taplin (d.1920), in the cottage just above the school on Enstone Hill.

BOLTON, EDWARD. Justice of the Peace, and 'chapel parson', of Litchfield Farm. His wife was the first president of the Enstone branch of the Women's Institute when it was formed in 1921.

BRASSEY, ALBERT (1844–1918). Owner of Heythrop House and the 5,000-acre estate given to him by his father, the railway magnate Thomas Brassey. He built the church at Heythrop and several cottages in Enstone.

BRAYBROOKE, BLANCHE. Born in 1872; wife of Edgar A. Braybrooke of Enstone House. Their son, a major in the Oxfordshire and Buckinghamshire Light Infantry, served with other Enstone men in World War II.

BROOKES, BEN. Agent for the Ditchley Estate; one-time chairman of Wootton Parish Council, and friend of J.H. Hughes.

BRUCE, JANET ELIZABETH. Scotswoman who built Drystone Hill House in 1923 and restored Brookside Cottages, Cleveley, resetting the 13th-century window and doorway at no. 1. She graduated from driving her open racing Amilcar, in helmet and goggles, to being chauffeur-driven in a Riley, but she preferred to make her local rounds on horseback, riding side-saddle. She objected so strongly to the building of Worth's Garage that she planted the coppice of trees around the Old Quarry (on the corner opposite the garage), to hide it from her view.

BUSHELL, THOMAS (1594–1674). Eccentric who built a fantastical 'waterworks', with trick fountains and grottoes, in the proximity of the house now called The Wells at the foot of Neat Enstone Hill, opposite the Drive side of the Harrow. It was visited by King Charles I and Queen Henrietta Maria in 1636. No trace of it remains, but Robert Graves wrote a vivid (though fanciful) description in his 1943 novel *Wife to Mr Milton*.

CAPES, EDWARD HENRY (Teddy) (1880–1967). Known to Mont Abbott as 'Gardener Capes' not just because he pruned hair, in his capacity as spare-time barber, but also because he was gardener to the Braybrookes at Enstone House. He lived at Capes Cottage, which still bears that name, next to Enstone House on the Oxford Road.

CLARIDGE, EDWIN (Neddy). Dairy farmer at Cleveley. Husband of Elizabeth Ellen, and father of Fred Claridge.

CLARIDGE, FREDERICK. Stockman at Cleveley, having previously served in the army in India. His wife was Minnie Annie (née Busby), who is recorded as having caught a trout with her hands while crossing the plank bridge over the stream between Cleveley and Church Enstone. Their 'seven unmarried daughters' charmed Mont Abbott and his brother Jim when they moved next door to Manor Farm Cottage, Cleveley, in 1940.

CLARIDGE, JACK. Rat-catcher. At one period he lived in the Fulwell cottage that Mont and Jim Abbott later moved into; at another, in the small cottage on Enstone Green next to 'down Alley'.

'COGGY,' *see* Knight, George.

COLLETT, CHARLES. Farmer, baker and miller, and father of Eric Collett; he also kept the Bell Inn. The remains of his watermill in Lidstone can still be seen. His bakery, in the hollow at the bottom of Neat Enstone Hill, is now known as Bridge House.

CORBETT, ELSIE. Pillar of the Women's Institute, and author of *A History of Spelsbury* (1962), about the village where she lived for over 40 years with Kathleen Dillon (in whose memory she dedicated her book). She was especially active in local affairs during World War II. The leader of the Liberal Party, Jo Grimond (later Lord Grimond), was her nephew.

CROLY, HENRY PENNINGTON, MRCS, LRCP (1877–1954). Doctor and surgeon, who lived at The Poplars in Charlbury. The doors of Charlbury Church are dedicated to him ('a beloved physician'). Whereas the other local doctor, William McNeight, demanded payment for each consultation, Dr Croly ran a popular 'penny-a-week' insurance scheme.

DAVIES, ALCWYN TOM (1916–1986). A much-respected farmer, and manager for J.H. Hughes at Long Hanborough.

DAVIES, ROSA. The wife, and since 1986 the widow, of Tom Davies. In earlier years she was a broadcaster and member of the BBC's radio repertory company. She became Mont's last, and possibly favourite, employer. He often referred to her as 'our Mam', which is what he used to call his own mother. Her daughter, 'Smiler', brought new joy and interests into Mont's latter years. 'Smiler' is now Mrs Gordon Elder.

DILLON, COLONEL ERIC. Tenant of Talbot House, later known as Enstone House. Cousin to the 17th Viscount Dillon. He died in 1946.

DILLON, HAROLD ARTHUR (17th Viscount). Antiquarian, curator of the Armoury of the Tower of London, and a trustee of the National Portrait Gallery and the British Museum. These responsibilities obliged him to travel to London three or four days a week for over 30 years—always 3rd class, for he was of a frugal disposition. According to John Graham (in his book *Ditchley Park, The House and the Foundation*), 'At the time of Lord Dillon's death in 1932 there was only one water closet [at Ditchley] and Lord Dillon habitually took his bath in front of the dining-room fire.'

DILLON, KATHLEEN NORA (1877–1958). Great-granddaughter of Henry, 13th Viscount Dillon. Lived at Spelsbury House with Elsie Corbett. She was awarded the Order of St Sava for her work in Serbia during World War I, and became county organizer of the Women's Voluntary Service in Oxfordshire during World War II.

'DOWN ALLEY.' A narrow path leading off Neat Enstone Green to a number of cottages, including the Dovecote, where the Abbotts lived. The Abbotts' cottage is now known as Trade Winds.

ENSTONE HOUSE. Formerly the Talbot Inn, from the family name of the Earls of Shrewsbury, the first owners of Heythrop. The house and land were first taken by the Jolly family (who gave their name to Jollys Ricks). They were followed by Squire Faulkner, Colonel Dillon, and the Braybrookes. Enstone House then became a private hotel, and since 1968 has been a residential home for the elderly.

ENTWISTLE, MR. Foreman for J.H. Hughes. He worked the farm at Rollright, though a contemporary has observed that 'he never stayed anywhere long'.

FAULKNER FAMILY. Mont Abbott's neighbours 'down Alley' (not to be confused with the family of Squire Faulkner).

FAULKNER, THOMAS ('Squire Faulkner'). Tenant of Talbot (Enstone) House. Besides owning the first motor-car in Enstone, he was also the last landowner in the district to plough with oxen.

GLOVER, GEORGE. Born 1869. Head teacher at Enstone School from 1902 to 1929. His three sons (George, Ernest, and Harold Wilson Glover) all won junior scholarships from Enstone School.

One of George Glover's pupils recalled that 'he was of the old style and not backward with the old cane'; but he was highly regarded, and a 1922 report from His Majesty's Inspectorate concluded: 'The Headmaster of this school and his wife work with energy and the children reflect their characteristics.' In 1914 Mr Glover was appointed teachers' representative on the Chipping Norton Education Committee. He was also a collector of taxes.

GLOVER, LAVINIA. Teacher, and wife of George. Initially listed as a 'Certified Mistress 3rd Div.', she was promoted to '2nd Div.' in 1907. Although the school had some 90 pupils, the only other assistant teacher was the notoriously unreliable Winifred Bolton. The records state that Lavinia Glover 'terminated her engagement as assistant teacher on 31 May 1924'.

GOODEY, JAMES WALTER. Farmer, of Stone Farm, Lidstone; his wife was Gertrude. F.W.G. Panting remembers him as a quiet soul—'But he could shout well if he caught you in his fields!' He died in 1973.

GREGORY, JOHN. Baker at Church Enstone mill where his name, scratched in the wall, is still legible. He later left the bakery and went to farm at Dunthrop, beyond Heythrop, where he had family connections. His son Frederick entered Enstone School in 1874.

GRIFFIN, WILLIAM EDWARD ('Spiffer'). Born December 1902, the son of another William Edward Griffin of Tew. He attended Enstone School, leaving in January 1916, shortly after his friend Mont Abbott.

HARLING, ERNEST HERBERT. Postman and proficient pig-killer, who lived at The Mount, Enstone. His wife was Kate, née Wearing. Their son Roy joined the RAF, becoming a flight-lieutenant and winning the DFC; he later became an airline pilot, and married Edward Barrett's daughter Joan in 1964.

HARRIS FAMILY. Mont Abbott's neighbours 'down Alley'. Granny Harris, a character and a gossip, used to end her scandalous anecdotes about local misbehaviours by saying 'Men be fools and the best on 'em be but middlin'.'

HARRIS, MOLLIE. Writer and broadcaster. She played the part of Martha Woodford in BBC Radio 4's long-running series *The Archers*, and also consulted Mont Abbott while writing her book *Cotswold Privies*. The book contains a photograph of Mont wielding his long wooden privy shovel or 'shittascoop', which was later donated by her to the County Museum at Woodstock. 'Ginger' (Leslie George Harris, 1912–1982) was her husband.

HARRISON, JACK. Woodman employed on the Ditchley Estate. He lived at Neat Enstone opposite the Green, to the side of 'down Alley'. Alec Stevens ('our Odd') was his grandson.

HATHAWAY, LEVI. Shepherd and local character, who lived in the cottage now called Hathaways, near the Crown Inn, Church Enstone. He died in 1958, aged 88.

HATWELL FAMILY. Showfolk who came to Enstone in the last week in May each year. Descendants of the original family still live in the Oxfordshire area, and still make a living by running and renting out fairground rides.

HAWES, SIDNEY (1882–1951). Tenant farmer, first at Church Enstone and then at Windy Hill, before taking over the tenancy of Fulwell Farm from Mr Lennox.

HAWTIN, ARTHUR ('Chisel'). Born in 1902; brother of Henry Ernest and schoolmate of Mont Abbott. His nickname dated back to his apprenticeship at the building firm Pye's. He was the eldest of Thomas Hawtin senior's sons, but it was his younger brother John Edmund (Teddy) who carried on the family undertaking business at Church Enstone.

HAWTIN, HENRY ERNEST. Coach-driver and mechanic, who started work at T.E. Worth's garage as a 14-year-old after leaving school in 1928. He served in the army in the 1939–45 war (in the course of which he married his wife Lilian), but returned to work at Worth's after the war. He died in 1987.

HAWTIN, JOHN. Employee on the Ditchley Estate, before he went to work for the council.

HAWTIN, JOSEPH. Parish clerk (like his father Thomas Hawtin senior), and father of thirteen children. He lived in Church Cottage, Enstone, and died in 1920.

HAWTIN, THOMAS JR. Son of Joseph; parish clerk, undertaker and wheelwright, like his grandfather of the same name. His son, Joseph E., also became sexton. He died in 1951.

HEDGES, HERBERT. Blacksmith at Neat Enstone; able to fashion a new iron tyre for a wagon wheel and forge the two ends together with his bare hands. He lived in the first house on the right 'down the lane', i.e. Chapel Lane. His shop has now gone, but was originally a two-up, two-down cottage, with an open shed at the side.

HEMMINGS, BILLY ('Bunny'). Rabbit-breeder. His 'hovel' was a tent on the allotments.

HIATT, CHARLES WILLIAM. Born in Cleveley in 1879, the younger son of William Hiatt. On being called up to fight in the 1914–18 war, he deposited all his belongings with the Ivings family at Mill Farm, Church Enstone. After the war he went to live at Mill Farm, and eventually died there.

HIGLEY, JOHN (Johnny). Shepherd in Enstone. He and his wife Susan had a son, John (born 1894) and two daughters, Emily (born 1896) and Lizzie (born 1898). He died in 1945.

HUCKIN, CLARA (née Healey). Cook at Enstone School. After being widowed she married Mont Abbott's brother Fred. She died in 1988, aged 92.

HUCKIN, EDWARD T. (Ted). Stonemason. He and his wife Kitty lived at no. 2 The Drive. He died in 1975, aged 76.

HUDSON, WALTER RAYMOND. Police constable at Enstone. A photograph of the opening of Enstone Village Hall in 1922 shows him wearing medals, indicating that he was an ex-serviceman. His wife was Rebecca Ann; their son Alfred Raymond George was born, baptized and buried in the space of 21 days in December 1912.

HUGHES, JACK H. ('Taffy'). Tenant farmer on the Ditchley Estate (which included Cleveley Manor Farm and Long Hanborough) and at Litchfield. He lived at Glympton. One of his colleagues remembers him as 'a wonderful farmer but a strict employer'. He died in 1977.

HUNT, ALEXANDER (Alex). Born 1902, the sixth son of Victor Hunt of Neat Enstone; he entered Enstone School at the same time as Mont Abbott.

HUNT, EDWARD (Ted). Farmer, born in 1894, the eldest son of Victor Hunt. When the Enstone Airfield was built on his land at Slade Farm, he and his family moved out of the district. His farmhouse has now been converted into two dwellings.

IVINGS, HILDA. Born 1901, the daughter of James Ivings; she was admitted to Enstone School on 13 September 1909, the same day as Mont Abbott.

IVINGS, JAMES (Jim) (1876–1975). Bullman. He started working a 10-hour day for Squire Faulkner at the age of 14, ploughing at Cleveley with four oxen for sixpence a week. He also found time to tour the pubs in the neighbourhood with his troupe of minstrels, playing the tin whistle, melodion, tambourine and triangle.

JEFFERIES, J.W. Saddler, boot-maker and coal- and coke-merchant of 17 High Street, Chipping Norton. Mont Abbott's father Thomas was an outworker for him in the early decades of the 20th century.

JENNINGS, TOM. Labourer on the Pratleys' farm; he lived at Church Enstone by the Square facing the Bicester Road.

JONES, JOHN RICHARD (Jack). Born February 1897; admitted to Enstone School in September 1905. He joined the Royal Navy, and died on active service in the Great War.

KEARNEY, J.K. Veterinary surgeon, who started his Woodstock practice before the 1939–45 war, and was joined in the 1950s by Norman Milburne ('Tim') Earle. The partnership then became Earle and Kearney, with Earle as senior partner. After Kearney's retirement, Earle was joined first by Geoffrey Butcher and then, in the 1970s, by J.S. Ware. This was when the practice became the Parkwood Veterinary Group, which still has offices in Woodstock.

KEEN, PHILIP. Born 1841, landlord of the Litchfield Arms, he married Annie (born 1840). Their daughter Clara was born in 1873.

KNIGHT, GEORGE ('Coggy'). Born 1897, the son of George Knight; Coggy lived in The Steps, a very old cottage opposite the Harrow Inn on the corner of The Drive and the main road. The cottage was demolished when the road levels were altered. A bit of a lad, he was once handed a summons under the elm-tree on the Green at Neat Enstone, and tore it up in front of the constable. He joined the Royal Navy and died in the 1914–18 war.

LENNOX, ARCHIBALD J. Tenant farmer at Fulwell, where he was succeeded by Mr Hawes.

LESLIE, CHRIS. Musician, who used to tour the local pubs with his brother John, under the name 'Banbury John and Fiddler Chris'. He was a teenager when he first met Mont Abbott at the Falkland Arms in Great Tew, where music nights were held every Sunday. He remembers how 'Monty' used to sit quietly in the corner—always immaculately dressed—till his turn came, when he would stand up and sing a 'fantastic range of songs, from folk songs to music-hall numbers, which he'd collected over his life'. Chris Leslie went on to play for some of the country's most successful folk bands, including the Albion Band and Fairport Convention.

LITCHFIELD ARMS. An important staging-post in the coaching days. By Mont Abbott's time, the inn was a large half-empty relic accommodating not just a pub but also various small businesses, such as those of Dickie Worth and James Joseph Adams, before they moved on to greater things. Described by Winifred Bennett as 'the finest building in Neat Enstone', it was demolished in the mid-1970s to make way for the Litchfield Close housing development.

LODGE, VICTOR. Possibly a son of David Lodge of Cleveley, who had four sons and two daughters at Enstone School in the 1890s. None is registered as Victor, but there was no other Lodge family in the locality.

McNEIGHT, WILLIAM R.P. Physician, who unlike Dr Croly did not operate a 'slate club', but required his fee to be paid at the time he attended a patient. Mrs M. Wearing recalls that when she was sick as a child and Dr McNeight was called, her sisters would pile books on top of the door so that they would fall on his head when he entered. He was evidently a severe man, and not as popular as Dr Croly. Dr McNeight lived in Crinan House, next to the White Hart in Charlbury.

MESSENGER, WILLIAM. Police constable. Originally from Churchill, he enrolled his three children at Enstone School after coming to the village in 1908.

NEWMAN, ABEL WILLIAM. Cowman, who lived at Woodford. After serving in the army throughout the Great War, he returned to the district to work as a road linesman. He had a son and four daughters.

OGLES, MARJORIE JOAN. Born 1923, the second daughter of Walter Ogles, postman, of Church Enstone. She went on from Enstone School to Charlbury School in 1934. During the 1939–45 war she left the village to become a nurse.

OLIFFE, LESLIE THOMAS. Carrier, of 18 Church Green, Witney, who married Mont Abbott's sister Dora.

PACKER, FRANK (1877–1967). Chipping Norton photographer who left behind a magnificent photographic record of the area and its people. He worked initially from his parents' boot- and shoe-shop in West Street. In 1903 he married Grace Todd, and several photographs show her—wearing a hat and looking somewhat alarmed—in the various early motorised vehicles that Packer purchased. Two years later he opened a photographic studio at 28 High Street, which had belonged to his grandfather, an upholsterer. Although the building has undergone several changes of use in recent years, it still bears the name Packer House.

PALMER, WILLIAM JACKSON. Clergyman. The son of a Lincoln bricklayer, he became curate of St Kenelm's in 1897, and vicar in 1904. In 1926 he was appointed rector of Saltfleetby in Lincolnshire, eventually retiring in 1951.

The vicar and his wife Kathleen were very well liked in Enstone. They employed a number of local girls, which had the effect of encouraging local lads to go to choir practice, as this gave them an excuse to call on the girls at the vicarage afterwards. Thomas Hawtin junior later married one of the girls.

PANTING, ALBERT (1899–1950). Son of William Panting, and brother of Tom, the postman. He lived 'down Alley', like the Abbotts, and served in the Great War. In 1937 he married Albert Stevens's daughter Dorothy.

PARSONS, MARGARET (Madge). Born in 1898, the eldest daughter of Natty and Katharine Parsons, she was an imposing figure who grew to be over 6 foot tall. She was a founding member of the Enstone Women's Institute (1921), and played the church organ at Enstone and Kiddington until she was 80 years old.

PARSONS, NATHANIEL ('Natty') (1872–1945). Churchwarden and landowner who farmed at Radford, as his family had done since 1812. His three sons went on from Enstone School to Bloxham.

PAXFORD, EDWARD (Eddy) (1877–1951). Postman, and son of Walter. In 1937 he was awarded a long-service medal for 45 years' service with the GPO.

PAXFORD, WALTER WILLIAM (1875–1957). Postman, who also kept a bicycle-shop at Spring Hill (above the Harrow Inn). Born in Lidstone, he started postal work at the age of 7, delivering letters after school, and retired from the GPO at the age of 77. He had a habit of reading people's postcards and would then inform people—in a very pronounced stutter—of the contents of their mail as he handed it over.

PEACHEY, FRED. Landlord of the Litchfield Arms. He died at Manor Cottages, Kingham, in 1951, at the age of 82.

PEACHEY, HORACE FREDERICK (1896–1963). Landlord of the Litchfield Arms in the 1940s, in succession to his father Fred. He and his wife, Annie, were still there in the mid-1950s. However, in its declining years the Litchfield Arms did not provide a living, and Horace Peachey had a side-job as coalman, sometimes assisted by T.E. Worth in the latter's early years in Enstone.

PEARCE, PERCY ('Pokey'). Born in 1906, the son of William Pearce of Neat Enstone. He was of an inquisitive nature, which—together with his Christian name—made his nickname inevitable. He and his mother Lou lived 'down Alley'. He worked on the Heythrop Estate and later at Shipton-under-Wychwood, and Frank Sheffield remembers him as 'wonderful at catching trout with his hands'.

PRATLEY, JOHN GEORGE. Hedger, of Fulwell. He had two daughters and a son, all born in the 1880s.

QUEEN HENRIETTA'S WATERWORKS, *see* Bushell, Thomas.

REGAN, FELIX (Phil). Born in 1893, the son of Owen Regan, he attended Enstone School with Mont Abbott, served in the Royal Navy, and died in the 1914–18 war.

REGAN, GERTRUDE. Born 1902, the daughter of Owen Regan, Gert was the first girl Mont Abbott ever 'proper-kissed'. She left Enstone for London and came back in later life as Mrs White, married and well-to-do. When at Enstone School, Gert's sister Chrissie was among those reported absent from time to time with St Vitus' Dance.

REGAN, OWEN. Born in India, the son of a sergeant-major in the 3rd Hussars. He became licensee of the Harrow Inn. A heavily built man, he was generally considered to be rather lazy. After his death in 1937, aged 68, his second wife Donaldina lived at The Thatch, Church Enstone.

SHEFFIELD, GEORGE FREDERICK ('Carter Sheffield') (1858–1935). One of 'they old carters' whom Mr Lennox advised Mont Abbott to learn his trade from, he was by all accounts a patient and helpful man. His grandson Frank recalls that 'people never heard our grampy swear!'

'George Sheffield's old book'—which Mont Abbott refers to in Chapter 16— was the Reverend John Jordan's *Parochial History of Enstone*, published in 1857. The former vicar of Enstone's description of the great storm of 1843 runs to some 7,000 words, and Mont paraphrased it for the purpose of his narrative.

SHEFFIELD, GEORGE ('Young George') (1885–1961). Son of George Frederick Sheffield, he was carter and later tractor-driver for Ted Hunt at Church Enstone. It was his wife, Emily Kezia (d. 1966) who shamed the men by capturing the greasy pig at the Enstone fête.

SHEFFIELD, GEORGE ('Little George'). Born December 1916; son of Young George and brother of Jack. He worked at Slade Farm from the age of 14 till he was

65. As a young boy he remembers being sent by his father to discover why Mont had not returned from work at Slade Farm one night. Finding Mont caught on the iron crossbars half-way down a well, Little George alerted his father, and they both returned to the farm with a rope and helped him out. Although Mont Abbott was later to tell Sheila Stewart, 'God alone knows how I bloody well made it' out of the well, he correctly remembered Little George being present when he regained consciousness. George Sheffield now lives on the Cleveley Road, Enstone.

SHEFFIELD, JOHN (Jack). Born 1918; son of Young George and brother of Little George. Mont called him 'Shuffel' and also 'Wive', because when asked his age as a child he found it difficult to say 'five'. He worked with Mont Abbott as under-carter at the age of 17, and sometimes (but particularly on Sundays, when Mont never worked) took Mont's place on the combine. A year of this labour was sufficient for Jack, however; he 'packed up with Ted Hunt at 18' and went to work for the county council on the road between the Bladon roundabout and the Bell Inn, Enstone ('all dug by hand'). When this work was interrupted by World War II, Jack Sheffield went to work for 13 years at Claridge's sawmill (powered by a sawdust-fired steam-tractor, and on the site now occupied by Chipperfield's Circus at Heythrop). Jack Sheffield lives on the Cleveley Road, Enstone.

SIMMS, ARTHUR GEORGE ('Smiler'). Postman, who lived at the second of the three tall cottages at the end of the Green Eye, Cleveley.

SNOW, GEORGE H. Baker and farm-worker. He and his wife Annie had two sons (Harry and William), and six daughters, including Annie (who is said to have ridden the only tricycle in the parish).

In 1927, when three of their daughters were admitted to Enstone School, the Snows were living at Leys Farm Cottage, as tenants of George Snow's employer Mr Ramsay of Leys Farm. Later they moved to one of the cottages opposite Litchfield Farm (where they were living in 1949, when the farm was sold), and in the 1954 parish register they are listed as living in Cleveley. George Snow died in 1965, aged 80; his wife Annie died in 1970.

SNOW, WINIFRED (Winnie). Born in 1907, the daughter of George Snow, she was working as a domestic servant at the time of her marriage to Albert Ward of Cleveley in 1932.

STEVENS, ALEC VICTOR ('our Odd') (1921–1990). Son of Albert (a former colour-sergeant who served in the Boer War) and Edith Stevens. He was taken prisoner at Tobruk in the 1939–45 war; on his release he retrained as a plasterer, and then joined Southern Electric. In 1948 he married Molly, who had come down from Sheffield during the war to work as a landgirl. They had a daughter, Sally. Mrs Stevens confirms that Mont Abbott used to help his mother in her unofficial capacity as part-time midwife: 'He used to fetch the doctor for Odd's mother when she had babies.' She also says that Mont had nicknames for the whole family (and indeed for almost everyone else)—not just for 'our Odd'.

TITCOMB, IVY. Born in 1902 at Lidstone, she was admitted to Enstone School on the same day as Mont Abbott (13 September 1909).

TWIGGS. The cottage at the roadside end of Manor Farm Cottages; it was named after Geoffrey and Christine Twigg, who lived there after Mont and Jim Abbott had moved on to Fulwell. (The name, therefore, was not current when Mont himself lived there.) There is an irremovable stain on one wall where Mont Abbott used to hang his hams.

VANCE, EMILY. Mistress at the Infants School at Church Enstone for 37 years. Winnie Bennett, whom Mr Glover selected to help Miss Vance as 'monitress' at the age of 12, described Miss Vance as her 'ideal teacher'. Emily Vance took classes 1 and 2, while Winnie Bennett taught the new arrivals in the same room.

VENVELL, JOHN HENRY (Harry). Garage owner, who became a major transporter of livestock. On his death in 1936, aged 63, he was succeeded by Hubert (1906–96) and Arthur Venvell. Hubert lived in the house between the school playground and the playing field, next to what is now called Venvell Close.

When Arthur died, his daughter Jean Millar inherited his half of the business. Venvell's ceased operating under that name in 1973, and although Millar's then took over the rest of the business, trading ceased completely in 1983.

WALKER, JACK. Long Compton horse doctor, who had no formal qualifications but considerable practical skill, and was therefore allowed to continue in practice under the supplementary veterinary register. His grandson is now a qualified veterinary surgeon in the Walker, Glanvill and Richards practice on the Enstone Road, Charlbury.

WARNER, SAMUEL. Farmer. He and his father first came to Enstone from Huntingdon, with three horses and a wagon; he worked first as a labourer, and then as a foreman for the Brasseys at Heythrop. When the Brasseys sold up, he acquired the Church Enstone farm from which the Sheffield children used to deliver milk to Mont Abbott's mother, after she had moved from 'down Alley' to Church Enstone.

WELLS, JANE (Jinny). Owner of the Old Shop on Neat Enstone Hill; her mother had kept the shop before her. Tall, thin, bespectacled and always dressed in black, she had a speech impediment which the youth of the village could not resist making fun of, asking for a variety of obscure items in order to hear her reply: 'I'm torry, but I don't tell dat tort of ting!' Her miserliness was legendary, and there is only one occasion on which she is known to have given anything away; when two girls called to say that their mother had just given birth to twins, she gave them one sweet each.

WORTH, THOMAS EDMUND ('Dicky') (1903–1985). Proprietor of Worth's Motor Services. He came to Enstone from Oxford as a young man, and started in business by mending bicycles in the sprawling premises of the Litchfield Arms when Horace Peachey was the innkeeper. Dickie Worth also used to help Horace Peachey in his secondary job as coalman; but as his motor business prospered, he was eventually able to buy up the Litchfield Arms. During the Second World War he became a 2nd lieutenant in the Home Guard.

Also available from Day Books

I Was Writing This Diary For You, Sasha

By HANA PRAVDA

Few diaries can have been written in more extraordinary circumstances than the one which a young Czech actress kept during the last months of World War II. Not only was she on the run from the Nazis, following her dramatic escape from captivity: she was also searching desperately for her husband Sasha, whom she had last seen when they were prisoners together at Auschwitz.

'*Almost unbearably moving.*' Daily Express

'*A most poignant tale of love and courage—terrifying, moving and ultimately life-enhancing.*' Derek Jacobi

Inside Stalin's Russia

The Diaries of Reader Bullard, 1930–1934

Edited by JULIAN AND MARGARET BULLARD

In October 1930, a former 'rebel and socialist'—as Reader Bullard described himself—arrived in the Soviet Union on a posting from the British Foreign Office. Although broadly sympathetic to the aims of the Russian Revolution, he was unable to ignore the evidence of his own eyes: and he recorded his experiences and impressions in a secret diary, which he considered so incriminating that parts of it had to be written in code.

'*A stunning portrait.*' The Independent

'*Fascinating. . . . A pleasure to read.*' Roy Hattersley, The Guardian

'*A wonderful find.*' Sunday Telegraph Books of the Year

A Brief Jolly Change

The Diaries of Henry Peerless, 1891–1920

Edited by EDWARD FENTON

The diaries of Henry Peerless provide a fascinating insight into one of the most important social trends of the past 150 years: the rise of mass tourism following the coming of the railway.

For 30 years Henry Peerless travelled all round the British Isles and beyond, by horse-drawn carriage, steam-train, steam-ship, bicycle and motor-car. The daily record of his journeys is not just a lively travelogue: it also paints a delightful picture of a whole class of people striving for diversion and pleasure at a time of unprecedented and cataclysmic change.

'*A remarkable find, beautifully handled.*' The British Diarist

'*Fascinating.*' Country Life

For more information about Day Books, visit:

www.day-books.com

All our publications can also be ordered direct through our website.